DISABILITY AND BUSINESS

DISABILITY
and
BUSINESS

Best Practices and

Strategies for Inclusion

CHARLES A. RILEY II

University Press of New England
Hanover and London

Published by University Press of New England,
One Court Street, Lebanon, NH 03766
www.upne.com
© 2006 by University Press of New England
Printed in the United States of America

5 4 3 2 1

Library of Congress Cataloging-in-Publication Data
Riley, Charles A.
Disability and business : best practices and strategies for inclusion /
Charles A. Riley II.
    p. cm.
Includes bibliographical references and index.
ISBN-13: 978-1-58465-522-0 (cloth : alk. paper)
ISBN-10: 1-58465-522-4 (alk. paper)
    1. People with disabilities—Employment—United States. 2. People
with disabilities—Economic aspects—United States. 3. People with
disabilites—United States—Economic conditions. I. Title.
HD7256.U5R55 2006
658.30087—dc22   2006016892

Listening to you, I get the music.

—Pete Townshend, "See Me, Feel Me,"
The Who's Tommy

For **Stephen Arthur Horne**

Artist, humanitarian, entrepreneur, and sportsman

Gentle Coz,

With passion and originality, without fanfare or compromise, you exemplify idealism and humanity in all you do, from art to commerce. The heroic service you offered to people with so-called mental disabilities was front-line disability advocacy of the most precious kind. You have been an unfailing source of moral, professional and aesthetic inspiration to me for longer than you realize, and this book is my tribute to you and all you represent.

With love and deep respect,
Your cousin Charlie

CONTENTS

PREFACE

And freedom tastes of reality
—Pete Townshend, "I'm Free," *The Who's Tommy*

Disability needs business just as business needs disability. Staring down the barrel of 80 percent unemployment in good times and in bad, the disability community can no longer rely on political activism or social networking to make a difference in the situation. The problem really is economic, and fixing it will take engagement with business, big and small. Progress will occur not on a charitable basis but through the standard commercial ethic of quid pro quo. This group, the largest minority by miles in the country, has to bring something to the table in return to gain inclusion and empowerment.

That same trade-off is where business stands to gain what it desperately needs: a genuinely new paradigm, complete with a revenue hike from the biggest niche market in history. We are talking about a whopping 101.4 million consumers by one count (from a study commissioned by Bill Gates, who was one of the first to recognize this gold mine when he saw it).[1] This book is published at what most of us hope will be the end of a recession, even as major corporations continue to post multibillion-dollar losses while their stock prices languish in the doghouse. The bankruptcy of original ideas is leashed to actual Chapter 11 proceedings signaling the demise of major companies, including most of the nation's airlines as well as pharmaceutical giants, accounting firms, retailers, and long-suffering manufacturers who have been hemorrhaging for decades. Their existing customer bases are dwindling and bored with tired marketing campaigns and the paucity of innovation. Another reason the outlook is persistently bleak is that there are macroeconomic forces inhibiting what had been thought of as progress.

The working-age population is shrinking, discretionary income is being swallowed by inflation, and depleted natural resources are limiting growth. Most companies are clueless about where to find the next mass sales and labor opportunity to grow economically. At the very least, they need to redress the mistake of overlooking people with disabilities as a viable, untapped source of consumers and employees. The sheer volume of people and dollars involved represents an opportunity that would be passed up only by the most illogical and myopic business leaders.

Making money on disability is a significant part of the argument of this book, most directly in the chapter on sales (go ahead, turn to chapter 4; who can blame you?), but it is not the only benefit. Integrating disability into your company's diversity strategy is a topic complex and massive enough to challenge the best minds in the marketing, public relations, information technology, design and architecture, human resources, legal, and management departments. It stimulates a long-range planning conversation that has the potential to transform the way your whole company does business, internally and externally. Each in his or her own silo can run the cost-benefit analysis and concoct a departmental policy that has the numbers that a manager would approve for implementation. But the stars of this story, as related in the best-practices section of each chapter, are sophisticated corporate minds who found interdisciplinary ways to integrate disability in a wide range of strategies—and make it pay its own way. Nobody can flat-out guarantee that discovering disability will solve all the problems faced by American industry, but the successes that have greeted the modest pioneer efforts are enough to suggest, even to a biased advocate-journalist, that there are rewards to be reaped by companies that step up to this challenge.

Business is facing more than just the pressure to post higher quarterly sales figures. The cause of the Dow's most recent drop goes deeper. It reflects a decade-long decline in trust. As soon as the forensic auditors finished with the energy sector (the Enron debacle), they were on to telecom (Worldcomm) and eventually a government-backed real estate sacred cow (Fannie Mae). Dozens of other scandals bobbed in their wakes. Consumers and investors lost confidence in the former darlings of Wall Street as reputations were stripped bare. A few companies preserved their image by clinging to ideology: Ikea, Virgin Airways, the Body Shop, Google, and Starbucks offer prime examples. Among them, Starbucks was also one of the first to build disability outreach into its marketing and hiring programs, and even redesigned the high counters to accommodate wheelchair users on both sides of the bar. Completing the job, Starbucks used its formidable public relations capabilities to get the word out as soon as the first cappuccino was drawn by a worker with cerebral palsy. The jump in sales can be quantified, but the response in terms of public trust can only be guessed.

The vast divide between disability and business suggests that both sides have failed. This is a book full of constructive suggestions for positive change, not a jeremiad. These pages are not filled with recriminations and tearjerkers, and, despite the political leanings expected of most of the disability community, this is essentially as much a probusiness book as it is a prodisability one. The premise is that the two sides are already capable of helping one another but have not recognized the ways they can make this happen. By concentrating on best practices and building the cost-benefit case, I am counting on managers' ability to discern the difference between inaction and taking the introductory steps that will yield results. This means abandoning the tired "right thing to do" mentality and all its demeaning clichés. As Gates declared when he launched Able to Work at the Microsoft campus in October 1999, "There are some things you do because it's the right thing to do. And there are some things you do because there is a market and that's good business to get into the market. I believe our technology can help people with disabilities and that's why I have forty people working in the accessibility field."[2] Let's leave the pity play, all the maudlin stuff about what can be done on behalf of these poor victims, to dumb television "reality" shows and get down to the brass tacks of how an extreme makeover of corporate culture can build trust and profits.

Nearly two decades ago, a remarkable encounter with a hugely successful consultant who divulged the future to the chairmen of such major corporations as American Express and Coca-Cola shaped the way I think about business and innovation. I was a lowly reporter at *Fortune* magazine when I got a call from the managing editor's office to get up there and take care of a raving discontent who had somehow made his way inside the Time Inc. headquarters and was camped out claiming that we had plagiarized his reports. I cooled off Andre W. Alkiewicz over an exorbitantly expensive lunch (how I miss my expense account) during which I learned he was the founder of Perception International and former managing director of the Hoppin, Watson investment bank. He had once been a British spy. He told me how he had managed to beat us to stories on telecommunications, information technology, and government regulation by as long a lead time as three years—his reports, down to the headlines, were almost exactly what we published. What reporter would not want access to that crystal ball?

Andre's wisdom came from what he called inferential thinking. He was a connoisseur of change. Signs of impending change contradict the status quo, which makes them aberrations. To some, they are an enormous source of irritation; to others, just peculiarities. However, the anomaly of today may easily become the norm of tomorrow. To dismiss it out of hand is the biggest mistake a planner can make. Judgment discerns which anomalies will have the staying power to become the new status quo. To make that call, it is necessary not only to observe how frequently an anomaly recurs but also to note whether it meshes with others. What at first glance may appear to be the end of the line in the development of these anomalies may turn out to be only a first stage in a far bigger and more encompassing change. Andre would cruise past the accumulated statistics and binary (yes-no) evidence of most corporate research and fasten his attention on a detail that seemed trivial. Out of that he would build a vision of the future for a whole industry.

After I left *Fortune* I collaborated with him at his think tank (highlighted by silver-service teas on the terrace of a vast stone mansion in the Connecticut hills), where we examined trends and approaching regulatory dangers for a select group of private clients. Andre's lessons in futurology for some of the nation's most powerful moguls were profound, and I was astonished throughout the writing of this book at how apt they are in the context of implementing disability-forward company policies. For him, disability would have proved an irresistible example of the U.S. economy's biggest anomaly, a whale gliding below the surface undetected, waiting for the harpoon guided by the sharp-eyed mariner whose wide-angle view from the crow's nest is essential. The originality of the disability perspective would also have appealed to him, including such elegant ideas as the way adaptation and accommodation spur progress, the cultural transformation of a corporation, the role of the user-expert, and the design technique of "wayfinding," all of which we will explore later in these pages. Disability and its static relegation to secondary status in diversity policies is a great example of Andre's belief that it is a fatal flaw on the part of managers to assume that past experience and the status quo are adequate guides to the future. A strong commitment in sticking to a plan, a lack of flexibility, causes a lack of recognition that the psychological, social, and political environment in which business takes place is in flux. We spent our consulting sessions with strategic planners who too often had such a narrow orientation that the big picture was unavailable to them. We used disaster scenarios to scare them out of the mindset that they knew exactly where they were going, because many failed to see that the destination of their entire industries had changed while they were not paying attention. Where those companies were going, no one was waiting with a welcome mat.

One of the essential tenets of Andre's radical thinking was his emphasis on intellectual capital, which fits right into the redefined role of workers with disabilities in what has been called the "knowledge economy." Intellectual capital, which is still a relatively marginal idea in corporate circles, was until recently considered solely as an exclusive attribute of top management. Thanks to the proliferation of information on every level of human resources, intellectual capital is no longer cloistered in the executive suite. It permeates the whole organization. Even the ultimate example of the stratified organization—the military—is adjusting to this phenomenon and, at this writing, is well ahead of business in doing so. This is not some generalized claim that people with disabilities are inherently smarter than everybody else or blessed with compensatory perceptive powers to make up for their "handicaps"—that would be falling into the "special" fallacy all over again. The progress that Microsoft, IBM, Cingular, SunTrust, Boeing, Motorola, and other companies have made in disability-forward management has depended overwhelmingly on the productivity of their "connected" workers. Whenever I consider the productive triumph of information over matter or distance I conjure the image of Stephen Hawking, the Einstein of our time and as seriously disabled, and awesomely connected, a person as you will ever find.

Is it so difficult to see around the corner of the future and make some reasonable strategic moves to survive? No. What is needed is intellectual breadth, curiosity, comprehension, and integrity. Not everyone, however, has these qualities. Acquiring them demands the application of a new kind of flexible thinking that is not intimidated by uncertainty. After the nomadic economy, we have passed through the agricultural and industrial economies and are now in the service economy. At every stage of human development we abandon certain functions of our productive work. These functions have been externalized, to the point that what will be left is the uppermost function of our brains: the economy of creativity. Individuals and corporations will have to change their intellectual bearings to survive as economic entities, develop new products and services that do not just follow from discoveries but precede them. In a total reversal of cause and effect, ideas will come first. Conjure the future and then create it. There is no way to leave 100 million Americans out of the picture. This book is dedicated to the proposition that, even if the ultimate "to be" cannot be fully divined, there is already enough light shed on the next century to cast sufficiently sharp shadows of things to come. Even though the final picture is not exactly in focus, to see just part of it allows for sound strategy planning to commence now.

· · ·

Some books are mined from libraries and archives. This one is based on nearly one hundred live interviews with sources on the corporate and NGO (nongovernmental organization) front lines, as well as my experience at the intersection of business and disability. I urged my inside sources at IBM, Cingular, SunTrust, Microsoft, and other major corporations to think through more than a recitation of current and past best practices to reveal the cutting-edge issues and ideas, frustrations, and imminent breakthroughs from their vantage points.

At the core of the book is a hard second look at what we really mean by "human resources," with particular attention to the way people with disabilities fit into a plan that puts their knowledge in place of brawn. Revising the design of the company in this way can enhance everyone's productivity, and does not imply that exceptions and concessions have to be made just to accommodate people with disabilities. "Special" is not equal. That concept highlights difference and pulls pity, or lowered standards, back into the picture. This is particularly true in the context of the legal and social backlash against affirmative action. The ground lost to poor performance poses a particularly thorny problem for people with disabilities, who never enjoyed the assistance of those policies but certainly face the stigma of being perceived as underqualified if they receive a leg up. The sense of urgency regarding this problem on the disability side is heightened by the second-guessing of the Americans with Disabilities Act (ADA) and its economic ramifications, a complex topic we return to in chapter 1.

After a recession, we need a recovery. As those of us who have hired people with disabilities on a regular and committed basis realize, recovery takes many forms. In addition to its most public connotation (going through detox, as dramatically exemplified by Elizabeth Taylor, Robert Downey Jr., and others), it applies to anyone who has missed work and is coming back from say, a chronic back problem or a heart attack. I found the "comeback kid" aspect of disability a great source of strength both for the individual (including myself) and for the organization. F. Scott Fitzgerald once famously declared, "There are no second acts in American lives." Although certainly true of Fitzgerald, who flamed out spectacularly after *The Great Gatsby* (another victory for alcohol), this pessimistic message of resignation is off base. It has been challenged time and again by the examples of those who start over again after spinal cord injuries, strokes, heart attacks, and other sudden-onset disabilities. Among the groups that certainly proved Fitzgerald wrong were the returning wounded veterans of conflicts, including Iraq, and the spectacularly successful postpolio "class" of overachievers (many of them now nearing retirement). They exemplify a larger trend of the whole labor force toward career redefinition as described by economists, including the back-to-work movement of baby boomers and the way in which recent metamorphoses of careers from one field to another coincide with a reinvention of the necessary skills. That echoes the reinitiation of one's career that is such an important stage in the lives of many people with disabilities, particularly those who incur their conditions at midcareer. As we found in my organization, a national magazine for people with disabilities that was entirely staffed by people with disabilities, there is nothing like the energy of a renaissance to lift the team. From micro- to macroeconomics, from the mom-and-pop shop to the multinational, the operative term at this stage in American business history is "recovery." Sales slumps or the lingering effects of terrorist attacks have taken longer to shake off than anyone expected. As of the spring of 2006, when I am putting the final touches on these pages, I don't know anyone or any business that is not in some way or another still "in recovery."

One of the ways the national economy can pick up the pace of its recovery is to make sure that business recognizes disability as a labor pool. Call it the "disability dividend." When the federal government was pondering the Work Incentives Improvement Act in 1999, one of the most effective pieces of evidence was a small study conducted by the Virginia-based non-profit NISH (formerly National Industries for the Severely Handicapped) that considered the cases of 1,910 workers with disabilities working in the food service industry on government contracts through the Javits-Wagner-O'Day Program. It showed that 75 percent of those who were on food stamps were able to discontinue their government benefits, and 76 percent of those on Social Security disability payments dropped or reduced their reliance on benefits. Multiply the $3,700 in savings per worker by the 10 million people likely to be affected by legislation that puts people to work, and the savings would be $37 billion a year in benefits payments alone. But that is not the whole story. In addition to the reduction in government entitlements (welfare, Medicare, Medicaid, food stamps, unemployment, Supplemental Security Income and Social Security Disability Insurance, and public housing), there is a payback in terms of federal and state income taxes as well as worker's contributions to Social Security and Medicare. That is just a broad-brush treatment of the type of incentive that business strategists love to identify when major policy shifts are considered.

Incentives come in different packages, many but not all of them based on money. Whenever I sat down with interviewees, the inevitable motivational disclosure seemed to arise: this is personal. I lived the disability business story for five marvelous years as the cofounder of a small business that employed members of the disability community and relied on sales to the community. Everything about the legal, human resources, marketing, public relations, office design, and management ground that this book covers was part of that experience. The climate of trust in the person with a disability as a "user-expert" that this book promotes, in terms of the trading zone in which people with and without disabilities meet (as defined in the first chapter), was the secret to our success as a team. My earlier adventures as a journalist prepared me for this immense and wonderfully complex topic. As a *Fortune* reporter covering politics and policy as well as other beats, I enjoyed the privilege of an inside look at corporate culture at major multinationals (including Time Inc.), and then I turned to the entrepreneurial life for a book titled *Small Business, Big Politics* that paved the way for many of the suggestions in these pages that will be useful to owner-managers. My current work with human rights advocates and ethics monitors through the nonprofit International Center for Corporate Accountability (ICCA) informs the critical thinking on the individual's relation to the corporation and presents the first of many opportunities for me to express my gratitude to the experts who guided my research. The founder and president of ICCA, S. Prakash Sethi, is not only one of the most original economists of our day but an indefatigable crusader on the part of the disenfranchised, an inspiration to me during the writing of every page of this book.

Two women literally made the book possible, and in my eyes they are almost twins in their fierce intelligence and profoundly humanitarian yet practical approach to disability. My brilliant editor, Phyllis Deutsch (editor in chief of the University Press of New England) exceeded her own high standards set in our earlier collaboration on the controversial book *Disability and the Media,* and brought to this project her wisdom, her astonishingly incisive line-editing skills, and, most important, the commitment to disability as an issue that is exactly what we need. The community owes her one if this book has its intended effect. It already owes an immense debt to my other pillar of support, the inimitable Tari Susan Hartman-Squire, who opened doors to corporate leaders and advocates just as she has opened doors for thousands of people with disabilities during decades of the most effective, tireless work on their behalf. A consultant and advocate who has been on the front lines since before the ADA, Hartman-Squire is in my opinion the preeminent figure in the arena of disability and business. She knows everybody, she is on top of every scenario, and she has had a hand in every one of the success stories to date, an astonishing achievement that could have been attained only when knowledge and passion are aligned. And this miracle worker is not even partly done with her good deeds. Tari's strategic hand is everywhere present in these pages. Through constant dialogue we pushed the envelope of this topic in ways that I hope other experts will find provocative, while never losing sight of the needs of the newcomer.

Through Tari, I met the dramatis personae of the corporate success stories you will encounter in these pages. For their time, their willingness to stretch their minds on tape, and for all they have done in this area, my thanks are extended to Ted Childs, Jim Sinocchi, and Millie DesBiens of IBM, Karen Quamenn of Medtronic, Branka Minic of Manpower, Mylene Padolina of Microsoft, Chris Fossel and Kimberly Reed of Merrill Lynch, John Studer of Procter & Gamble, Mary McCary of SunTrust, Amy Jones of Nordstrom, Kevin Foster of Motorola, Evan Furg of Universal Studios, Michael J. Caron of Avis, Joseph Cray of Nielsen Research, Michael J. Hartman of NASA, and Susan Palmer Mazrui of Cingular Wireless. In the public sector, let me salute the energetic and desperately needed efforts of my other sources, beginning with Alan Muir of Career Opportunities for Students with Disabilities, Roy Grizzard of the Bureau of Labor's Office of Disability Employment Policy, Ollie Cantos of the Bureau of Labor, Tom Donohue and Cathy Healy of the U.S. Chamber of Commerce, Carmen Jones, Eric Lipp of Open Doors, Valerie Fletcher of Adaptive Environments, Nancy Miller of Visions, Anthony Pfeiffer, Christopher Rosa, Professor Ruth O'Brien, Susanne M. Bruyere of Cornell University, Richard V. Burkhauser, and Ann Brash.

Side by side in the newsroom I learned about disability from my colleagues at *WE* magazine, whose capability and support for their often baffled editor in chief still push me. When we were pumping on all cylinders to meet deadlines, we blasted *Tommy* by The Who in the newsroom, and in tribute to those good old days I have lifted the epigraphs for each chapter from the lyrics. I will always doff my cap to my colleagues Fran Ahders, Fred Asong Eno, Jane S. Van Ingen, Robert Bennett, James Conrad, Dexter Benjamin, John Robinson, Terry Moakley, Casey Martin, the great George Covington, David McMullen, James J. Weisman, Tom Whittaker, John M. Williams, Lori Frisher, Mikki Lam, Ken Levinson, Dianne Pilgrim, Kitty Lunn, Francesca Rosenberg, Dr. Ruth Westheimer, Alexander Wood, and those we covered who became part of the family including John Hockenberry, Robin Williams, the late Christopher Reeve, Walter Cronkite, Andrea Bocelli, James Wolfensohn, Michael J. Fox, George Soros, and Mayor Rudolf Giuliani. The manuscript was nearly done when I was shocked by the news in July 2005 that we had lost one of our dearest coworkers, the gregarious Gordon S. Harper, who worked in our offices as a reporter, as a rainmaker, and even filled in as a fashion model. I remember the sunny day I drove Gordon home from his first day in our downtown offices along the FDR Drive in Manhattan. He was ecstatic to be part of *WE* magazine and charged up with ideas. He was my own age, and way better looking, so it was a shock to hear from his fiancée that he had "given up on life." I wondered what would have happened if he still had his job (our magazine folded four years ago). If I needed more incentive to make these pages that much more potent, Gordon's passing was enough.

Anger is a great motivator, too. This is usually the space where you read of the professorial author's debt of thanks for the support of his college and colleagues. I wish. My research was practically blocked by the unforgivable antagonism encountered in the halls of Baruch College, which has hampered a large-scale project of writing about disability (this is the second book of many I plan) to which I have dedicated a decade of my life. The antagonism is so vicious and persistent that I cannot tell if it arises from discrimination or plain stupidity. As the book was in preparation, small-minded academics denied every plea for research support, not only when I asked for time off to write but even when I made a petty-cash request to drive to a conference on disability and employment. "Intellectuals" whose political correctness is typically ludicrous in its deference to any other minority no matter how minor turned down my proposal to conduct a course on disability, one of the most practical ways to share and flesh out ideas before they are committed to paper. They also stared blankly at the job contacts for graduates with disabilities I brought back and were dismissive of my repeated warnings that the college had built an inaccessible Web site, proving itself yet again indifferent to the rights of our students with disabilities. Baruch falsely and hypocritically claims to rank first in diversity in the nation, but no institution is diverse if it leaves disability out of the equation. Nothing starts the adrenalin going like a barrier, as anyone in the disability community knows. Perhaps perversely, rather than blame my "colleagues" I thank them, and all the other pseudohumanists one encounters in academia who never will understand the importance of disability issues but whose prejudice fuels the fury that drove this book to its conclusion.

Thank goodness instead for the friends who know how much it matters to me to pull together a book that is both useful and intellectually rigorous. So often their contributions ensure that both purposes are fulfilled even as they keep my spirits up. Among the faithful, I owe heartfelt gratitude to Patrick Cullen, Lisa Hahn, Dr. Susan E. Goodman, Peter and Barb Peck, Asher B. Edelman, Raoul and Bettina WitteVeen, Brian Eckel, Paul Iskyan,

Teb Barnard, Gayana Jurkevich, Harry Brent, Rosemary Willhelm, and Lin Pulan, Lin Ke Qiang, Lin Qun Qing, Liu Ke Xin (my Chinese research team).

Closer to home, I am the beneficiary of a constant stream of ideas and support from my mother, Isabel C. Riley, my sisters Robin and Diane, and my darling wife, Liu Ke Ming, who was present for every exciting moment of the research and writing. My cousin and role model Stephen A. Horne, to whom this book is lovingly dedicated, distinguished himself on the front lines in this battle as an attendant in public mental hospitals during the sixties, and it is his sense of humanity and understanding that I honor. Our fathers were businessmen with big hearts, "way out there in the blue riding on a smile and a shoeshine," and I knew that if anyone was going to grasp the mix of idealism and pragmatism I strive for in these pages, it would be my gentle coz, Stevie.

Charles A. Riley II, PhD
Cutchogue, New York
May 2006

Notes

1. "The Market for Accessible Technology—The Wide Range of Abilities and Its Impact on Computer Use," Forrester Research, 2003, p. 1. See *www.forrester.com*.
2. John M. Williams, "Work: The Can-do Economic Revolution Is Heading Your Way," *WE* magazine, March–April 2000, pp. 47–48.

DISABILITY AND BUSINESS

Chapter 1

Handshakes, Not Handouts

Building the Business Case for Inclusion

How can we follow?
—Pete Townshend, "Sally Simpson," *The Who's Tommy*

Smack in the middle of the biggest economic boom in recent memory, I was running a national magazine targeting people with disabilities. We used their right to employment as the banner of our advocacy, and the stunning gains of consumers with disabilities as our pitch to advertisers. All around us people of all races, ages, and skill and educational levels were finding work. In four years, 21 million jobs were added thanks in part to the so-called New Economy, and the national unemployment rate was driven down below 3 percent. The magazine published an annual survey of hiring patterns that drew welcome sponsors and attention from the mainstream media.

But I was pulling my hair out. Year after year, the "work" report ran aground on the same rugged fact: people with disabilities were always left behind. Even at the peak in 2000, as the national unemployment rate dipped below 3 percent (it hovers around 5 percent at this writing, with oil at $75 a barrel), when every possible marginal labor pool was tapped and outsourcing was barely a blip on the radar, the numbers for people with disabilities were catastrophic. And infuriatingly static: the lead sentence of the story—it strains credibility—is the same today as it was then. While 30 million people with disabilities are of working age, between 75 and 80 percent of them are unemployed or underemployed. According to the Bureau of

Labor Statistics, there are roughly 120 million Americans who are considered "employed" according to SIPP (Survey of Income and Program Participation) data, and the most generous estimate of the number of workers with disabilities tops out at only 16 million. This has been the situation for well over three decades.

Pointing to one cause or another for the staggeringly high unemployment rate is relatively easy. Both the public and the private sectors share the blame, however unequally. On the one hand, obsolete government policies strip workers of their benefits as they reach a certain income level, acting as a proven deterrent to job searches. Less damnably, the major companies that otherwise participate in socially responsible hiring skipped this niche. Some are gun-shy of class-action lawsuits, while others have been creamed by ridiculous health care costs and are scared that workers with disabilities devour a disproportionate share of benefits. Most are far from putting together the equation between reaching a consumer niche and hiring from the community.

Let's start with the private sector. Somehow disability found itself split away from other minorities in business strategies. In terms of human resources, the corporate diversity initiatives that opened the doors to many minorities have largely excluded the applicant with a disability. The consumer recognition that kicked in after the civil rights battle over the right to work was won never materialized for people with disabilities—at least not yet. On a deeper level, discrimination rooted in fear has subverted what mechanisms are in place to advance the prospects of workers with disabilities. Try as many do to deny it, we still live in a stereotypical business hierarchy that privileges "attractive" sales reps (the Abercrombie and Fitch model), Gen X skateboarders who run the information technology departments (Google chic), and ex–football players who become chief executive officers (the *Fortune 500* poster boys in the corner offices). "Normal" is persistently defined by references to these physical types, as we will find in the chapter on office design. Decades ago the barriers hampering women and racial minorities were broken down through legal and political activism. Fearing the stick of lawsuits, fines, and boycotts, corporations complied with the laws generated in the sixties. The secondary wave of thinking on diversity has long since been apparent: profits are reaped by tapping minority markets. Once the carrot of sales joins the stick of regulation, the business case for diversity is solidly made.

But the disability niche is not even up to the stick stage. Comparable access to career opportunities for even the most qualified college graduates with disabilities remains overdue. Most of the major players in the obvious retail and service sectors that could ostensibly reach this market are still at the focus group stage. Neither business nor government has kept up with the progress from physical to cultural criteria in how we define disability, despite having grasped the significance of moving from race-based to culture-based diversity policies. Business needs to recognize that the disability community long ago shifted gears from viewing itself based on a medical model to a sociopolitical view that leaves physical considerations in the background. The first step is to redefine corporate strategies according to this change in thinking. The aim of this book is to follow through by spelling out the *fiscal*, legal, and moral rationales for inclusion, and then using best practices to show the way to finish the job, launch the career, and close the deal. This is a guide, not a manifesto, and the steps it recommends are not based on politics or altruism but on standard business practices, because they make good business dollars and sense.

What has kept corporations from recognizing the opportunity that disability offers? Lack of information is the first problem. Gathering a reliable statistical abstract of how much people with disabilities work and shop is vital. The demographic blind spot in this area has been a persistent obstacle to addressing the problem from a public policy standpoint, and it undermines attempts to get business leaders on board as well. When they are asked to try something different, there is comfort in numbers. Emerging research, conducted by a former advocate turned corporate consultant and Nielsen Entertainment's—the gold standard of market research—V. P. Joesph Craigh has at least partly rectified the lack of compelling evidence, especially in the area of marketing. The concept is simple: use national disability conventions as a magnet to draw companies to conduct focus groups with the strategic leaders, trendsetters, key influences, and opinion makers. The difficulty with most of the skimpy data available from economists, however, is that it splits into grim confirmation of the worst fears about the worker with a disability, on one side, and a far brighter picture of the consumer with a disability on the other.

Freakonomics

Even for seasoned experts, the economics of disability in the United States simply do not add up. But nobody doubts there is an absolutely massive customer base, almost too big to be styled a niche, waiting to be tapped. People with disabilities have been vastly undervalued as customers. Many have multimillion-dollar insurance settlements anchoring their assets. Others are more modestly if securely bankrolled by monthly benefit and insurance checks. If the preliminary research is any indication, they shop like hell online and loyally pay a premium to companies for extra service. If you are a connoisseur of business trends, they are right in the bull's-eye of three major movements: the knowledge worker's rise as predicted by Peter Drucker in 1968 and inflated by the computer age, the demand-driven consumer rights revolution that has grabbed economic power away from producers, and the boomer generation with all its clout.

Yet the fullness of this promise is undermined by the kind of unemployment and income figures posted by single mothers with a high school education. Faced with this incongruity, forecasters have backed off the whole sector, and, consequently, the corporate strategists who rely on their graphs are on hold. All the while community cheerleaders in the la-la land of nonprofits have, if a moment of candor is permitted, foolishly adhered to the traditional fundraising syndrome—"the dreaded rubber chicken dinner." As Tari Susan Hartman-Squire, a marketing consultant based in Los Angeles, whose EIN SOF Communications is the leading force behind some of the more profitable campaigns in disability marketing, sums up the problem: "The benchmark was set by the ADA, but the next phase is to use consumer lifestyle and choices to help build the business case. We must cut across the paradigm that the disability community is asking for a 'financial handout' as opposed to extending a 'fiscal handshake.' When push comes to shove, major nonprofit organizations may still want a rubber chicken dinner, but it delivers no customers' return on investment and doesn't help a corporation's bottom line. It's a dance. Disability organizations are in the process of redefining themselves and their self-perception of making this all more businesslike."[1]

It is time to get on the dance floor, with business calling the tune because it is business that pays the piper. Neither federal nor state government programs, variations on welfare, have made a dent in the unemployment situation, which they are exacerbating by their usual, dumb heavy-handedness. In a parallel display of incompetence, many nonprofits are running on empty when it comes to impact or ideas. They demonstrably hurt the cause by throwing those same old black-tie galas Hartman-Squire despairs of, windfalls only for celebrities who nab $35,000 appearance fees and caterers who enjoy a ten-times markup on every bottle of plonk. These ritual boondoggles just defer the collective guilt another year with a pity pitch. But try explaining that to the twentysomething who has just learned from his neurosurgeon that the spinal cord injury he sustained in a car accident a week before college graduation means his career prospects have, according to the current prognostications, just plummeted. So what if Denzel Washington circles the Waldorf ballroom glad-handing donors to another project to cure paralysis? Thanks to his physical therapists and anything he has read beyond the medical level of *Reader's Digest,* the new addition to the disability community realizes that paraplegia cannot be cured. He just wants to know if he will ever launch a career, finish college, go out on a date, have a family.

The promises of rhetoric and science fiction hurt more than they help. Real hope is going to come from economic progress. Just like the kid in the wheelchair, decision makers in businesses both big and small need straight, yes-or-no answers to the basic questions about disability. For employers and sales managers this is either a market segment they want to get into, or not. A basic calculation of costs against benefits will help in making the choice. Grants administrators or government gatekeepers have a relatively easy task by comparison. All they have to do is match the agenda of the donor or institution with the supplications of the applicant and the "bang-for-the-buck" problem is solved, no matter what the outcome. This will not suffice for business, where results count.

Before we write off the nonprofits, however, there is an important new role for them to play that several are just discovering. A byword of this book is the value of the "user-expert" to businesses seeking an informed understanding of the needs of either the consumer or the colleague with a disability. The best repositories of information about the community are unquestionably the established nonprofits. They need to undergo a metamorphosis to be ready for their own self-fulfilling prophecy—the economic phase in the disability rights movement. The smarter organizations have evolved from medical to political and on to economic mission plans. In the case of the National Spinal Cord Injury Association (NSCIA), for example, the original function fifty-six years ago at its founding was to provide clinical and rehabilitation services for civilians who survived their spinal cord injuries (veterans had their own service organizations). The second phase in the organization's history was political advocacy, as it joined in the legislative fight for accessibility, antidiscrimination measures including the ADA, and other public policy issues. Now the NSCIA means business. Just as this book was coming together, its Business Advisory Committee (BAC) was brainstorming a landmark study of corporate intentions and reputations in the disability community. Its highlight was a hybrid between a "report card" and a "white paper"—a first for the disability community, inspired by the NAACP's annual report on corporate reputations and economic impact in the black community. "We're not as organized as our other diversity counterparts, so this White Paper Report has been a good stretch goal," says Marcie Roth, NSCIA executive director.

This is just the beginning of a major transformation of the functions of service and grassroots organizations into agents of economic change. The new disability nonprofits are going to be effective third-party players between corporations and the government in the same way that nongovernmental organizations (NGOs) are filling this gap in other human rights accountability and environmental areas. They can ensure that corporations do the right thing when it comes to disability, at least in part by acting as consulting experts to business leadership. Eventually they are going to supplement the ineffectual government agencies that have traditionally kept an eye on business. Monitoring big business is a tricky but important job, often mistakenly left to agencies that are incompetent (flat-footed government regulators), ethically dubious (industry associations charged with cleaning up their own messes), or unqualified (the media, on the two counts of lack of expertise and conflict of interest). One of the only reliable ways to measure the performance of a company in terms of an issue like disability awareness is to turn to a nonprofit with a solid background in the advanced understanding of the problems at hand and with no ties to the company. For some years the National Organization on Disability in Washington, D.C., the former President's Committee for the Employment of People with Disabilities, and various major nonprofits associated with one disability or another (Easter Seals, the MS Society, United Cerebral Palsy, Just One Break, the Job Accommodation Network, and others) have honored corporations for their work in the field, but too often the recognition was tarnished by the obvious fact that the corporation had made a hefty donation to the cause. "There's no such thing as a free lunch," Jerome Belson, a frequent giver to disability causes and the former chairman of my media company, once growled as he prepared to pick up yet another Tiffany trophy inscribed with his name at a reception in Manhattan for Easter Seals that he had essentially paid for with a seven-figure check, also inscribed with his name. This old-style tax deduction stuff is overdue for change. The future of corporate-nonprofit partnerships is going to be a more equitable exchange at the bargaining table instead of the banquet table. The NGO will confer expertise and validity, and the corporation will bring careers and a commitment to disability as part of diversity. One of the first lessons the NGO can offer business is a candid assessment of the risks and rewards involved in getting into the disability sector, in terms that business understands.

A basic tenet of decision making in the for-profit world, taught early in the business curriculum, is SWOT (strengths, weaknesses, opportunities, and threats) analysis. It is time for disability to take the SWOT test. The strength part is a layup. Posting $1 trillion dollars in aggregate income and a massive head count of 54 million (or 100 million, if we use Mr. Gates's figure), the upside is scarcely questionable. On the basis of volume alone disability represents the largest minority market around. A fraction of that was on the table when the black or gay markets were in question. Just ask Nike, McDonald's, or Absolut how those campaigns turned out.

The weaknesses are broken down into strikingly different categories. The main drawback is that disability is largely unknown as a business phenomenon. The ADA is hazy to the point of incomprehensibility. Many still assume people with disabilities are too poor to count as a consumer niche and too sick or lazy to work, based on the horrendous unemployment rate and the attendant income gap. Disability organizations are still leading with an 80-percent-unemployment-rate plea, combined with an untapped-consumer-potential message, that is confounding to corporations, foundations, and the press. Meanwhile the indelible impression left by an amputee panhandler outside the subway stop deters the marketing director en route to the office. It has never been easy for a minority community to emerge from the deficit left by anecdotal or first-person observation. Attitudinal barriers are damaging but impossible to quantify.

For serious students of the problem there is a pressing need to crunch the numbers. When strategies are devised, particularly in the executive suites of major companies, there is a fundamental need, even call it a craving, for data. This lacuna has posed a massive obstacle for those pushing hard in the field of disability marketing or employment, because the numbers they need simply have not been available. Any marketing intern could Google you precisely how many black women buy feminine hygiene products, or how many gay guys boarded cruises to the Caribbean last winter, thanks to studies conducted by the Association of Travel Marketing Executives and Marketresearch.com, but nobody could deliver a basic twenty-page demographic report on the movies or mutual funds preferred by customers with disabilities. Until now. Because the business case for inclusion requires quantitative justification, consultants in the disability field, such as Tari Hartman-Squire's EIN SOF Communications and Nielsen Entertainment's Joseph Craig, who launched the "Disability Community Market Research Initiative," are focused on crunching the numbers. Some of their top clients across a variety of sectors (restaurants, telecommunications, banks, Internet service providers, pharmaceuticals, travel) just tabulated the results of a series of focus groups in conjunction with national disability organizations. By plugging the data gap, the focus groups (which are ongoing) are reducing a significant strategic barrier. Here is the pitch as Kevin Bradley, the director of diversity initiatives for McDonald's who conceived the Business Advisory Committee of the National Spinal Cord Injury Association, delivers it: "If I held up five twenty-dollar bills and said one is from an African-American consumer, one from a Hispanic customer, this from a gay consumer, one from a single mom, and one from a customer with a disability. Which dollar came from which customer? Do you really care? Which will you give up? Which will you want to go into your competitor's cash register?[2]

The opportunities are manifold, and most arise from the expected rewards of leadership. Being first to tap a massive market spells profits and customer loyalty. IBM has always scored high on disability-consumer-trend reports because it got to the users first. Similarly, Medtronic, thanks to Karen Quamenn's leadership, has capitalized on its early lead in more disability-specific medical technology. Moving into the vanguard on the employment front will bring corporations a powerful group of dedicated workers. The best practices hailed in the pages that follow are examples of leadership in action. In many cases, companies (especially entrepreneurs) could be eligible to be rewarded by government support, including subsidies. The most spectacular example of building solid relationships with the disability community that translated into real support in this regard was Cingular Wireless as it approached the merger with AT&T Wireless with a multibillion-dollar venture. Because of Cingular's track record of providing far more accessibility than other wireless carriers, the merger approval meant that people with disabilities could get more accessible services over a larger geographic region. The rest is history. This case, which we consider at length in the chapter on management, represents the high-stakes payoff for being out front on disability that investors, executives, and bankers cannot afford to ignore. Hiring often spins higher volume sales. The benefits to corporate image are also a part of the opportunity package, particularly in a time of devastating ethical scandals that draw regulatory ire and alienate activist consumers and investors who can tumble sales figures and stock prices.

The traditional threat, posed by direct competition, is tellingly absent from this analysis. Once I had taped about half my interviews with decision makers who have taken the lead on disability, it was surprisingly clear that they had no worries whatsoever about losing ground to their rivals. The whole disability idea is so novel that the usual rules and paranoia do not apply, and most were more than happy to share the secrets of their success with others in their industry. It is not unusual to find human resources and even marketing advocates from rival banks, for example, gathering at conferences or industry events to learn about each other's best practices. A more substantive threat remains the possibility of ADA suits and regulatory action as well as the lingering concern over the costs of health benefits. According to a 2005 study, the average company has thirty-seven suits pending against it, costing $8 million a year in fees or damages. More than 10 percent of large companies lose a ridiculously high 5 percent of their gross revenues to legal fees, proving that lawsuits are expensive even if the company wins. And there is nothing on the fiction shelves as strange as the accumulation of charges one encounters on the typical HMO bill. Later in this book I will explore the threat to a company's share price posed by socially responsible investment, a brand-spanking-new idea borrowed from the latest thinking in corporate accountability that could, properly advanced, light a fire under some of the nation's chief executive officers. Finally, having launched a small business and watched it crash and burn, experience has taught me that there is the risk of being too far ahead of the curve and not gaining recognition for it. The isolation and exposure of the pioneer (as the joke goes, the one with the arrows stuck in his or her chest rather than in the back) can be all the more hair-raising in an economy such as the current one. We have to respect the macroeconomic uncertainties plaguing even the huge businesses that could afford large-scale disability initiatives. The worst of these are tricky health care and benefit policies, almost all of which are in a permanent state of flux related to the politicized mess of Social Security and universal health coverage. Hopefully in the years to come, the work disincentives will be leveled by progressive implementation of the Ticket to Work and Work Incentives Improvement Act, and by better public policy initiatives.

Doing the Math

Navigating the fog of legal obscurity, government stupidity, and corporate oblivion is tough without the beacon of reliable data. Most of the numbers on employment, income, and net worth are dated and suspect, but for now they are all we have to go on. According to the latest SIPP data, working-age people (sixteen to sixty-four) with a disability are far more likely than nondisabled to receive means-tested income (bureaucratic code for government benefits) and less likely to receive earned income from salaries and wages or asset income from investments. Once on the job, as with other minorities, there are persistent wage gaps between workers with and without disabilities. In 1994–1995, the last year for which these numbers are available, the median monthly earnings of men with no disabilities was $2,190, while men with nonsevere disabilities pulled in $1,857 and those with severe disabilities made $1,262. Women did even more poorly. While nondisabled women earned $1,470, those with nonsevere disabilities made $1,200 and with severe disabilities only $1,000. Overall, people with disabilities earned nearly 57 percent less, $779 per month, compared with $1,368 for people with no disability. By comparison with any minority group, these decade-old numbers are abysmal.

The blame is variously assigned by economists from contending schools. They are more interested in the long-term public policy debates over benefits and job stimulation than in the nitty-gritty of selling and hiring day to day. The landmark Americans with Disabilities Act (ADA) was passed and signed into law in 1990 upon assurances by its supporters that it would turn the employment debacle around. Now there are economists who (it sounds like heresy in this context) skewer the ADA, arguing that it has been ineffectual and remains unenforceable. Some of the anti-ADA voices are the usual conservative suspects who have problems with the generosity and leniency of government benefits programs. But many moderates who have studied the numbers and are struggling with the policy problems also wonder, uncomfortably, if the ADA has failed. In one of the most clearheaded essays on the economics of the unemployment problem, Mary C. Daly and Richard V. Burkhauser trace the source to Washington's bingeing on benefits and predict trouble ahead as the aging boomers incur disabilities. Burkhauser, Susanne Bruyere, and David Stapleton, are investigators at the massively productive Center for Economic Research on Employment Policy for Persons with Disabilities at Cornell, where Andrew Houtenville is head of the related statistics team, probably the most impressive place to check in on recent economic thinking on the topic. The two "income transfer" programs most to blame are Social Security Disability Insurance (SSDI) and Supplemental Security Income (SSI) benefits created in 1935 by the Social Security Act and administered to this day by the Social Security Administration. The seeds of the current downturn were sown in the eighties, when the unemployment rate among people with disabilities failed to respond to the overall boom in the American economy and federal benefits coincidentally became easier to obtain. As Burkhauser and Daly observe, the gap between job creation and the employment of people with disabilities (some of whom had worked but were now opting out and taking benefits) steadily grew, favoring the dropouts:

The trend towards rising caseloads and expenditures began in the mid-1980s. However, the pace of growth increased during the 1990s . . . The number of beneficiaries of disability transfers increased following eligibility expansion and liberalization in 1984. While benefit rolls increased slowly over the rest of the decade, employment rates also rose through the business cycle expansion of the late 1980s. It was not until the start of the 1990s, following additional easing of SSDI and SSI benefit eligibility, the passage of the ADA, and a marked slowdown in the national economy, that benefit rolls rose rapidly and employment rates fell. These trends did not reverse during the 1990s expansion.[3]

Burkhauser and Daly coolly conclude that the bungling (my adjective) efforts of the federal government in its most recent attempts to help out on the fiscal front have done more harm than good, even to the extent that the ADA looks untenable to them. Their charts clearly show that employment declined after its passage. The dominant impact of public policy leans far more toward "income transfer" (code for welfare) than toward any business stimulus to hire more people with disabilities. Lamentably, this is the precise opposite of what was meant to happen with the passage of the ADA, a law intended to reverse the tendency of public policy to equate to income transfer. The law was supposed to support companies and individuals and protect employment. Yet it is tough to argue with the numbers, which not only show the steep decline in employment against an almost symmetrical rise in benefit enrollment but point as well to the prospect for the situation to be exacerbated because of the confluence of three looming factors. As the retirement age is pushed back to sixty-seven, the relative value of both the SSDI and the SSI benefits will increase, making the package even more enticing. This converges with a spike in the percentage of the population aged fifty and over, exactly the stage at which the onset of disabilities naturally drives up the number of applications for benefits. To amplify the effect, the gap between employment rates and benefit applications is sensitive to the business cycle, so the longer the economic malaise that began in 2001 lingers, the higher the number of recipients is expected to rise against the fall in jobholders. If change does not intervene soon, this pattern threatens to lock in for generations.

The Cliff

In good times and in bad, studies by advocacy groups show that 80 percent of the unemployed people with disabilities would work if they could do so without losing their health care.[4] The "cliff," as it is known to insiders, is the limit at which one's health benefits drop off once income rises to a certain level. It is essential for employers and managers to understand this from the perspective of a person with a disability. Going over the benefits cliff is the prime worry keeping many who are qualified from seeking work. They fear losing government benefits that, over the long term, are valued far more highly (and have greater psychological weight, vis-à-vis a sense of security) than a typical salary and benefits package in a volatile economic climate. Those very benefits can make the difference between living independently in their own homes, with community-based sevices, and being warehoused in nursing homes and other institutions. The public policy dimension of this problem is considerable, and there is only so much the private sector can do to remedy it without considerable changes being made in the basic rules for SSDI. Presidential candidates since 2000 have been waving tax and other incentives in front of voters to convince them that wholesale changes in federal rules are unnecessary, but the unemployment rate refuses to budge and voters with disabilities wisely do not become excited about a thousand-dollar tax credit for work-related expenses (the Gore campaign in 2000) or Bush's New Freedom Initiative measures that apply Medicare benefits to paying for personal service assistants. By allaying the cost of transportation or nursing, these election-year initiatives, in addition to buying votes, are meant to persuade people with high costs of living that going to work can make fiscal sense. It's a typical Washington ploy, displaying inside-the-Beltway naïveté regarding the rational basis for going to work in the first place. President Clinton's "big idea" was the Ticket to Work and Work Incentives Improvement Act (TWWIIA), legislation that promised to lighten the Social Security Administration's scrutiny of those who return to work so that they could retain benefits. It failed miserably. As one banker involved in disability issues nationwide said to me on condition the quote not be attributed, "It was just another Washington boondoggle. Who needs all this stuff? Why can't they just go to work?"[5]

When someone on SSDI receiving assistance on a variety of treatment and drug plans weighs whether or not it is worth it to take a job, it is not a year-by-year calculation of what helps him or her stay ahead of the game. Giving up benefits is a long-term, big-ticket decision. The current controversy over Social Security offers a window on the angst of an even more extensive baseline of Americans when it comes to their long-term financial well-being. It should illuminate the emotions and logic that all too often deter people with disabilities from taking a job. With major economic and population trends pointing to the greater accrued value of the federal handouts, clearly many people with disabilities are opting out of the workforce.

From an economist's point of view, this points to an urgent need to rethink the eligibility requirements for benefits, because current policy is shunting people with disabilities into the categories of low-skilled, poorly educated, and inexperienced workers—the lowest in the pile. Consequently the break-even point (cliff) for eligibility stays so low. Marginal tax rates on benefits could increase and still not affect the behavior that leads to choosing them. Unlike the situation for other minorities, however, there has never been an effective initiative by which government rewarded employers with procurement contracts or direct grants-in-aid for hiring people with disabilities. While the federal government and its rules certainly play a major role in the economic welfare of people with disabilities, that role does not include policies that have helped many other minorities by giving employers who hire them preferential access to procurement contracts, capital, development funding, or other significant stimuli. For small businesses especially the prospect of incentives offers a good reason to watch Washington more closely. For now, it is important to keep an eye on the person with a disability, on his or her situation as partly determined by government policy. Practically the only government program that has had any impact in countering these trends is vocational rehabilitation, which is generally administered on the state level. Usually associated with severe disabilities, vocational rehabilitation (VR) is offered to over a million people a year, and roughly one-fifth graduate (or are "rehabilitated") to a job. Placing 200,000 people in jobs is nothing to sneeze at, of course, but the problem with focusing too closely on the cheery news from VR is largely a question of the type of jobs for which it prepares its clients. For our purposes, it is important to aim higher than menial jobs in the food and maintenance areas. As one activist said, not for attribution out of respect for the effort and frustration of the VR counselors, "I'd hate to slam them all wholesale, but it is a huge waste of money and they end up doing more harm than good."

Double Vision

Current policy and practices are costing Washington and big business dramatically more with every passing year. According to the General Accounting Office, participation by working-age people in Social Security disability programs has grown from fewer than 4 million people in 1985 to 6.6 million people in 1995 to 11 million today. The inflation-adjusted cost of cash benefits rose 66 percent, from $23 billion in 1985 to $53 billion in 1994, and then went through the roof to $87.3 billion in 2002. In addition, the cost of providing Medicare and Medicaid to these beneficiaries skyrocketed from about $48 billion in 1994, when the aggregate of health and disability benefits topped $100 billion for the first time, to $226 billion. If the Republicans stay in office, they are sure to turn their attention to the drain on public coffers and eventually cut benefits. That will slow the growth in the buying power of the community. But even before it hits corporate sales, the decline will have affected businesses. Executives have long since turned anxious about the ballooning costs associated with disability. From 1983 to 1993, disability compensation payments grew from $10.4 million to $23.4 million while compensation payments to survivors rose only slightly from $1.5 million to $1.9 million over the same period. Data after that may be unavailable, but it is not hard to extrapolate. More alarming, employers' self-insurance payments and medical and hospitalization costs tripled in the same decade.

It is not exactly an economic anomaly, but there is a symbolic disjunction between the guidelines for SSDI or SSI benefits and those for the ADA, which offers a far broader definition of what it is to be a person with a disability. The inability to decide who actually has a disability underscores the lack of understanding of the needs of the community. Those who apply for benefits go through a five-month waiting period, and are screened at both the federal and state level by medical and vocational consultants. The standards may be federally mandated, but there is a surprisingly wide variance state to state in how easy it is to score approval, with Louisiana and New Mexico about twice as difficult as Delaware, New Jersey, and Rhode Island according to recent reports.

The two programs, like Medicaid and Medicare, serve different constituencies even though they share a health-based eligibility system. The payouts are financed by a payroll tax (of 0.90 percent in 2000) paid by employees and employers on a maximum of $76,200 (in 2000, but adjusted to reflect national averages). Recipients must have worked in Social Security jobs for at least one-quarter of the period after age twenty-one up to the year of disability and for five of the preceding ten years. The benefits are allotted based on past earnings. The population that gets SSDI benefits is better off (more than twice the household income), better educated, and usually older than the average SSI recipient, who has less work experience and whose income must be less than the federal benefit rate ($512 per month or $6,144 per year in 2000) with resources less than $2,000. The maximum monthly federal SSI benefit is $512, or $769 for married couples filing jointly. That is the figure for which 7.7 million individuals are giving up their attempt to find work. Half receive SSDI, 37 percent receive SSI, and 13 percent get both. Every time the screening criteria are liberalized, the benefit rolls swell; this was true even during the boom economies of the 1980s and 1990s and definitely during the recessions. At those low monthly rates, nobody is getting rich on disability benefits.

Who is to blame? The Social Security Administration? The HMOs and insurers? Those who framed the ADA and its fuzzy mandates? The ADA is the target of many economists, including Daron Acemogulu, Josh Angrist, and Thomas Deliere. How about the liberals and the "moral hazard problems" of benefits that come with taking away the incentive to work? They are the culprits according to John Bound and Timothy Waidman, while David Autor and Mark Duggan say the choice of benefits of employment are a result of higher replacement rates for benefits and the declining economy. Anybody just want to blame the lousy economy? Edward H. Yelin, a researcher at the University of California/San Francisco, is an expert on employment trends for people with disabilities who has written dozens of academic articles (often funded by the Social Security Administration as well as arthritis research organizations) and, best of all, a hard-hitting and valuable book that is not shy about calling the unemployment situation a crisis. He thinks the answer may lie in rethinking how disability and work can go together in their own "dynamic":

Displaced from employment opportunities a little more each year, and with progressively less access to transfer payments, the well-being of persons with disabilities is gradually being eroded. The noisy politics that followed the attack on the SSDI program in 1981 ultimately served persons with disabilities far better than did the quiet politics of the last few years, for it is often easier to fight off a frontal assault than to parry an accretion of small losses. Hidden by the subtle workings of the labor market, persons with disabilities bear a disproportionate share of the costs of industrial change, and most of us never notice . . . In the long term, the plight of persons with disabilities is tied to more general trends in the economy, but much can be done in the short term to keep these persons employed by making the fit between the rhythms of disability and the rhythms of work more rational. Ironically, the decline of the manufacturing sector occurred, at least in part, because industrial-strength working conditions are no longer successful. In that sense, what was bad for General Motors was bad for all of us, but it was devastating for persons with disabilities particularly older and nonwhite ones.[6]

Another school of economists has directly questioned the numbers themselves, contending that the unemployment picture could not possibly be as bad as the federal data suggest. One collection of research essays, *The Decline*

in Employment of People with Disabilities: A Policy Puzzle, includes so many essays that argue the numbers are flawed that, rather than gather conclusions
and recommendations as most such volumes do, the editors chose to leave
the whole dispute open and submit the conflict to the reader for resolution.[7]
The particulars of the discrepancy are too esoteric to take up your time here.
The debate over definitions of "disability" and "work" alone goes on for hundreds of pages, and naturally the definitions affect outcomes of any statistical measurement. The agenda for the economists is focused on public policy
recommendations rather than on business strategies. When the editors
finally do admit that the disability community is losing ground economically, they go out on a limb and suggest policy initiatives that might help:

> Increasing the investment in the human capital of people with disabilities and re-
> ducing physical barriers seem like sensible approaches to increasing the employ-
> ment of people with disabilities and reducing their dependence on government
> benefits . . . The bottom line of this book is that the unprecedented fall in the em-
> ployment rate of working-aged people with disabilities in the 1990s was a direct
> effect of the intended consequences of public policies. To better integrate working-
> age people with disabilities into the workforce, increase their employment, and re-
> duce their dependence on SSDI and SSI will require changes in these policies that
> make providing jobs less costly for employers and the relative gains from work over
> disability income supports greater for those with disabilities.[8]

The theory is great, but nobody is holding his or her breath waiting for
Washington to make any of this happen. In the real world, where the answers need to be found for business problems involving productivity or
growth, only the notion of developing "human capital" is worth further exploration. All this points to a familiar division between public- and private-
sector responsibilities, and those in major corporations along with entrepreneurs are in good company if they find themselves baffled or put off by
regulations that effectively provide incentives for people with disabilities to
stay home. But this book is not a primer on disability and policy; it is a battle plan for business. Washington's ineptitude must be taken as a given (as
usual) so that we can move on to what the private sector can do on its own.

A Cultural Divide

In the specialized human resources field known as diversity management,
the stagnant rate of employment for people with disabilities suggests they

are out of sync with other minorities. Even though the rhetoric of corporate diversity is a perfect match for the language we use to describe the status and needs of people with disabilities, it is a rare organization even in this day that includes the term "disability" in its policies. Back in 1996, when I started *WE* magazine, we briefly tried a campaign within corporate circles, especially through the Conference Board and trade groups for advertising and computers, to amend race- and gender-specific corporate diversity statements to include disability as a cultural phenomenon. As this book headed to press in the autumn of 2005, a sixteen-page advertorial in the *New York Times Magazine* featuring the diversity efforts of a dozen companies, including the *Times* itself, used "disability" exactly once, in the section describing the Bayer Corporation (notably, a pharmaceutical company with a vested interest in staying on the right side of a major market). Everything else was race, ethnicity, and gender.

The transition in disability studies from a physical, especially medical, definition of disability to the cultural one is precisely parallel to the shift in corporate diversity thinking from race- and gender-based categories to cultural ones. That trend, which gained momentum with gay rights in the seventies, has led to a more sophisticated environment inside organizations that need to promote teamwork or at least cooperation. Under racial and gender classifications, differences in appearance and other physical characteristics were at first thrust to the foreground. Even when used as incentives for hiring or promoting, this flatly emphasized the notion that physical characteristics shape a person's identity. So does the "medical model" against which disability advocates have fought for so long, because it puts the disability before the person. Just as "people-first" language was a crucial step in disability rights, so is the recognition that a cultural view of disability is as important to diversity policymakers as their recognition that "Asian," to take one example, is not a skin color but a cultural orientation.

Less than two decades after the passage of the ADA, the assessment of whether disability is making inroads within diversity management or maturing as a market ought to be made by applying the standard of cultural recognition. Once again, the fuzzy definitions make it harder for chief executives to know what they are asked to support. As Hartman-Squire notes, the lack of a defined "lineage, group identity, or heritage" that one finds with African-Americans, for instance, works against the disability community. "Marketers and recruiters haven't yet been able to get their minds around the disability niche yet because only recently have activists and scholars identified the culture. In many instances, the disability community has not yet internalized its own identity as a culture, and consequently gives mixed messages to business, so business can't find a cookie-cutter, 'one size fits all' way to approach it. Further compounding the issue is that most people with functional limitations don't self-identify as part of the 'disability community,' so that makes it much harder to target marketing messages."[9]

The best thing that could happen to disability planning at companies that never did anything about it would be to skip the medical and political phases and get right down to identification of disability as a culture that is open for business. One of the most successful ideas in place at disability-forward corporations is the cultural affinity group for disability (as well as parents or family members of people with disabilities). As we will see in the chapter on management, this type of forum for cultural issues involving disability has proved invaluable at such corporations as Microsoft, Bank of America, SunTrust, Cingular Wireless, and Northwest Airlines.

The Trading Zone

Progress will begin when rank-and-file corporate staffers begin perceiving each person with a disability as a customer or a colleague instead of a beneficiary of charity. To achieve this, I propose the creation of a trading zone. It begins as a place inside the company where people with and without disabilities exchange information, knowledge, and cultural insight. The equation holds only with the perception of disability as a culture that can be approached (pursued, even) as a market and talent pool. Both sides of a trading zone define their territories, impose limits that secure their own comfort zones, and agree on the rules that apply in the interactive area.

Many disciplines, particularly those that boast of diversity, are divided on close inspection into subcultures. The historian of science Peter Galison wittily delineates the division of physics into theoreticians and experimenters, logic and image, who find common ground in the laboratory.[10] The trading zone for them, as in the anthropological and economic examples with which the concept began, is a focal point of coordination that does not prevent the subcultures from remaining, on a global or macro level, independent and divergent. The trading zone is an agreed-on place of translation as well as exchange that works when the relationships it hosts are symbiotic. As two groups become trading partners, the more frequently they interact the more freely they communicate, and, over time, contact yields understanding leading to mastery or fluency in each other's lingo and, essential to business, trust.

Diversity and parity are far from identical. This is not the place for a full-blown recap of affirmative action and its track record in business, in large part because it never extended to disability anyway on any substantive level. By now, even in academia, its anachronistic stronghold, affirmative action is far from a term of endearment in the diversity community. Trading zones do not in and of themselves solve the equality problem, but they do permit direct collaboration based on an agreed sense of equal value between goods and an implicit faith in the importance of some kind of continuity in trade itself that binds different groups. For the sake of preserving one of the main arguments of this book, that disability culture has its stand-alone importance (let alone its own inner diversity), it is important to emphasize the ways in which a trading zone permits the sustained autonomy of subcultures even as it allows for economic survival. Corporations are redefining their identities in terms of maximizing the meaning of what they do, enhancing their reputations in terms of accountability and adding validity as much as value. I do not want to rely on the ethical justification for adding disability to the culture, because this deflects the fiscal rationales. Economists who have studied disability have recommended, using a different metaphor, a similar concept. Yelin, for example, calls it a "safe harbor":

Systematic intervention for the individual through medical and rehabilitation services has had limited success and has been very expensive. I believe public policy can be much more effective in improving the employment situation of persons with disabilities by intervening on the other side of the template, by fostering working conditions conducive to the maintenance of work and by focusing employment efforts on those industries with the potential to expand their work forces. In effect, I am arguing for a safe harbors policy, in which public policy systematically describes the industries and workplaces that can and do hire persons with disabilities, and assists them in doing so, while fighting discrimination against such persons in firms not giving them their proportionate share of work. Some employers have taken it upon themselves to initiate a nascent version of a safe harbors policy. Called disability management, the policy is intended to reduce disability compensation premiums by preventive measures, including putting persons with disabilities into work environments in which they can thrive.[11]

Where is the trading zone? It must be in both the workplace and the marketplace. For a brief period, wild-eyed theorists of the Internet suggested that the best of all possible meeting places for workers and consumers with disabilities and their nondisabled counterparts would be the cybercommunities they created with online forums, shopping, and message boards. Removing the (largely visual) markers by which people with disabilities could be discriminated against, this utopia was meant to level the playing field. It reminded me of the caption in a *New Yorker* cartoon that showed a Labrador with his paws on the keyboard grinning in front of a monitor and making an aside to a watching puppy: "Nobody knows you're a dog on the Internet." By removing all the physical barriers to accessibility—"the drag of actually going to the office or store," as the Web evangels described it—the telecommuter and online shopper could conduct business online without ever being spotted as a person with a disability. Think of the convenience! But the isolation is not empowering. Self-identification is one of the crucial issues throughout this book. In the chapter on human resource management we will delve deeper into why some people with a disability do not care for the label. "Passing" is always an option at work, and one of the reasons the unemployment figures might be off is simply the reluctance of thousands of people, especially those with invisible disabilities (such as epilepsy), to self-identify. As Alan Muir, executive director of Career Opportunities for Students with Disabilities (COSD) and the nation's leading expert on moving college students with disabilities into the workforce, notes, "There is a great level of misunderstanding as to how difficult disclosure is. Companies want them to disclose but it can't be the 'gotcha' thing, and no serious candidate is going to wake up one day and just say 'I'll disclose.' It will take a lot of work to assure employers and candidates that self-identification is a positive thing."[12] On both sides of the trading zone, the fear factor is strong. Breaking it down will take an unprecedented level of understanding and willingness to change.

One of the great repositories of novel trends in business is the *Harvard Business Review,* which annually presents its list of breakthrough ideas concocted, with much fanfare, by its editors in conjunction with think-tank experts and management consultants from the World Economic Forum held in Davos, Switzerland, each year. One of the most intriguing ideas in the 2005 list is "a taboo on taboos" involving ideas and language that had previously been left unspoken or lost under what the linguist Steven Pinker called "the euphemism treadmill." The article explaining this idea never mentions disability, but it is not hard to see how disability could fit into the strategy of a company that is conquering its fear by talking about the world as it really is, and that is completely impossible without bringing up disability. "The challenge is to enable full and frank discussions of touchy topics without creating a hostile environment. The best place to start, perhaps, is a public acknowledgement of what is not being talked about, followed by education about what is in and out of bounds (with the emphasis on 'in')."[13]

"In" is where we are headed. The entry-level job seeker and the chief executive officer must be in on this. All the different departments of the corporation, from human resources to marketing to public relations to information technology to legal, from customer service to corporate communications, have to be in, as well as managers and supervisors. So should the nonprofit disability organizations, service providers, government policymakers, and school administrators (high schools and colleges) that prepare the workers of the future. Disability has been a taboo for too long. The ideal trading zone is a place of visibility for both the disability community and the nondisabled business partner. It is a place for handshakes, not handouts.

Notes

1. Personal interview with the author, June 2005.
2. Personal interview with the author, October 2005.
3. Richard V. Burkhauser and Mary C. Daly, "United States Disability Policy in a Changing Environment," Federal Reserve Bank, San Francisco, Working Paper 2002–21, September 2001, pp. 1–6.
4. N.O.D./Harris 2000 Survey of Americans with Disabilities.
5. Personal interview with the author, October 2005.
6. Edward H. Yelin, *Disability and the Displaced Worker* (New Brunswick, N.J.: Rutgers University Press, 1992), p. 153.
7. David C. Stapleton and Richard V. Burkhauser, editors, *The Decline in Employment of People with Disabilities: A Policy Puzzle* (Kalamazoo, Mich.: W. E. Upjohn Institute for Employment Research, 2003).
8. David C. Stapleton and Richard V. Burkhauser, "A Review of the Evidence and Its Implications for Policy Change," in *The Decline in Employment of People with Disabilities*, pp. 399–403.
9. Personal interview with the author, June 2005.
10. Peter Galison, *Image and Logic: A Material Culture of Microphysics* (Chicago: University of Chicago Press, 1997).
11. Yelin, *Disability and the Displaced Worker*, p. 155.
12. Personal interview with the author, August 2005.
13. Leigh Buchanan, "A Taboo on Taboos," from "The HBR List: Breakthrough Ideas for 2005," *Harvard Business Review*, February 2005, p. 43.

Chapter 2

Playing by the Rules

Disability for the Legal Department

And learn all you should know.
—Pete Townshend, "Amazing Journey," *The Who's Tommy*

The most urgent responsibility of business toward disability is mastery of the handful of laws governing discrimination and accommodation in the hiring process and on the job. Preeminent among them is the Americans with Disabilities Act, signed by President George H. W. Bush on July 26, 1990. Just to give the newcomer a notion of how significant that date has become in the community, it is annually marked by advocates as "independence day." But you won't find many small-business owner-managers celebrating. In their eyes, the problem has always been that the ADA was set down in broad brushstrokes, the language of legislators eager to appease as many constituencies as possible. Arguing that the costs of accommodations would be exorbitant, the surprisingly massive small-business lobby fought the bill tooth and nail on its way to the Oval Office. Some large businesses are delighted that Congress left plenty of massive exceptions, especially substantial donors to PACs such as airlines and long-distance bus companies. Those loopholes were wide enough to drive a bus through. Uncertainties regarding the law restrain hiring. The loose wording and inconsistent court decisions have left much of the business community guessing the meaning of the key phrases and terms, including "reasonable accommodation," "fitness for duty," or "job-related and consistent with business necessity." The pages that follow track the law point by point in its current interpretation, using its text, commentary by noted legal experts in the field of disability, and case studies to pin down what the ADA means today for your business. Its full text is provided in appendix C.

A few of the most common myths about the legal dimension of disability ought to be dispelled at the outset. A condition does not have to be life threatening to be a disability. It is precisely the idea of living and working with a disability, sans drama, that is vital for managers to grasp. At some point, probably a decade from now when diversity really does become inclusive, we are going to realize that there have been many more people with disabilities working among us than we thought. They are just colleagues who are reluctant to make a big deal about it and draw attention. They didn't need the ADA to get a job or move ahead, and they felt little connection to any "community."

As "passing" demonstrates, a disability need not even be visible. Sorting out what is or is not a disability is important. Temporary conditions, including a broken arm or a healthy pregnancy, are not disabilities, nor is a predisposition to illness. The ADA definition of disability is in three parts: "An 'individual with a disability' is someone who has a physical or mental impairment that substantially limits one or more major life activities, has a record of such an impairment, or is regarded as having such an impairment." The first and largest category is basically covered by the list of mental and physical disorders that limit major life activities such as walking, hearing, speaking, seeing, working, caring for oneself, lifting, standing, performing manual tasks, and, pay attention please, *learning*. The frequent causes of limits to such activities are cancer, heart disease, diabetes, hearing loss, blindness or limited vision, arthritis, speech disorders, dyslexia, ADD, ADHD, bipolar condition, HIV infection, amputation, and spinal cord injury (paraplegia is lack of leg movement, while quadriplegia refers to loss of full control of the arms and legs although many quadriplegics use their arms to a certain extent). These lists may be throwbacks to the old medical model, but they are graphic reminders of how wide-ranging the possible disabilities can be among people who might answer a want ad. The second part of the definition is more problematic, given today's medical rules and the ever widening privacy zone they give patients, while the third part is downright enigmatic. A "record of impairment" means the person had a recognized, documented disability in the past. This can be as straightforward as having been treated for cancer and still being covered by the ADA even though one has been cancer-free for years. The summer before this book went to press, the world's most watched person with a disability on the job was Supreme Court Chief Justice William H. Rehnquist. Images of him with a cane and a Nike cap walking back up the drive on his way home from the hospital were in all the papers. Rehnquist defied the vultures of the media and the partisans gunning for his retirement by gritting out the ebb and flow of his treatment to the very end. Janet Battaile, an editor in the Washington bureau of the *New York Times* and a cancer survivor, wrote a super essay celebrating Rehnquist and the "chemo kids" in Washington—Judge Edward R. Becker, Senator Arlen Specter, Justices Sandra Day O'Connor, Ruth Bader Ginsburg, and John Paul Stevens—all of whom were working proof of the productivity of Rehnquist's "just do it" mentality. As Becker told Battaile for the *Times* piece: "I was on the bench all morning. I'll be back this afternoon. The bottom line is, you can be under chemotherapy and work seven days a week. You get some fatigue. You take a nap and work through it. The last couple of years have been the most productive I've ever had in my life."[1]

Image Consciousness

Not every condition covered by the ADA inspires the same admiration. On the negative side, the most prevalent example of the comeback is fraught with moral overtones especially in the puritanical atmosphere of today's nervous corporation, and that is recovery from drug or alcohol abuse. The law cautiously makes clear the exclusion from the ADA umbrella of those who use illegal drugs or abuse alcohol. Less problematic for some in terms of morality, but still stigma ridden, is the case of the worker who has spent some months in a psychiatric hospital and is entitled to protection under the ADA. This is one of the litmus tests of the level of sophistication in disability culture. Even those who readily acknowledge the status of a wheelchair user occasionally struggle with the inclusion of mental with physical disabilities. The phrase "going postal" has entered the vernacular for the murderous backlash that, deep down, many people fear from disgruntled coworkers with mental problems. The media and movies reinforce the lethal wacko stereotype. The smartest, most successful businessman-turned-advocate I know, Alan Muir, who heads the nonprofit Career Opportunities for Students with Disabilities, sighs when the conversation turns to the problem of getting corporate America to understand pscychiatric disability. He says, "This will end up being the last bastion of stigma. Folks are starting to understand learning disability, but I am not sure we will ever get past the way traumatic brain injury or severe emotional problems cut deep to the core of the conscious and unconscious fear factors that arise if you feel you are in harm's way."[2]

For those, like Muir, who work in the field, this partition between physical and mental was long ago removed. They are decidedly in the minority, however, and the lack of progress is clear to anyone who recalls the failed vice presidential candidacy of Tom Eagleton in 1972 and sets it side by side with the stream of ADA complaints involving wrongful dismissal on psychiatric grounds. In cases comparable to Eagleton's, lingering and all-too-public medical records overshadowed careers in ways that would be actionable today. One other reason the "record of impairment" clause is important is that it protects those who have been misdiagnosed.

The whole "danger to others" problem is broadly misunderstood, especially from the legal point of view. For a variety of reasons, some of them dating to the Dark Ages, epilepsy is one of the invisible disabilities that incurs the most discrimination. More than 2 million Americans have the condition, and 80 percent of them have it under control thanks to medications such as Topamax, but that does not stop employers from invoking the "danger to others" clause in the ADA to avoid hiring them. Since seizures tend to come at night anyway, the risks are low. Every state issues driver's licenses to people with epilepsy who are seizure-free. Yet the unemployment rate for self-identified people with epilepsy is extremely high, and many prefer to "pass." It is one of the classic examples of misunderstanding hidden disability in the workplace.

The final part of the ADA definition pertains to being "regarded" as having a disability as evidenced in the attitudes of others toward the worker. This can be so broadly construed that, in the eyes of many scoffers, it strains credibility. For instance, a hair colorist who is rumored to have AIDS, even if there is no condition that impairs a life activity, *can* sue for discrimination. Congress inserted the "regarded as" (and the Supreme Court has backed it) because employers, colleagues, and society, can *make* a person disabled. As the infelicitous yet sensitive text of the bill reads, "Society's myths, fears and stereotypes about disability and disease are as handicapping as are the physical limitations that flow from actual impairments." The "regarded as" provision of the ADA comes closest to the experience of racial discrimination. The most despicable of many recent examples of its persistence was the class-action suit against Abercrombie and Fitch that alleged what any teenager working for Abercrombie, the Gap, Victoria's Secret, Old Navy, or any number of similarly culpable retail chains could tell you: if you are attractive and white, you get a sales position up front where the prospects for commissions are likely to be sweet. The winners of the suit were African-Americans, Asians, and Latinos, who won $50 million in damages in 2004. But another group should have been included. Are you obese? Do you stutter? Limp? You're in the stockroom, if you even get a job. Abercrombie and Fitch dodged the ADA implications of its violations and sweated out a brief barrage of negative press (curtailed by the obvious reluctance on the part of magazines to lose ad pages). But according to a former student of mine who is a store manager in Manhattan, the practice if not the policy with regard to people with disabilities is utterly unchanged. Any evidence of physical disability consigns you to somewhere in the back of the store, and conspicuous disability puts you behind the stockroom doors. English of Caribbean descent, and reluctant for me to use her name as she is a full-time assistant manager, she finds it hypocritical yet interesting that attractive, twentysomething African-Americans and Asians now have no problem securing the prime selling spots near the front door even as she has, under orders, relegated physically less "perfect" sales reps to distant corners (specifically, mature workers and those with disabilities).[3] Where they go in the store has everything to do with image.

Abercrombie got off easy. The collateral damage to the retail industry as a whole was minimal, so Abercrombie did not get spanked by any of the trade associations that can in other legal or ethical situations act as unofficial regulatory influences. As industries are unlikely to hold the feet of their own to the fire, this is a job for the nongovernmental monitors mentioned in chapter 1. A public report card on Abercrombie would have given the civil cases greater resonance with the general consumer and spurred improved behavior. As we shall see in the jump from the marketing to the public relations chapter, the significance of spreading the message at this early stage in the evolution of disability awareness in business cannot be underestimated.

As a media professional, I paid close attention to the "regarded as" provisions of the ADA (too often overlooked by business thinkers) because we directly dealt with the ways in which people with disabilities were publicly regarded. The question is more than skin deep. Inside a disability-conscious company, this ought to translate into a vital element of the "trading zone" in which disabled and nondisabled staffers meet. The manager who understands "regarded as" in its broader sense is clued in to the important attitude of nondisabled team members toward those with disabilities. The framers of the ADA included this difficult but essential provision because perception is a part of the workplace environment. It influences the attitudes of people on both sides of the trading zone and, more than just an atmospheric effect, can factor in such nitty-gritty decisions as who gets an assignment, a raise, a job, or a pink slip. These are the points of entry for legal problems. The "regarded as" clause in the ADA could be viewed either suspiciously or progressively, as another example of vague Washington law writing or as an invitation to reconsider the ways in which members of a work-force view one another and how to direct perception in a constructive way.

The flip side of "regarded as" is the extremely sensitive issue of "self-identification," which is not mentioned in the ADA but in current employment conversations about disability is one of the most important legal and ethical questions to be raised. After all, the advantages called for elsewhere in this book stem from identifying a worker as having a disability. Finally, and as a reminder that the ADA was the belated echo of sixties-era human rights legislation, there are protections in the law for those who associate with people with disabilities and those who fear retribution if they raise a complaint. Under Section 503(a) it is considered discrimination if a worker who has made a charge or participated in an investigation involving an ADA complaint—the equivalent of a whistle-blower—is disciplined or harassed for doing so. Companies of any size need to be prepared for a complaint with a set procedure and policy in place. Even in a small business, this is not the type of situation that can be quelled by a quiet chat behind closed doors and a call to the family attorney. This provision of the ADA makes it possible for whistle-blowers to act from within companies that drag their heels on ADA compliance.

Detecting Discrimination

The ADA has five titles or sections pertaining to different types of organization. The most important for business purposes is Title I, which prohibits discrimination by employers with fifteen or more on staff (down from twenty-five originally). Title II applies to the public sector, prohibiting discrimination by state or local government or any other "public entity." Title III is of commercial interest primarily because it mandates access to public accommodations such as restaurants, hotels, and theaters. Title IV governs telecommunications. It has mainly been of benefit to those with speech or hearing disabilities while having its impact on major carriers. A grab bag of provisions is in Title V, the most important of which offer guidelines on the recovery of legal fees and immunity against retaliation for plaintiffs.

The threat of lawsuits is the first concern of most businesses, and the bulk of the complaints involve Title I. While the pace of civil actions has diminished in the past five years as court rulings have tended to favor companies, approximately fifteen thousand cases are argued each year. Two thousand are usually settled, and only 10 percent end in judgments in favor of the plaintiffs. The scoreboard read much differently in 1990, when the passage of the bill unleashed an initial surge of successful suits. Almost as soon as they could, plaintiffs who had been waiting for the legislation to pass came out of the woodwork. Within the first five months of the ADA's enactment, 3,358 charges of discrimination were filed with the Equal Employment Opportunity Commission (which is in charge of administering the act). The largest group of cases involved wrongful dismissal (46.1 percent); roughly the same percentages were for reasonable accommodation problems (20.4 percent) and hiring discrimination (15.4 percent); and only 9 percent were about harassment in the workplace or denial of benefits (3.4 percent).

The current judicial trend is to support the employers, especially in the politically sensitive area of small business. By 2004, the courts were shooting down nine out of every ten complaints, much to the distress of activists who chewed their lower lips as the Supreme Court set the tone in a series of decisions that curtailed the expectations of future plaintiffs by trimming the ADA back to the bone.

Discrimination is categorized under seven headings, all of which share the characteristic of isolating and excluding the individual with a disability from the rest of the workforce. The first category covers situations such as prohibiting a worker from putting in overtime because of a heart condition or keeping a salesperson off the floor because she is an amputee or has a facial disfigurement. It reads: "Limiting, segregating, or classifying an applicant or employee in a way that adversely affects him or her because of a disability." The nub of course is in proving that the classification is "adverse." Whether it is on the basis of having a disability or the perception of a disability, discrimination is actionable if it "limits" or affects any of the following: job application or hiring, annual reviews or promotions, firing, layoffs and right of return from a layoff, leave of absence or sabbatical transfers, salary, fringe benefits or bonuses, training (including selection for conferences), job assignments, or any of the "terms conditions and privileges of employment." Among the latter, of interest to either the human resources or marketing departments as well, are the recruitment and advertising efforts of the company. There is a massive need for editorial revisions in the human resources postings and policies of large corporations in this country. Sometimes it is not just the text of the company manual that needs work. I've visited companies where a perfectly apt job posting (disability-friendly, on paper) is tucked way up in the corner of a bulletin board so far from wheelchair eye-level that it would take an osprey's vision to make out the words in the biggest font. Sharp companies not only see to it that this never happens. They also put notices of job openings or ADA policies on tape or in a voice mailbox, and of course the Web site should have alternative-format versions as well.

The second category of discrimination covers contracts with vendors, recruiting agencies, or other businesses that deal with yours, so that neither party in a contract can discriminate against or breach the privacy of a person with a disability. For large corporations, especially in this age of outsourcing and globalization, this is an incentive to examine the working conditions on the shop floor of the subcontractors. Often, a subcontractor's entire output is produced for one major company, the Wal-Mart, the Starbucks, or the Home Depot proprietary arrangement that gobbles up merchandise. These multinationals must realize that their buying power gives them tremendous leverage for improving workplace standards around the world. Their vast sphere of influence entails accountability with regard to the rights of the workers employed by the subcontractors, and it is important for the big corporations to include ADA-style disability provisions in the codes of conduct that they sign with subcontractors. A disability-forward organization is one that wields this power to create a culture of inclusion not only intramurally but through the satellite organizations that depend on it. Doing the right thing? Then pass it on.

The third category involves standards and policies, particularly as manifested in the writing of employee and management manuals. The company's policy on disability rights should be posted on employee bulletin boards and included in employee handbooks on personnel policy. It should be discussed in orientation briefings and training sessions. It needs to be worded carefully. While some companies have updated their human resources documents to reflect post-ADA progress, too many lack specific references to disability or fail to reexamine old provisions that are potentially violations of the law. Even if a policy appears "neutral," it could place the worker with a disability at a disadvantage. A favorite example is the requirement in many job descriptions of the forty-hour week, which can be problematic for people with certain mental conditions. In other cases, an ADA complaint can be filed if a companywide policy does not have a legitimate impact on the job tasks of the person with a disability. If social or recreational activities are sponsored by the employer, they had better be accessible and not foster a climate of hostility. Although many companies require employees to have a driver's license, why should a blind computer programmer have to comply? The ADA can be invoked in such a case.

The fourth category extends coverage to those who have a relationship or association with a person with a disability, and was included in the law because the parent of a child with huge medical bills, for example, should not be dropped from an applicant pool because of the recruiter's fear of the added burden to the company's health care coverage. While "family relationship" is clearly spelled out in the case of a spouse, child, or parent, all of which are recognized by the law, the more loosely worded "relationship or association" is a hot-button issue especially among gay employees or those who are troubled by the controversy surrounding gay civil unions and marriage. Courts seem to recognize cohabitation as a "relationship," while social "associations" such as membership in an advocacy organization would entail coverage under the law. Using these definitions, for example, a legal associate bucking for partnership at a white-shoe firm whose mother is under treatment for late-stage Parkinson's cannot be denied promotion because the other partners are worried she will be absent or distracted by her role as caregiver. Neither can the restaurant assistant manager who asks for a promotion whose live-in companion has AIDS. Both are well within recent judicial interpretations of the law's phrases. Elsewhere in this book we delve into the cultural aspect of disability, which is directly invoked by this extension of the ADA to associations. Membership in an advocacy or service organization, attendance at sports events for athletes with disabilities, and participation in the many disability community events would all be indicators of such an association in its broader sense. These may not be completely valid in the eyes of the courts, but the point is to take the ADA as a cue for a concentric expansion of disability rights in a corporation. Rather than view the association with disability as a legal point of vulnerability, it ought to be welcomed as a broadening of the corporate reach. Incidentally, the "reasonable accommodation" requirement, which we turn to next, is *not* applicable to the employee with a relationship to the person with a disability. In general, discrimination is demonstrably on the decline in the workplace. According to the latest National Organization on Disability/Harris Poll, released in 2004, 22 percent of employees with disabilities reported encountering discrimination on the job, down from 36 percent in the 2000 version of the same poll.

Hiring

The first step in the minefield of ADA compliance is the one that requires the most courage. There has been so much ballyhoo over the errors that one can make in hiring a person with a disability that many in the field of disability employment believe that this on its own has helped to keep the job rate down. Ollie Cantos, a chatty blind Philippine attorney, is the Bush administration's ambassador to big business for disability recruiting. As he says, the litigious state of affairs has immobilized many human resources managers. "In walks a person with a disability who is otherwise qualified, and immediately bells go off. If we do hire, we could be sued, and if we don't, we'll also get sued, or we'll be caught in one of those drive-by class-action suits. So let's not do anything," he warns.[4]

There is a way through the minefield. If the recruiting process focuses on the job and its needs rather than on the medical status of the applicants, most of the rest follows logically. Carefully and clearly delineated job requirements (for a receptionist, sitting for long periods, for example) that are consistent with business necessity are a good way to avoid the misunderstandings or discriminatory gestures that lead to lawsuits. The writing of the "essential functions" should include a wide range of factors such as attendance, performance measures, physical requirements, sensory requirements (peripheral vision is necessary to operate many moving machines). It is never a bad idea to include open-ended statements such as "the requirements include, but are not limited to," or "additional tasks may be assigned." The standard forty-hour week and companywide vacation and sick leave policies are within the rights of the interviewer to explain and expect, even though, as we shall soon see, flextime is a major employer technique for accommodation.

Don't Go There

A recent college graduate who has applied online for an auditing position at a major public accounting firm turns up for the interview on crutches. The interviewer is alert to the basic provisions of the ADA but a little hazy on the particulars. What can she ask or do, and what is off limits? Section 102(c)(2)(A) dictates that, unless the company is also conducing an agreed-upon preemployment medical examination, she "shall not conduct a medical examination or make inquiries of a job applicant as to whether such applicant is an individual with a disability or as to the nature or severity of such disability." That rules out a bevy of questions that in the past have been used to screen *potential* heavy users of the medical insurance programs or workers who will not be accepted by peers or pull their own weight—two myths about employees with disabilities that advocates have striven hard to put to rest. There is a long list of questions the ADA prohibits, and, just as important, these questions are also forbidden when checking an applicant's references. Among the questions:

- Do you have a health problem?
- Have you ever had surgery or been hospitalized?
- Have you ever sued a company or filed an ADA complaint?
- Do you drink alcohol or take prescription drugs?
- What kind of regular exercise do you perform?
- Will you need time off for medical treatment?
- Have you ever visited a psychiatrist or psychologist, or been treated for a mental disorder?
- Have you ever received worker's compensation or disability benefits?
- How many days of work did you miss for illness last year?

Many of these questions go against the grain of what we all know are long-established patterns in recruiting. As a former varsity hockey player for an Ivy League team, for instance, I can attest to the prominence of my continuing participation in the sport in my first corporate interviews. The problems do not just arise from what is said at the interview either. Social functions are a major part of corporate recruiting. There is not an investment bank or law firm in Manhattan that does not feature an open bar for its summer interns or associates and potential recruits, who in the evening hours quite openly demonstrate to their managers their preferences, and quaffing ability, in terms of the grape or the grain. As uncomfortable as such events may be for people in recovery from alcoholism, whose Perriers with lime often betray their anonymity, they are nothing compared with the softball and basketball games that are also a major part of company outings. In Manhattan, it is not unusual in the summer to hear the whistles and shouts of a pack of runners on a company scavenger hunt running through the avenues of midtown meant to build team spirit among new recruits. I have never seen a wheelchair racer among them.

There are limited legal exceptions to this "don't go there" zone. If an applicant has a disability that is "obvious" *and* could have an impact on his or her work, the interviewer is allowed to ask how the applicant would accomplish the job. For instance, the receptionist in the high-tempo New Haven offices of Gist, the pre-press company where my magazine's photos and design files were readied for the printer, is a below-the-elbow amputee with plenty of buttons and keys to push. In addition to her computer duties (word processing and logging and tracking hundreds of jobs on the schedule), Angela Belli operated one of those vast phone consoles that route calls from frantic editors like myself through to any one of the seventy staff members buzzing from workstation to desk to proofing room in the chaotic glass studio behind her. In her job interview, her boss (a super Yale graduate named

John Robinson, who took pride in having her on board) *would* have been well within the ADA rules had he asked her to demonstrate how she would do all this (he never did). Salesmen often have to lug their samples around, and a mobility problem might prompt an interviewer, within the law, to ask how someone who uses crutches or is a quadriplegic how he or she would manage that. There is a further caveat, however: make sure that if more than one applicant shows up, among them one with an obvious disability that turns out not to have an impact on the way that applicant would function (such as the receptionist who handled the calls with such apparent ease), the demonstration must be required not only of her but of *all* applicants for the job. This is not as far-fetched as it sounds. Many large companies use group interviews, especially in searches for internships or entry-level positions. They put teams of interviewers on the job. The group dynamic poses some thorny ADA-related questions, because one inappropriate question in this context could be liable, and privacy is all the more crucial.

Along the same lines of the responsibility for subcontractors and their policies, companies need to be aware of the threat of lawsuits to them if they use a temporary worker hired through an agency that is in turn in violation of the ADA. Although most employment agencies are up to speed on these rules, a business can be liable without being aware of the problem because the company itself is in compliance. It is fascinating as well as reassuring to note that one of the most frequently cited examples of superb disability awareness is the temp giant Manpower, which has for a decade been among the top companies to work for in America for people with disabilities. Although the awards the company has received have not been enough to ward off a few ADA suits for wrongful dismissal, on balance the company's willingness to work with vocational rehab programs and take on some of the tougher placements (severe disabilities) keeps its halo polished. In the words of Branka Minic, director of workforce development in Manpower's Miami office, "You have to bring those that are not participating in the workforce into the workforce. I'm talking about people with disabilities. We know there are millions who want to work, but are not; women coming back to workforce, young people out of school, immigrants, public assistance recipients, all these groups' unemployment is higher than normal. Manpower is interested in people with disabilities because that's our strategic position."[5]

Until now, we have focused on the straightforward hiring process. Sometimes the seemingly sure progress from a great interview to an offer to the final step of starting a job goes awry. When this involves disability, more land mines have to be avoided. Employers do have the right to make a *post-offer* medical examination a condition of hiring, but only if all applicants, regardless of disability, submit to the examination. The company can impose conditions on hiring, or even withdraw an offer, but only under specific circumstances. The company would have to show that the disability would make it impossible or unsafe for the applicant to do the job, so that it is "job-related and consistent with business necessity," or poses a threat to the health or safety of others in the workplace (a lightning rod in HIV/AIDS cases), or that the company is not able to make sufficient accommodation to enable the applicant to do the job. At this point, red flags are rising left and right, and the risk of an ADA complaint is imminent. The company cannot back out of an offer because the applicant's medical history poses a risk that benefits claims will arise or because there is "speculative risk of a future disabling problem." In the event that there is a postoffer medical exam, the results and any medical history have to be kept in a locked file and treated as confidential. The supervisor or manager can be informed about any accommodations or restrictions, just as the staff nurse or safety officer can be informed (or any government official inspecting ADA compliance), but the actual test results are not permitted to be shared with a supervisor or manager. Even in a small company, the medical and personnel files have to be kept separate. The doctor or person conducting the exam gets a job description that spells out the essential functions and can be asked if the disability limits the candidate's ability to do the job, and what accommodations are needed. The ADA is even tougher on postemployment medical examinations, which not only have to be universally administered but may only be required of a worker with a disability when an "inquiry is job-related and consistent with business necessity." The area in which these examinations are prevalent involves alcohol or drug abuse. In a different scenario, if a worker requests an accommodation, the company can require a medical examination to determine need.

Compensation

We get past the interview stage, and we are ready to consider an offer. The ADA directly prohibits discrimination in terms of compensation and benefit plans. As is still the case with women, people with disabilities earn a significant percentage less than their nondisabled peers. Various organizations have pegged that figure at between 30 and 60 percent less. This clearly indicates that some companies have exposure to ADA complaints, but, as with women, pinning down a company to a pattern of discrimination is difficult. When such a case is successfully argued, it can cost a company dearly. Morgan Stanley paid out $54 million in fines, back pay, and damages in a 2004 gender-bias class-action suit. Those companies that are unsure of whether they are in compliance should conduct payroll audits, but salary stubs are not the only way to track the gap. Figuring out compensation means taking into consideration the usual factors such as seniority, educational level, performance, and so forth. Perks count, too. Just because a person is a wheelchair user does not mean that the health club membership should not be offered. Whatever training or conferences are available to some workers must be open to those with disabilities, and they must be accessible both in terms of facilities and in terms of the format of the training materials. Off-site training, recreational, or social events have to be held in accessible venues. So does web-based training.

Some benefits weigh more heavily than others for recruits from the disability community. One of them is guaranteed under the Family and Medical Leave Act (FMLA) of 1993, which stipulates that with appropriate medical documentation, verifiable by a company physician, an employee can make a request for up to twelve weeks of unpaid leave, at the end of which the employee must be reinstated to the same or equivalent position. At that point, somewhat to the consternation of corporate legal departments, FMLA and ADA overlap, and the employer has to comply with the ADA rules for any "fitness-for-duty" medical examination upon return as well as with the rules about any need for accommodation.

The dollars-and-cents part of the ADA that bedevils many human resources professionals is health insurance. The Equal Employment Opportunity Commission (EEOC) says that the decision to hire cannot be affected by concern about the impact on the employer's health plan, and that new hires must have equal access to that plan. Disability-based insurance distinctions *are* allowed, however, if the employer's bona fide health plan already makes them.

Reasonable Accommodation

After the employee accepts the offer, the next step is accommodation. In a later chapter we'll consider all those cool architectural and design ideas that turn modes of accommodation into means of enhancing the workplace; let's concentrate here on what the law requires. When the ADA is lambasted in the press or in private, the reason often has something to do with the burden placed on a small business to build a ramp or alter bathrooms. The law requires the employer to make "reasonable accommodation" except in circumstances that would cause the business to "suffer undue hardship." Both phrases are subject to broad legal and ethical interpretations. Accommodation means different things to different people. Some see it as synonymous with *cost*. Others realize it means *change*. This poses a problem for businesses that have a set way of doing things and prefer the status quo. Some organizations are more adept at change than others. No company can afford to turn its back on higher productivity, and this—not the avoidance of lawsuits—should be the real goal of accommodation.

The most obvious legally required minimum accommodations are architectural features, such as the ramps, parking spaces, and large stalls in bathrooms that most of us now take for granted. They make facilities accessible so that the employee with a disability can perform the "essential functions of the job." Such features are required by law not only for employees but also to make public facilities accessible to customers. Reasonable accommodations must be made to workers who are hired on a temporary, part-time, or probationary basis, not just full-timers. As with enhanced productivity among the workers, the cost-benefit balancing act of accessibility for retail businesses and restaurants depends on the increased sales that access brings. The capital expenditures that accommodation and accessibility necessitate were the anti-ADA battle cry of small business during the lobbying fight before the bill was passed and when full-scale enforcement began in 1994. As disability advocates are swift to point out, the costs have been far less onerous than were predicted by anti-ADA forces, and the gains in productivity or sales have in most cases more than made up for them. According to the Department of Justice, 19 percent of accommodations cost nothing at all, and 69 percent cost less than $500.

On an individual basis, under the law, the individual with a disability must request a reasonable accommodation—no complaint is possible without such a request. The boss is not expected to diagnose an employee's condition. Instead, the boss should be paying attention to the job, the tools, and the environment in which it is done. Its essential functions are assessed, and in consultation with the individual requesting the accommodation, as well as the supervisor, the employer identifies a solution to the problem. Often there is a star performer, especially in a manual job, whose approach to the task can be assessed and used as a benchmark for trying out accommodation ideas and finding the part of the job that is most difficult. A person with a disability is often the "user-expert" who is best qualified to solve the problem in coordination with the company. All this should be carefully documented in a paper trail that includes the reasons for denying a preferred accommodation, such as whether it poses problems for other employees or customers. Sometimes the solution is equipment or design alteration, but often it involves scheduling or changing the routine. The current thinking among policymakers has shifted from architectural accessibility to innovative scheduling, reflecting the significance of the shift from physical to mental disabilities. As Roy Grizzard, assistant secretary of the Bureau of Labor's Office of Disability Employment Policy, points out: "It's important for the employer to be flexible and to think outside that old nine-to-five box. If Joe and Sam don't want to quit but can't put in forty hours a week anymore, why don't we put them together to do one job?"[6]

The company is permitted to determine whether the cost of the accommodation, which need not be state-of-the-art equipment as long as it is effective, would impose an "undue hardship." Size matters, of course. Small businesses have a good deal more leeway in this area than big corporations. The law states that an accommodation may be too costly, or disruptive, if it imposes an undue burden on the financial resources of the employer. The final arbiter of this is the EEOC, which investigates and rules on cases when complaints are filed. The law adds that in the case of small businesses with limited resources a compromise can be reached, with the employee chipping in to cover part of the cost of expensive equipment (covering $1,000 of a $5,000 computer bill, for instance).

Although figuring "undue hardship" may look like a typical David and Goliath situation, where major corporations have to comply and small businesses can often get off the hook, one of the factors involved is also the type of business. This aspect of the law changed rapidly as computers became a more pervasive part of the job, even in "low-tech" industries like construction. Small software and computer-design firms are at one end of the spectrum. They have a tremendous capacity to retrofit workstations to make them veritable wonders of accessibility, an in-house advantage over, for instance, a car maintenance shop that has been running on the same computer for a decade (the other end of the spectrum).

Some regulatory relief was promised to the small-business lobbyists as the ADA was marked up on its way to the 1990 vote. Under Section 44 of the IRS Code, a concern with under $1 million in gross receipts or fewer than thirty full-time employees is eligible for the Disabled Access Credit (DAC). That can mean as much as $5,000 a year in tax credits for expenses incurred in making the company ADA-compliant, up to $15,000. Many firms use the DAC not only for hardware (new equipment or architectural modifications) but for services, such as sign language interpreters or readers for those who are blind. There are other ways to take the sting out of compliance financially, such as applying to health insurance companies to cover the cost of assistive technology, or to state or other nonprofit sources for assistance to buy equipment, or to vendors for discounts. It is not uncommon for a person to take some of the equipment he or she used on another job or at home along to the new job, such as a telecommunication device for the deaf (TDD), a customized phone or software for the computer. As the ADA implies, the impact on a business is not always fiscal. If the accommodation upsets the way work is done, or has an effect on the work of others, this is part of the "hardship" that needs to be addressed. Jealousy about preferred parking and other morale problems don't count, but in a team situation a shift in schedule could put too much of a burden on the others.

Supported Employment

One extreme form of accommodation is a controversial measure known as "supported employment." This poses a special set of legal circumstances. The wide range of so-called mental disabilities still presents a frontier for employment, addressed by "supported employment" situations that provide menial jobs for thousands of workers with McDonald's (the McJobs Program), Wal-Mart, Home Depot, Marriott (through a foundation dedicated completely to people with disabilities), Kentucky Fried Chicken (Project Pride), Boeing, and other major corporations. These are high-profile programs that get mixed reviews from advocates, who view them as merely a slight upgrade from the old "sheltered employment nightmare." The problem is not just that the jobs don't pay well. They operate in a parallel economic universe, usually less competitive and more closely tied to government agencies, philanthropic organizations, and rehab or health care providers. On the positive side, it is undeniable that such programs pave the way not only to independent living (getting those employed off the SSDI rolls) but to fulfillment, although they tend to distort the disability picture for those outside the community by presenting low expectations and high self-congratulations. Supported employment usually helps those who are developmentally disabled, mentally ill, or have had a traumatic brain injury. It starts with a vocational rehabilitation therapist working for the state, who focuses on skills and past experience and tries to outfit the worker for a particular job. The agency follows the worker to the Wal-Mart and coaches all day long, beyond the typical on-the-job training that all new hires get. The "follow-along" support can last months, and is a means to ensure the employer of quality control as well as the minimization of any risks attending the hire. One of the most important aspects of having the coach on site is the opportunity this provides to instruct coworkers in interacting with a person with a disability. It is training for the rookies in disability etiquette and thinking, and a (taxpayer-funded, thank you) means of providing a personal guarantor of the trading zone we have been trying to establish between the disabled and nondisabled sectors of the company. The communication problems posed by workers with mental retardation or head trauma, to take two common examples, can be formidable.

Not all of the mental disabilities require supported employment, to be sure. Among the developmental disabilities are not only retardation and Down syndrome (which can cause retardation) but a variety of other conditions that simply cause someone to learn more slowly than average. Such conditions are more complicated from a work standpoint than the far more common bipolar, panic, or obsessive-compulsive disorders, which affect about one in five adults. Obviously this is where privacy concerns have skewed the job statistics, as most workers are cautious about disclosure. As a manager, it is important to realize that most of the slower learning or mastering of tasks involves the way a person processes information. The accommodations mandated by the ADA assist in concentration, screening out distractions in the environment, tempering criticism and negative feedback, managing schedules and deadlines so that stamina and the side effects of medications can be under control, and carefully monitoring what has come to be known, in this productivity-centered era, as multitasking. The next gradation along this spectrum is the category of learning disabilities, which are estimated to affect 15 percent of the workforce. Such employees struggle in basic skills (reading, writing, math), and the accommodations they require are usually geared to tailoring the job requirements to meet their abilities. Not surprisingly, on their own they are unlikely to file ADA complaints, and advocates are generally so bent on finding them jobs that they are unlikely to initiate class-action suits to protect their rights.

Disabled on the Job

As experts in the field point out, work itself often causes disability. Historically this often meant gruesome tales of industrial injuries, but the recent toll is, if less bloody, then more widespread. One type of unexpected fallout from the Internet explosion was a trail of casualties left by keyboard and mouse designs that required hands and wrists to expend more motion daily than they normally do in a month. Last year alone, 250,000 repetitive stress disorder (RSD) cases were diagnosed, mainly involving computer use, which now accounts for 70 percent of occupational injuries, and the estimated cost to business has been conservatively figured at $20 billion. Setting aside the health-care-policy problems posed by RSD in recent years, this has become one of the most scrutinized testing grounds for a new breed of ADA cases. On the one hand, because so many people have RSD (as many as 10 million), its status as a disability is not as hard a sell anymore among skeptics, who are now more likely to have experienced it or to know someone who has. One could even argue that RSD has helped broaden awareness of disability in general. Educated and otherwise indifferent young professionals incur their injuries on the job and then face the need to alter their habits or redesign their computers to stave off further aggravation and lost productivity. On the other hand, the epidemic proportions of RSD have, in the eyes of some, sapped corporate resources that would otherwise go into disability initiatives benefiting other groups, and have diluted the sense of what constitutes a disability.

Along with RSD, the boomers are the other big story in ADA circles. With the retirement age receding further into the high sixties, and with retirees whose pensions were blown on multimillion-dollar accounting scandals coming back out of retirement, the prospects for employees becoming disabled during their career are far more likely. Companies that have invested time and money in training an employee should consider ways to get that employee back on the job as soon as possible after an injury. Although the ADA is silent on the specifics, it is not a bad idea for companies to have a set policy for return-to-work situations. Many ease the transition through telecommuting or part-time duties. Retaining good workers after they incur a disability is an important part of the company's policy on inclusion.

Disability is not static. At hiring, a condition may be at a certain stage and then either diminish (for instance cancer) or grow more severe (HIV becoming AIDS, arthritis growing worse, vision loss, the way ALS or MS can kick in at a certain age). The ADA applies at every stage. This is more of a problem for the supervisor, who follows with accommodations as the ability to do a job changes. Many encourage the employee to include company doctors and nurses in the medical care, although privacy rules are complex on this issue. The test is whether the medical measures are "job-related."

Unions

Going to bat for workers who are victims of discrimination used to be a job for unions, but the disability community and organized labor have historically been ill at ease with one another. Some would say the community scarcely needs unions, which have rapidly become pale shadows of their former selves, particularly in the wake of crushing political defeats. They still represent about 24 percent of the manufacturing workforce and 12.5 percent of workers overall. The main intersection between the community and the unions is the Industry-Labor Council on Employment and Disability, which represents more than 140 corporations and 400,000 workers.

What collective bargaining agreements often call for is not always in sync with disability rights. The ADA has been in conflict with certain contracts of the nineties particularly, which later had to be amended. Some companies follow the easier path of the collective bargaining agreements and try to avoid accommodations. One of the best studies of this split is Susanne M. Bruyere's article "The Implication of the ADA for Labor Relations, Collective Bargaining, and Contract Administration."[7] Its brief history of unions and disability focuses on one particular issue: Seniority is sacred to unions, and the kind of flextime schedule or "light duty" that may seem a reasonable accommodation is not easily handed to one union member who has less seniority than another. Nor is the spirit of assistance as alive as one might suspect, so that additional duties assigned to one coworker to accommodate another might be problematic. Going around the union to work out accommodations directly with the employee could violate both the employer's pact with the National Labor Relations Act (NLRA) and the worker's status in the union. But then we have the old confidentiality problem—who knows what medical questions could arise in such a meeting?

What is the best option for enforcing ADA provisions in such cases? Some suggest a committee of management and union representatives just for ADA situations, such as health and workers' compensation cases, and requests for accommodations. This is analogous to the on-site or intramural organizations that play a major role in the coming chapter on management. While one aspect of the agenda of such organizations is sure to be ensuring compliance with the law, their broader mission is cultural. As we are about to see, the ADA is only the start.

Agenda

- *Know the law* and its current interpretations.
- *Review, audit, and revise company policies and personnel actions* to go beyond ADA compliance.
- *Maintain a paper trail* of every company action on disability and accommodation.

- *Keep up with court decisions* on ADA cases not only in your industry but in general.
- *Don't forget that the policies and actions of subcontractors and temporary agencies* you use are your responsibility.
- *Regularly convene a standing committee* on accommodations and ADA compliance.

Notes

1. Janet Bataille, "Very Much Alive, Thank You," *New York Times,* July 17, 2005, Week in Review, p. 3.
2. Personal interview, August 2005.
3. Personal interview, September 2005.
4. Personal interview, August 2005.
5. Personal interview, October 2005.
6. Personal interview, August 2005.
7. *Journal of Rehabilitation Administration,* special issue, *Americans with Disabilities Act and Employment: Does It Work?* vol. 17, no. 3, August 1993, p. 123.

Chapter 3

The Way In

Human Resources

There's more at the door.
Pete Townshend, "Welcome," *The Who's Tommy*

The gatekeepers to a disability-forward corporation are a new corps of human resources professionals who know the ropes when it comes to recruiting from the community. The expertise required extends well beyond the "don't go there" mentality of the ADA rules we just covered, that paralyzing temerity which has dominated human resources (HR) for nearly two decades and done so much damage to the job prospects of people with disabilities. Rather than legal and social taboos, the HR expert keeps up with a constantly advancing set of cultural guidelines and fresh ideas to boost the company's presence in the community and nab the most productive and loyal employees. For those who are adept at surfing corporate trends to advance their own recognition inside the hierarchy, disability is a godsend. It is at the evolutionary stage where race and gender were in the seventies. This could be a career maker for a junior HR executive who is sharp enough to zero in on what will be the next significant phase in the diversity saga. Many of the most prominent figures in HR built their reputations on success in attracting talent from the African-American, Latino, gay and lesbian, or mature communities, including Ted Childs at IBM, Renaldo Jensen at Ford, J. Frederick Candy at Pepsi, and Mylene Padolina at Microsoft. There is an empty place in the long HR hall of fame for the portrait of the first executive to elevate disability to this level.

The time is ripe. All the experts agree that the prospects are there, and so is the demand. Bringing them together continues to be the problem. Economists expect that the pace of retirements will create 10 million openings in the United States in the next five years. Diversity hiring will fill the usual 20 percent of those openings, but the pace at which jobs are expected to be added will tap out the usual sources, including the most rapidly growing ones (Latino and Asian). The hue and cry in the media and on the floor of Congress over outsourcing will exert three intimidating pistons of pressure on companies to hire at home: regulatory, shareholder, and consumer. The onus on HR will be to uncover a reliable domestic talent pool. Some of the *Fortune 500* have already started to look in the direction of disability, but they got lost. The often-lamented scarcity of qualified applicants is an excuse used by many as a way out of posting better numbers in this area. Lack of jobs is the symmetric excuse heard among recent graduates who grumble about not being placed. If this script sounds familiar, then you must know your diversity history, because the same complaints were heard especially about women three decades ago. For those in the lead (we will consider a few of the success stories in the pages that follow) the best results are gained by focused recruiting campaigns, just like the ones launched in the seventies to bolster the percentages of women, African-Americans, gays, and, later, Latinos and Asians. The proven methods use outreach, internships, mentoring, sponsorships, and community initiatives that court younger workers with disabilities. There is also good news at the other end of the career arc, as many companies have recognized the value of older employees who return to work after incurring a disability. These constituencies bring along their own bonus, by the way. Instead of nervously wondering how to behave when they turn up looking for a job, make the logical leap between the jobs you offer them and increased sales, and you will have grasped the end point of this process.

Where do you start? The most successful corporations go to the sources. IBM, Microsoft, SunTrust, and the Bank of America, among other companies, find candidates at the employment fairs where the entire pool is composed of entry-level applicants with disabilities. The best attended of these are sponsored annually by Gallaudet University, the National Technical Institute for the Deaf, the Job Accommodation Network, the Office of Disability Employment Policy of the U.S. Department of Labor, and, on more modest scales, the career services offices of universities, such as the University of Minnesota and the University of California system, that are stronger in the disability area than others. While most of the public universities have one type of token disability services presence or another, and among the privates it is hit or miss, not all colleges are created equal in this regard. My own is hopeless, for instance, despite its midtown Manhattan location, business orientation, and overblown claims to being "the most diverse college in the nation." One important sign of competence is the presence of disability in the curriculum and among the student activities, in the form of disability studies programs (although not usually available as a major), clubs, and administrative services. As with any other minority, the best talent is attracted to a college that has a proven commitment to its needs, and such a campus in turn produces the highest-quality job candidates. There is a much greater chance of finding an outstanding graduate with a disability at Berkeley or the University of Illinois at Urbana/Champaign than at Yale. Another straight-shot source is the local vocational rehabilitation office. These are run by the state, and some are steadily improving in terms of offering up-to-date skills training for, admittedly, mostly lower-level positions. Standard employment and temp agencies are problematic. Unlike race and gender, disability is not a category that can be requested or spoken of, owing to the ADA guidelines. Until it joins race, homosexuality, and other cultural "markers" embraced by the key word "diversity," it will be next to impossible for the massive online job services to have any impact in this area. Most corporations and placement agencies use nonprofits as a way around this. When candidates come from, for example, the Office of Disability Policy's (ODEP) Workforce Recruitment Program (WRP), Employer Assistance and Recruiting Network (EARN), or COSD, it is clear to the recruiter that they have a disability even if they can't say so directly and the company can't ask. Online résumé submission is bounced through the nonprofit to, say, the IBM human resources department, where it can be coded, legally, for diversity based on the intermediate source.

Some companies arise again and again in the conversation on disability and employment. Among the strongest are those in the tech, telecommunications, and banking sectors, partly because they have all the tools to make knowledge-focused jobs accessible, and more significantly because they long ago discovered the profits that accrue from recognition in the community. Disability and technology go way back, and when you talk about history it is inevitable you will arrive at Big Blue. According to company annals, IBM hired its first employee with a disability in 1914. Four decades ago it invented remote controlled-keyboards and voice-activation tools, and has been churning out assistive technology products since. Today it is considered one of the most aggressive recruiters in the community, thanks in large part to the outspoken Ted Childs, vice president of Global Workforce Diversity with worldwide responsibility for workforce diversity programs and policies. A high-level HR executive at a monster corporation like IBM was exactly what the community needed in the alarming nineties, when the employment-trend lines started to plummet after the passage of the ADA. In turn, I would respectfully suggest that disability was exactly what permitted Childs to complete the spectrum of cultural diversity that has distinguished his own career, which is recognized nationally by the HR profession as its equivalent of what Warren Buffett is to finance or Steve Jobs is to marketing (it is a constant complaint in HR that the stars are not nearly as recognized within the company or in the press as their counterparts in other departments). Childs had already made his mark in the African-American community. During an eighteen-month service leave from IBM from 1982 to 1983, he served as executive assistant to Dr. Benjamin L. Hooks, head of the NAACP. He won the coveted *Working Woman* citations for his efforts in advancing the cause of women at IBM. Disability is the capstone of his run. He has won just about every award and honorary degree an HR executive can be nominated for, including the top-employer citations of the disability media and nonprofit service organizations. All this is publicity and trade gossip. Inside the walls of IBM, where it counts, he has had the ear of chairmen Lou Gerstner and Samuel J. Palmisano as well as the board, which he briefs annually on his disability progress. In other words, he has the clout to elevate disability to strategic heights it does not attain in other major companies. And, much to his credit, he has used it. Just since 1999 IBM has spent $3.6 million on accommodation, including state-of-the art architectural and technological IT upgrades on fifty buildings worldwide. According to a recent company survey, about 6,580 IBM employees, or 2 percent of the workforce of 329,001, are self-identified persons with a disability. Even more impressively, 47 percent are in what the company calls "core" positions, including engineering (electrical, mechanical, industrial, and software), information systems and information technology support, business administration, technology development, marketing, and sales. Most companies waffle when asked point blank how many people with disabilities are on the payroll, but IBM is openly proud of its efforts.

When I ran *WE* magazine and we named the Top 10 Companies each year, Childs and Millie DesBiens, his media-savvy assistant, made sure we were aware, several times a year, of all that IBM was doing in the recruiting area. They had done more than enough to earn the number one spot two years in a row (he was vocally disappointed the year IBM was bumped to number two by Microsoft). Curious about how his programs worked on the inside, at his invitation I attended a two-day company summit at the eerily ascetic Palisades Executive Conference Center up the Hudson River from

Manhattan, where IBM holds many of its training sessions. All the management players in IBM's disability effort, both HR and sales, would be there, and even though I was identified as press this was not a media show but a working meeting on how HR, engineering, management, and sales would work together in a global "action plan." The agenda began with pep-rally speeches from honchos. Then it was time for a panel on "best practices" that included presentations from a senior White House policy adviser as well as the Royal Bank. There were proprietary briefings on the gee-whiz accessibility tools and information technology coming out of the amazing lab in Austin, Texas, where IBM develops its disability products (unnecessarily closed to me, because the briefings would have been incomprehensible anyway). Much of the two days was spent on country reports on staffing (Japan, Australia, Canada, Latin America, South Africa), but the most revelatory part of the two days was probably the seamless segue from HR into design and marketing strategy sessions. From the first minute it was clear that HR, product development, and marketing were singing a trio in close harmony. It was also obvious that Childs was putting the pressure on the HR managers to raise the ante: "I have a challenge for you," he excitedly told the executives at the first session of the conference. "We don't know exactly how many of our people have disabilities. I would like to double the number we do know before the next meeting. We're going to put our best thinkers on this case."[1] I was briefly tempted to pipe up and suggest that, with all those IBMers swirling their computer mice forty hours a week, carpal tunnel alone would probably take care of that increase, but I kept my mouth shut.

Among those "best thinkers" is Jim Sinocchi, cochair of IBM's People with Disabilities Global Executive Diversity Task Force. He was a major presence at the conference, and his is the name you are most likely to encounter when you Google "IBM and disability." A wheelchair user, he works in the press office, which prompts me to leap ahead a space or two and alert you to the chain of HR, marketing, and public relations in the company's disability strategy. As Sinocchi says, "You hire people with a disability for the same reason you hire anybody else—because they have the skills and talent to get the job done. Do you want to miss out on hiring a talented employee just because she uses a wheelchair, or because she walks a little differently, or because she can't hear?" In addition to writing releases and being IBM's most visible employee with a disability, Sinocchi heads in-house recruiting programs such as Project Able for computer professionals, and Lift and Entry Point for students. It seems as if all major corporations have to apply catchy names to outreach efforts, just as the White House labels military operations with goofy names, but they have garnered results. Entry

Point collaborates with the American Association for the Advancement of Science to place students with disabilities in industry jobs. Project Able started in 1999 to help those who had already begun their careers in IT to move upward. Between those two, IBM has hired more than 350 interns and full-timers, a very strong showing.

Out with the Old

What IBM gets and most other companies do not is the manifold value of aggressively adding disability to diversity policies. As with other minorities, most recently the "mature" group (over forty), the transition from politely avoiding the topic to ardently bringing it up is best accomplished when outdated and harmful assumptions are laid to rest. The worst of these linked disability and inability, or lack of qualifications, a common misperception of all minorities in the prediversity days. Gradually, with increased visibility of organizations such as COSD, and the United States Business Leadership Network (USBLN), corporate America is learning to dissociate disability from a presumed lack of experience, education, or training. Statistically, most job seekers with disabilities, even those who have been in the unemployment ranks, did hold jobs. The majority, 70 percent, incurred their disability during their working years, so that the once prevalent notion that people with disabilities do not know what it means to put in a full day's work is not only a disservice but rubbish. It has taken time, and a series of widely publicized NOD/Harris Polls, but the canard that people with disabilities don't want to work is also gradually fading. It is occasionally revived by the obsessive efforts of media blowhards like John Stossel who latch onto egregious cases of the exploitation of the benefit system and play them to the hilt. One of the toughest prejudices to break down is the persistent suspicion that a person in recovery from alcohol or drug abuse is not really a person with a disability. Taking this a notch lower, there are still many who regard AIDS, despite what the Supreme Court says, not only as a "fake" disability but as a threat to fellow workers. Along those lines, one of the stereotypes that workers with disabilities have always had to battle is the notion that the office environment is somehow less safe thanks to them, or that they pose a medical or safety hazard. While these myths hang on, there is still work to be done on the educational side by HR professionals.

The basic literature on hiring people with disabilities is straightforward and little changed since the passage of the ADA in 1990. Most of the HR rule books available inside corporations or through trade associations offer a sober take on the privacy and antidiscrimination provisions of the law. The caveats have been in place for nearly two decades, so HR interviewers are by now familiar with the constraints that the ADA stipulates, particularly the proscription against asking directly about a disability or medical condition. Companies that have moved to more advanced thinking on disability have, instead, addressed the mind-set of the interviewer. In addition to the assumption that people with disabilities are incapable of handling certain jobs, there is a tendency among many who have no experience in this area to assume that the company might not have any jobs that would be right for a person with a disability. The trouble with this prejudice is simply that, first, it ignores the fact that a job is a job, and then it categorizes the interviewee as someone who needs to be put into a "special" spot. It would be impossible to instruct interviewers not to be judgmental—their job is in part a moment-by-moment string of judgments that must be made quickly—but these should not be *medical* judgments, especially as there are few recruiters who have graduated from Harvard Medical School and would be able to make them. Along these lines, the Department of Labor's Office of Disability Employment Programs recommends that nondisabled interviewers keep a lid on their imaginations and emotions, including the tendency to indulge in amateur medical diagnoses or psychotherapy when meeting a person with an unknown but apparent disability. As compassionate as these suppositions might seem, they pull the focus away from the skills and capabilities of the interviewee and focus on the medical condition. The ODEP checklist also warns: "Don't speculate or try to imagine how you would perform a specific job if you had the applicant's disability."

People who are unused to disability tend to get hung up on the little "miracles" of everyday life—the sort of thing that used to sell vaudeville tickets in Helen Keller's day, when people would pay to watch her take her tea. These are humdrum details to people with disabilities, who are just eager to be hired because their computer skills or natural salesmanship qualifies them for the job, not because the human resources department wants to see if they can drive to work. A more valid concern turns on the company itself: Are we really as accessible as we say we are? Or will our setup make it harder for this person to do his or her job, and advance in his or her career?

Recruiting begins even before a position opens. Web sites and printed materials that offer job postings should be in alternative formats that are accessible, and efforts should be made to link or forward them to service sites with disability constituencies. Employers big and small ought to develop a rapport with the local disability organizations, NGOs, training programs, and government offices where employment counseling is offered. Most universities now have a well-staffed office of disability services, dedicated in part to adjudicating requests for note takers or extra time on exams, and with the building awareness of COSD there are increased linkages with career placement offices. Even the U.S. Chamber of Commerce has some wonderful programs and resources, under the leadership of Tom Donohue and workforce development staffer Cathy Healy, who also serves on the USBLN board of directors. These would also be perfect prospects for liaisons to corporate recruiters who could rely on the campus connection to identify hot prospects. Along with internships and other on-campus recruiting efforts, the more contact recruiters have with the disability community on the college level, the more likely the pipeline will have started to flow once the positions are open. Along these lines, major corporations ought to know where the best students with disabilities tend to go to school, because, as with most minorities, certain colleges attract the best and brightest because they in turn have built an identity for being more disability-friendly. While Gallaudet may be the Grambling of deafness, and the Perkins School for the Blind the Wellesley of blind students, other disabilities have their favorite campuses. History favors the strong track record of the University of California system for liberal arts majors who are wheelchair users or have other physical disabilities, and the Georgia Institute of Technology along with the Rochester Institute of Technology are famous for attracting top-notch computer geeks, while the University of Minnesota, renowned for its disability consciousness, is probably the best source for candidates with the all-round humanities background many recruiters seek.

Nor should recruiting be confined to the usual college campus cattle call. One of the most solid ways to make sure people with disabilities are involved in a company is through executive search firms, who should be directed to nonprofits, ODEP, EARN, or COSD as a way to legally ensure that candidates with disabilities will be included in any diverse applicant group. Another way is to make sure subcontractors employ people with disabilities— many multinationals set the standards for their subcontractors when it comes to whom they hire, for how much, and under what conditions.

The best practices of IBM, Microsoft, SunTrust, Cingular Wireless, and a select handful of others aside, it is no exaggeration to say that the efforts to place people with disabilities at major corporations have so far been a failure. The often desperate efforts of government and nonprofits to remedy the employment gap have cycled through well-intended initiatives, programs, and theories at an exhausting pace since the relative success of returning injured veterans from World War II raised public consciousness of the issue.

For patriotic reasons, companies were more likely to hire them than they are people with disabilities today. There is no point in rehashing the history of one fruitless theory after another. Instead, let's look ahead to the tip of a private-sector agenda pointed toward the future for a new generation of qualified candidates.

Think Different

The experts who broker the jobs are surprisingly bullish. Some of them are for-profit headhunters or HR consultants in the game for the fees as well as the social good. Others are with NGOs targeted at disability and business, the best of which are staffed as well as supported by involved pragmatists with corporate track records. This means they have the expertise to make the fiscal case for hiring their candidates, and the contacts that make it happen. They dash back and forth between the HR leadership of Fortune 500 companies and a core group of college placement offices. The message they carry is one of encouragement, despite the historic trend lines. Unlike the bureaucrats who have blown smoke at this problem for years, the new breed of advocate-entrepreneurs have a focused view of the job market and career trends. Although the electricity bills for their modest offices are often covered by grants from the ubiquitous ODEP, they have few kind words for either federal or state officials. (When one of the prospects they are cultivating lands a public-sector position, they alter that tune, especially if the job is on the management ladder). Accustomed to viewing the government as the employer (or customer) of the last resort in a "real" capitalist economy, they consider the jobs that count to be fast-track positions with major corporations. Even small businesses, including the many disability-specific entrepreneurs who tend to hire within the community, lack the validity and cachet of a Merrill Lynch or Procter & Gamble (number one and two on *DiversityInc*'s 2005 Top 10 companies that hire people with disabilities). The minimum-wage "transition" of vocational rehabilitation "graduates" is not for them, either, even if that phenomenon posts greater numbers overall and reflects a historically more accurate reality than their ambitions allow. These disability employment specialists, the sharpest of whom combine professional experience in high-stakes commerce and national advocacy, are determined to see a top-down breakthrough in the employment picture, led by the white-collar prospects of college graduates with disabilities. The rationale for their high expectations is worth pondering.

I joined the movers and shakers in the disability employment field in the summer of 2005 at a two-day annual conference of the nonprofit Career Opportunities for Students with Disabilities (COSD) that laid out cutting-edge strategies for matching companies and college graduates. The setting could not have been more "medical model," even if the agenda was pure disability culture. We gathered behind the glass facade of the immaculate, high-modernist headquarters of Merck's worldwide research division in the heart of Boston's Longwood medical district. During coffee and lunch breaks we could see legions of white-coated doctors and researchers out on the sidewalks, baking in the July heat as they swarmed Harvard Medical School and a dozen area hospitals. Inside, the high point for the nearly two hundred diversity consultants, corporate recruiters, government bureaucrats, and counselors from colleges across the nation was a raucous keynote delivered by Temple Grandin, an industrial designer with severe autism. One of the stars of the disability pantheon, she is internationally famous for designing the slaughterhouses in which millions of cows are turned into Big Macs each day. Grandin's virtuosic performance was the perfect précis of the whole conference and the broader effort it represented—upbeat and wide-ranging, a success story and a harangue, alternately clear as day and contradictory as anything. She was boasting about her latest project, retooling the notorious Denver Airport, a budgetary rat hole down which $500 million had already been poured for the privilege of now-legendary tales of flying Tumi suitcases thanks to faulty bar code programming. A blazing antiestablishment triumph in and of herself, she echoed the Bill Cosby–esque sentiments of many other speakers at the affair, urging students with disabilities on to a greater sense of responsibility and economic self-reliance. Some of the pills were bitter indeed. The hosts from Merck winced as Grandin teed off on the high costs of prescription drugs, but the crowd was eating it up. She swaggered like a ranch hand back and forth onstage in her boots, denim shirt, jeans, and big silver belt buckle, waving casually to a set of PowerPoint slides that basically had little to do with the crablike scuttle of her highly opinionated meditation on getting jobs, the importance of pharmacology (take that, Tom Cruise!), thinking in pictures, the merits of the *Wall Street Journal,* and the imperative of restoring etiquette (not to mention spirituality) to society. Another audience might have found the non sequiturs trying, but this choir laughed on cue. Some of the screed was in code. The "Aspergers" were not a sitcom family but people with the high-functioning type of autism that affects an estimated one million people in the United States. Grandin counseled the counselors, "Don't get too hung up on labels. Brains have problems . . . They get through college, but they're not getting jobs. They're majoring in the wrong things. We need to build up the talent in things they are good at and get them jobs."

That hit the bull's-eye. Having arrived expecting more bad news and excuses, I had already been pleasantly surprised to hear from one corporate recruiter after another (Merrill, Lockheed Martin, Microsoft, Procter & Gamble, NASA were all there in force) that openings were readily available. "We have the jobs. Where are the candidates?" asked Microsoft's Mylene Padolina, senior diversity consultant, echoing her corporate counterparts. Every recruiter had unfilled openings and had arrived in Boston hoping to narrow the chase for the qualified college graduates with a disability down to viable candidates through the intermediaries in the room. The fickle finger of blame was drifting away from big business and toward the schools, with a hint of impatience about the students themselves. The missing graduates seemed to be lost between the campus service offices that get them across the stage at graduation and the career placement offices that are supposed to get them in the door at corporations. The disability services counselors and career placement officers needed coordination. Moreover, participants argued, the shots ought to be called by a disability-forward career placement officer rather than a coddling disability service counselor. Progress depends on results, despite cross-campus politics. Conferences of this sort are always elaborate exercises in networking, but the thesis about putting career placement first was adding new urgency to that custom.

Meanwhile onstage, Grandin, who had been kicked out of most of the schools she attended for beating up kids or otherwise acting out, was all for a subversive approach: "Never mind the interview process. That's for the talkers. We have to get through the back door. Sell your work, not your personality." She had scored her first major commission, a Swift slaughterhouse, by presenting her portfolio to the wife of an insurance agent who worked with the company. Then she had turned the inward focus of autism into a weapon of stunning efficiency to make herself unique in a competitive field, the solo practitioner to whom the whole corporate world goes when the job is too big and complex for the others. And she was funny about it, too. A number of project managers were present from NASA, which had scheduled another meeting in town to coincide with the conference. NASA has for the past two decades enjoyed a stunning reputation in disability circles for internships and career advancement. Grandin, who had just noted that Albert Einstein and Carl Sagan would have been diagnosed as autistic in our time, gave a couple of the NASA managers up front a grin and delivered a great line: "I hope the folks from NASA won't mind if I call it the world's largest sheltered workshop for the socially challenged." The jibe was greeted with knowing laughter. Placement counselors from colleges around the country were furiously taking notes.

This breath of fresh air was needed. Many of the people in the auditorium were spending their working days (and weekends) worried about what is to be done *with, to, by,* and *for* their "clients." This is the blameless but incapacitating fault of the disability services mentality, derived as it is from nursing and caregiving. Grandin was doing her best not only to alleviate it but to turn it around, because ultimately, if the college counselor lacks confidence in the "product," the sales pitch to the company is likely to be compromised. My apologies for referring to college kids with disabilities as "product," but the implicit statement is similar to those made in other chapters of this book that emphasize the importance of placing trust in the person with a disability qua expert. One of the most memorable autobiographical bits of Grandin's talk took us inside the working environment where she felt safest and most productive, a neat trick considering her role in designing work environments. "I'm not a talker," she admitted more than once in an hour-long lecture. "So I feel comfortable in the construction trailer, on-site." There is no irony in the point, though. Finding a niche, for which in her case there had been "no barrier to entry," is the essential stratagem from which the rest unfolds.

Business trends can be embodied in rare and memorable individuals. Grandin is walking, talking proof positive of the vaunted "think different" exordium of the old Apple ad campaign. "I am what I do, not what I feel. My mind works like Google for images," she explains. The solutions she provides for some of the rawest, thorniest design problems in the nation's dwindling industrial economy depend on this uncanny aptitude for picturing a system before it is even drawn, much less built to the tune of millions of dollars. One of the incongruities she offered was that just a day after advocates who work primarily with deaf and blind clients had spent hours urging the attendees to saturate their software and office environments with text captioning of all kinds, Grandin on behalf of "Aspergers" (and dyslexics as well as those with other learning disabilities, one could add) was all in favor of getting rid of words in deference to images. A blind college placement officer next to me sighed and closed his notebook, a reminder yet again of the difficulty of finding the pan-disability solution.

But the applicability of many of Grandin's points was not lost on those who shoulder the brunt of this daunting task. All eyes in a gathering of this kind are on the major corporate attendees. Merely mentioning the name of one brings polite little bursts of spontaneous applause during not only the banquet, which the sponsors pay for, but throughout the presentations as well. They are more than sponsors. They are there to affirm a commitment to hiring and promoting people with disabilities. Their best practices may not be as far out as Grandin's more emphatic suggestions, but they do harmonize with her main points about skirting the customary career paths, zoning in on the niche, fostering an environment of comfort and communication, and encouraging the unique talent. Much to the glee of the NGOs pushing them to hire more, they are starting to become intensely competitive about being viewed as the nation's leading player in this field, which beats the old collegiality of the few regular corporate representatives who would annually pat each other on the back for doing so much for the community. The candidates will be the winners if major companies start to vie with one another for top honors in this new diversity category. This means that the companies are beginning to want credit for their efforts, and it behooves the colleges and NGOs to mobilize their own forces, and the media, to keep up that applause. The pittance spent on an engraved plaque for the HR director's office may be one of the best investments in the NGO's budget. Looking ahead still further, a similar competitive atmosphere will push colleges to do more on their end.

Friends in High Places

Major corporations that "go big" in a diversity category acquire reputations the way they add subsidiaries—after a huge gulp, they hoist the banner. Against this impersonality, it has frankly been reassuring to meet some of the individuals behind the scenes who are the necessary inside advocates on behalf of disability. One of the gentlest and at the same time most influential is Chris Fossel, a vice president at Merrill Lynch who presents a business card that is, intriguingly, not from HR but from Client Account Services. He turned up in Boston as a quiet sideline observer, along with Kimberly Reed, a diversity champion (yes, that's her title) who recruits for Merrill's Global Private Client Group. Both she and Fossel have offices in New Jersey. They are the point people for disability at Merrill, which employs a whopping 50,600 people worldwide. Institutions as vast and complex as "Mother Merrill" (its affectionate nickname in the eighties during the bull market, when the perks were particularly lavish) host recruiting events on campus and also encourage intramural networks of people with disabilities. Fossel is the volunteer godfather to the professional affinity organizations inside Merrill that are disability-based. They are ammunition for the recruiting pitch, rather like fraternities that host would-be varsity athletes on campus visits. The first affinity group Fossel led was a group of hard-of-hearing operations personnel frustrated at being stuck at entry level long after those with less seniority had moved up. Fossell became involved in their meetings in Denver in the 1990s and immediately perceived the need to go deeper. Merrill has a long-standing reputation for parlaying this kind of inner responsiveness into client services that make a buck. In this case it was a service package for deaf clients that was launched with some fanfare at about the same time. Hiring deaf retail brokers and call-desk personnel was a necessity to back up the products and services the company was initiating, so HR, banking, and marketing had to work together.

Sitting at a table with Fossell and Reed, I left a few questions about motives and identity unasked. Reed, a young, loquacious African-American (raised in Westchester, Pennsylvania), is the epitome of the diversity recruiter, a born ambassador who would go over well on college campuses where Merrill hosts receptions for seniors. Fossel, however, is a white guy, probably in his forties (just like me), with no apparent disability. Eyebrows raised? The question of the recruiter's identity is a complex one. On looks alone, neither Fossel nor Reed is ideal for the job of recruiting students with disabilities if you subscribe to the theory that the recruiter and candidate ought to somehow mirror one another. By that widely held tenet, Merrill also ought to send out one of its deaf employees. Visible disabilities would score higher on the charts of demographic appeal, simplistic as it sounds.

For a powerful example, take John Studer, an associate director of human resources at the Cincinnati headquarters of Procter & Gamble. During thirty-three years inside that colossus, one of the most corporate of corporations, he has seen major changes in the situation of people with disabilities, some of them because of his own efforts. He spearheads the task force for recruiting candidates with disabilities (one of the only companies to take recruiting so seriously) and spends a week a month on the road visiting college campuses. A Falstaffian company man with a visible disability (missing his left arm), he has that unblinking loyalty to Procter and Gamble (P&G) one finds in the professional class all over Cincinnati. He was ready to pull from his wallet the folded card bearing the company mission statement. In his case, the company comes first, the disability agenda second. When I met Studer at the COSD think tank, he was still assessing the impact of the acquisition of rival Gillette, and quickly noted that the huge hearing aid battery market would add to the vast ranks of consumers with disabilities P&G already claimed. He may be HR, but he's thinking like a marketer. If I were prepping a graduating senior for an interview with him, I might actually urge a touch of restraint vis-à-vis the Grandin-style individualism and "think different" line. At P&G, understanding the strong corporate culture and conforming to it count. It's P&G culture first, disability culture second. Yet Studer is in Boston, and on the road, to assert P&G's commitment to disability, and the consumer product giant was one of the first to host a COSD gathering. The rewards for entry-level candidates are famous: starting salaries of $70,000 steadily mount to $100,000 for fourth-year-managers (with MBA). The first example of profit sharing in the world, P&G has spawned an estimated three thousand millionaires, largely because most of them stay with the company their entire careers. "We tend to promote from within," Studer quietly explains.[2]

Follow the Leader

These corporate pioneers, even the most experienced of them, need a guide to the tricky disability terrain. Their guru is the indomitable Alan Muir, who created COSD, I am tempted to say, in his own image. At just over three feet tall, perpetually in motion and as funny as he is persistent, he is tough to resist. Like so many of the great coaches in sports history, he is an authority because he was a star. In Muir's case the game is high finance, and his bench assignment is to find jobs, not just in finance but definitely in white-collar areas, for the tens of thousands of students with disabilities who graduate from and the 1.2 million enrolled in suburban U.S. colleges each year. It is hard to think of anyone more perfectly cut out to handle the task.

Muir in the go-go eighties was a hard-charging banker in the commercial lending division of Chase Manhattan bank, using his considerable charm and tactical skills to extend the urban bank's reach into suburban Suffolk County on Long Island. His accounts ranged from $5 million to $500 million. In the sixteen years he spent in the trenches he mastered several aspects of corporate culture and developed an eyewitness appreciation of what operations managers require from personnel. His clients ran the gamut of small- to midcap manufacturing and service concerns, a cross section of the American economy and its recruiting needs. His own career development relied on developing the survival instincts one needs to progress through the byzantine ways of a huge bank that was blowing up into an even more gargantuan empire thanks to a cannonade of mergers (from Chase Manhattan to Chemical to JPMorgan Chase). As Muir picks his targets among major multinationals today, the old Chase lessons on how one prompts action inside a major bureaucracy come in handy.

Many who drift into diversity later in their careers started out swimming in the mainstream. Only during his last two years at the bank did Muir become involved in issues of disability, serving on the worldwide diversity committee. Those were the days, he notes, when disability was a long way down the agenda. "We spent a lot of time talking about all the other issues, and disability stayed last on the list so it often never came up during meetings. Then, gradually, it became number two as the culture changed." Knowing Muir, he pulled it up to that level personally.

A major life change occurred in 1999, when Muir's wife was offered a position as a certified nurse midwife in Tennessee. What's a fast-talking New York banker to do in Knoxville? He embarked on a seven-month, self-directed job search, meeting with what he estimates were seventy-five or more recruiters. Even with a tight résumé and a terrific track record as a high-ranking producer for one of the world's elite commercial banks, the doors were not flying open. Muir decided to do something to address the situation. He headed to the University of Tennessee, where he knocked on the door of the career services office. He strategized with the director, Robert Greenberg, to start integrating disability into the university's burgeoning diversity initiative. When the university took him on, they let him devote a fifth of his time to career services, the rest to disability services. He embarked on an ambitious and invaluable research project, roving the nation in person to meet with other career services counselors as well as employers to assess the current needs of both students and recruiters. He blazed the trail. "Nobody was doing this at the time, making the attempt to integrate these companies who were hot to trot on hiring graduates with disabilities and the qualified candidates who were ready to be hired." The insights from his fact-finding mission were abundant and would forever pave the road of career development for students with disabilities. Foremost among them was the perception of a crazy gap between businesses that were interested in disability and students who were scrambling for their first career-establishing jobs after graduation. Even those universities that have, for decades in some cases, been recognized as bastions of high disability consciousness were not securing the campus visits of major recruiters, or if the recruiters were there, it was like a scavenger hunt to find students with disabilities. Why? Because disability was part of a separate on-campus entity overseen by disability services, which was too busy keeping the kids going in school through accommodation and hand-holding to care about job hunting, let alone career development. Career services, the point of contact with companies, was not effectively aware of the candidates with disabilities in the campus pipeline or the addition of disability to the diversity conversation. Muir began to fume. He had ardent converts on the line in the human resources offices of Microsoft, Procter & Gamble, IBM, Exxon-Mobil, and his old employers JPMorgan Chase, but they were complaining that they felt like they were on a wild-goose chase recruiting candidates to gear up their disability programs. It was time to build the bridge. The result was COSD, a nonprofit that is unique in the nation and a stellar example of how much can be accomplished by a brilliant business mind that is trilingual, fluent in the lingoes of disability culture, big business, and academia.

Muir started with what he had at hand. Convinced that his business contacts would come through with the jobs, he turned his attention to students (or, as he puts it, "I adopted the student's point of view"). He collaborated with Greenberg to launch an ambitious, disability-specific training and research initiative that would completely shift the employment counseling functions, such as they were, away from the on-campus disability services office to career services. If this sounds like another one of those headache-inducing stories of internecine campus politics, it isn't. What Muir accomplished reflects a philosophical reorientation from the medical model toward self-reliance. He recognized that as valuable as disability services counselors can be in the effort to accommodate students during their early years on campus especially, this was not necessarily conducive to jump-starting careers at the other end of the four years. The current manifestation of Muir's approach is different from that of all the other well-intentioned proponents of college recruiting, who spend most of their time cajoling corporations into making more of an effort. Muir pushes the kids to take on internships and find mentors, to fatten their résumés and demonstrate before they graduate that they can grit it out on the job day in and day out. As he candidly observes: "There is a supply-and-demand side to this problem. Companies actually have a heavy demand for new recruits with disabilities, but often the supply of ready talent is lacking. The students need to understand themselves as well as business. Retention is not always the company's fault. We have to realize that the students may not be quite expert enough or capable enough to maintain their performance in the work environment for a long period."[3]

To do this, Muir raised money from the state vocational rehabilitation authority, the former President's Committee on Employment of People with Disabilities, and the current ODEP. Rather than set up shop as another standard-issue service organization for disability issues, Muir became a consultant ferrying cutting-edge training and recruiting ideas between big business and academia. He began convening university college placement officers, employers, and government agencies at the annual COSD conference.

The honor roll of host companies is impressive: Lockheed-Martin, IBM, Microsoft, SunTrust, Merck, Blue Cross Blue Shield of Massachusetts, P&G, Motorola, Nordstrom, Exxon-Mobil, and NASA. By 2005, he had a roster of 250 universities, colleges, and community colleges along with more than a hundred companies, a vibrant mix of nonprofits and private-sector heavy-weights that is extensive enough to patch regional or seasonal misconnec-tions between supply and demand (to use his formulation). As he says, "We know what the system is, and we have to figure out a way to make it work better. We also know what the capabilities of the students are. It's a matter of working within that framework." For now, he is confining his efforts to big businesses rather than the entrepreneurs that supply them; small busi-nesses have not exactly been knocking on his door anyway, because they cling to long-standing fears of the disability rights movement and they don't have time. He realizes that by enlisting the Fortune 500 he sets up more than just a "trickle-down" effect—it's a full-court press on both the smaller suppliers and the colleges: "The big companies don't mind exerting a lot of pressure on folks they work with, particularly the universities. We have quite a few schools referred to us by the employers who ask the tough question: How many graduates with disabilities can you get for interviews? If nobody at the school gives them a straight answer, if they hem and haw on this, they won't get that relationship they need. That is where COSD comes in."

When Muir goes after a corporate commitment, he does not repeat the mistake made by many advocates who try to chase down the CEO and buttonhole him or her into making a dramatic gesture. "From my banking career, I know you can't just go to the chairman or the board members. I stay with the one passionate person inside the company who acts as a one-person wrecking crew. Then I see how far up the ladder I can get. We get a lot of change done that way—from the inside up."

Some of the methods COSD offers have a time-honored patina. Muir is committed to internships and mentoring, for example, as a way of filling a résumé as well as weaning the candidate from the overprotection of family and disability services. "Many students don't come from parents with dis-abilities, so they are already in a bicultural family that often just want them to 'pass.' They need a mentor with a disability to bring them up to speed." He invites recruiters to on-campus workshops so they can adopt the stu-dent's perspective.

Muir's tactical forte is innovation. Among the ideas he is dying to try out is an efficient online database, not limited to a particular school but nation-wide, that can be a trolling ground for companies looking for a particular match among candidates with disabilities. That will provide the direct conversation between recruiters and students that is erratically available across the country's colleges today. It will be free for students, on a fee basis for companies. Building from this, he wants to set up a virtual university to coach students on the basics of writing résumés and cover letters, setting up internships and interviews, and the more disability-specific issues, such as how to handle the often excruciating question of self-disclosure. The advantage this would offer to recruiters is the legal comfort zone of knowing they are dealing with a candidate with a disability, abnegating the awkward self-identification problem. I worry that Muir's portal will get lost in the excesses of online recruiting, where Monster is more than just the name of a leading site—it's a mentality. Competing with Hotjobs, Craigslist, or Monster is not for the faint of heart.

Muir has been in the game long enough to know that the good guys are not always winning. If there is one area in which he is not so confident, it involves the laggards:

> I am concerned about the ones who are getting lost in the shuffle, and I want universities to be mindful of their situation. In the long run, on the national scene what will end up being the last bastion of stigma, even after folks understand learning disabilities, is the area of psychiatric conditions and brain injuries. I am not sure we will ever get past that, because they cut deep to the core of the conscious and unconscious fear factors employers harbor, that suspicion you are in harm's way. Deafness, blindness, the tangibility of some disabilities somehow make it easier. But "going postal" comes from the invisible, and when you really can't see it you definitely don't understand it. In the end, employers will go where there is need. As long as there are well-prepared, highly experienced graduates with disabilities out there moving up the career ladders, then they are more likely to hire others.

Where the Jobs Are

That's what is happening at Microsoft, one of Muir's favorite examples of disability recruiting (and a massive booster of COSD). While IBM is inclined to go it alone in this area, Microsoft is a joiner. Since the inception of the U.S. Business Leadership Network, Microsoft has been a major player in this, the most effective and interesting of all the business groups involved in disability. We will return to this alliance of major corporations later in this book, because they have done a great job of disseminating best practices on the management side. Microsoft is always a presence at ODEP, COSD, National Organization on Disability (NOD), American Federation of the Blind

(AFB), the annual California State University Northridge (CSUN) Conference on Technology and Persons with Disabilities, the newly forming Youth to Work Coalition, NSCIA's Business Advisory Committee, and other organizations' job fairs and diversity conferences, including their annual paid congressional internships in Washington, D.C. Messages from Bill Gates, attempting to humorously link his eyeglasses to assistive technology, have run in many disability publications. The company dispatches Mylene Padolina, a personable and well-spoken HR manager specializing in diversity (Asian descent, no visible disability), to tout the company's progress, and it works because in the community the company's name is golden.

Back in Redmond, Washington, where Microsoft is headquartered, disability is part of corporate strategy. Some of the measures are, in my opinion, too old school. The company probably overrelies on a slick video, insipidly titled *Windows of Opportunity*, that since 1999 has been regularly thrust upon candidates and employees as part of the company's effort to "sensitize." I am probably not the only one who is sick of these fairly predictable productions, which remind me of required driver's ed films, but many in HR make their living at creating and dispensing them, and Microsoft's version actually won a ton of awards.

Microsoft is more interesting when it pushes the strategic envelope, as it has for some time. The earliest recorded stirrings of disability awareness at the company began in 1988, two years before the passage of the ADA, when Microsoft perceived the potential profits in viable products for the unknown assistive technology market. To its credit, the design of Windows 2.0 included technology well ahead of its time for users with a variety of disabilities, after a slew of problems beset Windows 85. Just staying in the technological dimension of this brief history, Microsoft products have all along been admirably ahead of the regulatory curve. Consider the fact that the passage of Section 508 of the Rehabilitation Act, which occurred a full decade later, was "crunch time" for the software, hardware, and online industries. From 1988 on, Microsoft has made accessibility awareness a constant goal companywide, rapidly expanding the means of addressing it from technology product groups (potential profit centers) to human resources and community affairs.

Just as IBM has its solutions development wizards for accessibility in a lab in Austin, Microsoft has a formidable Accessible Technology Group, which has gobbled up research dollars but also generated revenues in the millions since its inception in 1992 (the company will not release accessibility-specific figures). With that built-in revenue, it is not hard to figure out why Padolina shows up at MIT job fairs: Microsoft needs engineers with disabilities. According to Ellen Mosner, the publicist for the Accessible Technology Group, "From a single full-time staff position that oversaw accessibility issues in 1992, Microsoft's Accessibility Technology Group (ATG) has grown to nearly forty employees and consultants who work with product developers, assistive-technology vendors." The in-house ATG also collaborates closely with various product groups, including those responsible for the blockbuster revenue generators like MS Office, to ensure that accessibility is considered from the first design stages through product upgrade cycles. One of the crucial steps is incorporating advice from users with disabilities, including the Microsoft accessibility advisers and beta testers who fit certain user profiles (blindness, deafness, difficulty handling a mouse or using a keyboard). They are constant presences at the growing number of accessibility conferences including CSUN Technology and Persons with Disabilities and Closing the Gap. They also take an active role in regulatory issues, most of which concern the revision of Section 508 standards that make technology accessible. Microsoft helped develop the voluntary product accessibility template (VPAT), which is used by its rivals and smaller firms to describe how products support Section 508 requirements.

Leveraging its leadership on the tech side helps Microsoft recruit candidates with disabilities. One lure is the state-of-the-art accommodations you get when you arrive. Then company representatives go out and sell it: "Microsoft believes that everyone has potential—sometimes people just need the resources to realize it," says Sarah Meyer, senior manager of community affairs. "Over the past five years, the company has funded a variety of projects that address this issue, including an initiative that helped demonstrate to employers methods for recruiting, hiring, and retaining individuals with disabilities (Institute for Community Inclusion); a Technology Business Incubator project to fund entrepreneurs with disabilities (Community Options); High School–High Tech sites in Denver and Los Angeles; National Center for Accessible Media at WGBH-Boston (who created the DVS® system used for *Ray* and other movies and TV shows) to work with corporations to educate them about accessible Web design; Living Independently in Los Angeles AKA LILA (a Geographic Information 'Asset Mapping' System based interactive database to identify and map resources for people with disabilities); National Organization on Disability's Start on Success internship program; and Accessibility Concept Research and Accessibility Product Development at universities in the U.S., United Kingdom and Sweden."

Much of the advantage that Microsoft has established is found at the early end of the recruiting process. The company, which has always had a youth-oriented slant on HR, has a massive outreach program involving disability. It starts as early as grade school and high school students with disabilities, who receive internships, job shadow programs, and technology training. Microsoft has probably had more bang for its buck from internships than any other company in disability recruiting. By the time the student with a disability reaches the college level, the program accelerates, and takes a rather interesting turn in that it involves government agencies and national nonprofits. Microsoft is eager to join NGOs and the government in addressing the problem of the underemployment of people with disabilities.

The partnerships with nonprofits and government make sense from a practical standpoint. As with any disability recruiting effort, privacy is an issue, and the identification of viable candidates is not always as easy as it would appear. This is where the American Association of People with Disabilities (AAPD), a loosely constructed nonprofit based with 100,000-plus members, comes in. According to publicist Sarah Meyer, the AAPD and Microsoft launched a joint federal internship program, Expanding Tomorrow's IT Workforce, that enlists government agencies to generate IT internships. The program was modeled on congressional internships supported by the Mitsubishi Electric America Foundation (MEAF). Each year ten college students sign up for an eleven-week program, at $25 an hour and an inestimable boost to their IT careers (just having Microsoft on the résumé adds to the starting salary anywhere else, one should remember). They can get college credit for their summer at, for example, the Departments of Homeland Security, Education, Labor, Transportation, and Health and Human Services, or at FEMA (no jokes, please), the FAA, U.S. Patent and Trade, and the National Science Foundation. They also end up on the scouting lists of Microsoft engineering recruiters, which means there is a job opening at the end of the process for the most talented among them.

Another shining example of best practices in this area is SunTrust Bank, the 53,000-employee commercial bank with $172.4 billion in assets headquartered in Atlanta. It is no accident that, exactly coincident with the recent push for more employees with disabilities, SunTrust had the full-court press on for more clients with disabilities. For blind clients, the company rolled out Braille and large-print statements at no extra cost, and hustled to make the online banking accessible to JAWS and other text-to-voice programs. For deaf clients it made the online services automatically use visual confirmation of transactions and backed this with 24/7 access to teletypewriter (TTY) phone service. In certain states where SunTrust is a major player (Florida, Maryland, Virginia), government support for assistive technology was matched with the bank's Assistive Technology Loan Fund Programs to engineer low-interest purchases of computer equipment, home improvements, lift-equipped and hand-controlled cars, power wheelchairs, electric scooters, and even hearing aids. Bringing this full circle to hiring, in Virginia the small-business clients qualify for reduced interest rates for capital expenditures on equipment or services to accommodate either staff or customers.

The phrasing of SunTrust's diversity initiative mission statement is instructive: "More than just race or gender, diversity can mean a single characteristic, experience or idea that makes one person similar to or different from another." Even more fascinating is the order of the initiative's five priorities, starting with marketing and moving through human resources, management, and community relations: "Increase market share in growing segments; attract and retain the most talented and productive workforce; create an atmosphere of respect and inclusion with zero tolerance for harassment; foster beneficial community relationships; provide equal business opportunity for minority and women suppliers."

From an employee who noticed that there was a need to have branch personnel who could use sign language, the SunTrust program has matured rapidly. By 2004 the company had recruited more than one hundred staffers with disabilities, many of whom work in the call center and in operations in Richmond, Virginia. That is also where you find the office of Katherine McCrary, the point person in the SunTrust disability initiative. Her job in HR was created by the CEO when the premerger bank was still called Crestar. As her career morphed from human resources (in charge of temporary staffing at headquarters) into the current authoritative role on disability policy, it crossed the borders of HR into marketing, management, community relations, and strategy. Her brief from the start was to combine recruiting with these areas. The problem at the outset was one faced by many in HR when it comes to disability. "They don't know where to go to get the candidates, because there has been no one-stop shopping place for talent. You have Easter Seals and forty other organizations to call, and it's too much for the HR person, which is why so many give up. Employers want it simple. They want to know where to go. That is why we support and believe in Alan Muir and COSD, and are proud to host his 2006 conference."

That is also why she invests much of her time, with the company's support, in her activities as the national president of the U.S. Business Leadership Network as well as in her efforts inside the country's major HR professional association, the Society for Human Resources Management (SHRM, with 200,000 members). She is one of the nation's most plugged-in executives in the upper echelons of disability activism. She recognizes that if progress is to be made by people with disabilities, big business will have to be involved. She observes, "It's the employers that need to take charge of this issue. Corporate America is on the demand side of the equation. If you are a lead employer or involved, then your community knows that and they are going to drive their business to you and work for you because you are known for being disability friendly."[4]

McCrary has pulled out all the stops to propel SunTrust to the front ranks. Her version of disability-mentoring day is an extravaganza, mobilizing the whole corporate suite and around fifty college juniors and seniors with disabilities to "tour the footprint" of SunTrust headquarters each of the past three years. The mentoring goes on all year round, and McCrary has even orchestrated arrangements by which new hires with disabilities have as many as six mentors simultaneously, her sly way of introducing disability issues to a broader coterie inside the company. She runs a centralized company fund for accommodations of about $10,000 a year and points out that she's never been able to spend all of it—her anecdotal proof that accommodations are not nearly as expensive as the anti-ADA lobby says. Most accommodations cost less than $500. Another $50,000 is for the annual salaries of interns with disabilities. At this writing, two of the year-round interns who are training in the commercial banking sector are blind.

Someone has to write the checks for all this benevolence. SunTrust Chief Executive Officer L. Phillip Humann seems unable to deny McCrary any request, because, as the chairman's letter on disability states, there is a direct line between diversity-fueled hiring and attracting new accounts: "SunTrust recognizes that recruiting and hiring people with disabilities is a business strategy that works for several reasons: we are able to tap into a generally under-employed segment of our communities and hire very capable individuals to work in key business lines. One very positive outgrowth of this recruitment activity is that we learn from our employees about their disabilities and are able to develop products and services that are friendlier to customers with disabilities." Adds McCrary, "It's smart business."

Agenda

- *Hire from the community* to which you hope to *sell.*
- *Send out your best managers with disabilities* to attract candidates.
- *Link recruiting to strategic planning* in product development, sales, finance, and operations.

- *Go to the focused sources for candidates,* including organizations such as COSD and colleges noted for disability.
- *Don't be shy about using in-house affinity groups and product development* as recruiting bait.
- *Interns and mentoring* are proven measures.
- *Make sure accommodations are in place before* launching a disability effort.

Notes

1. Welcoming remarks, IBM Leadership Conference for People with Disabilities, Palisades, New York, September 24, 2000.
2. Personal interview, August 2005.
3. Personal interview, July 2005.
4. Personal interview, September 2005.

Chapter 4

Show Me the Money

Marketing with the Disability Community

Right behind you I see the millions.
—Pete Townshend, "Go to the Mirror," *The Who's Tommy*

Time for the profit part. One of the vast, unaccountable marketing secrets of our time is the massed buying power of 54 million Americans
(Forrester Research doubles that figure) who are out there with an aggregate income of a trillion dollars a year to spend ($220 billion in discre-
tionary income) and the ridiculously few companies who have "discovered"
them or bothered to cater to them. Even the more conservative estimate of
the aggregate, $796 billion, offered recently by Packaged Facts, a Manhat-
tan-based market research firm, is vastly larger than the African-American, Latino, and women's markets combined. This immense pie, which
grew between 1990 and 2000 by 25 percent (thanks to aging baby boomers,
faster than the buying power of any other subgroup and still expanding),
has been in the oven for what seems like ages while alert companies dish
up their slices of delicious profits. Those who have been in the forefront
have certainly enjoyed a high rate of return on investment, and the litany of
success stories would be impressive except that the lineup has not changed
much over the past decade.

The paradigm for adroit target marketing, akin to the vast success enjoyed by Absolut vodka with gay consumers, was offered nearly a decade ago
by Kmart, which was goaded into including a child using a wheelchair in
one of its advertising circulars by a vice president who was also the parent

of a child with a disability. The response was measurable not only in the thousands of letters the company received but in an undeniable boost in sales that came directly from families with a disability connection. Kmart has been riding that early success ever since, as has Nordstrom, which in 1987 started to include wheelchair users in its ad campaigns (a third of its models are people of color or have disabilities) as part of a noble diversity-marketing initiative that has paid off in tracked purchases totaling in the millions from customers with disabilities. "Our intent in showing models with disabilities was not to market specifically to that segment of consumers but simply to show a diverse mix of people in our promotional materials," says Nordstrom's Amy Jones. "People with disabilities are a part of the diverse makeup of our customer base." The company backed up the campaign by making the stores and Web site state-of-the-art accessible and offering seminars on ADA compliance as well as such specifics as garment tailoring for wheelchair users. Nordstrom also wrote some welcome checks to Career Opportunities for Students with Disabilities (COSD), the American Foundation for the Blind, Special Olympics, and the National Multiple Sclerosis Society. Every committee or organization that puts disability and business together seems to have a member from Nordstrom, including the Business Leadership Network and the Employer Subcommittee of the former President's Committee on Employment of People with Disabilities The first TV ad featuring a person with a disability was a Levi's 501 jeans ad that debuted during the 1984 Olympics. That was followed by a series of a dozen McDonald's spots, including those featuring Paralympic athletes in the company's mainstream Olympics promotion, launched in 2004 (and just announced to be renewed for 2008, with the athletes' images gracing the likes of cups, bags, and tray liners).

Mattel similarly won the hearts and wallets of the community with the introduction in 1997 of Share A Smile™ Becky®, Barbie's doll friend who uses a wheelchair. Becky had thunderous global press with five hundred news hits around the world, sold out almost instantly in two weeks, went back into production, and brought inestimable added sales from heads of households, teachers, disability activists, and grandmothers who are also part of the demographic. When Becky got stuck in the Barbie Dream House elevator, which was not wheelchair accessible, Mattel shipped a model to the father of "Universal Design," the late Ron Mace at the University of North Carolina, to assist with making the house wheelchair accessible.

Some companies grab their market share by accident. When Chrysler brought out the snub-nosed, retro PT Cruiser in 2000, one of the first constituencies to catch on and make it a surprise best seller was the tightly connected group of wheelchair users who drive. They found the Cruiser perfect for modification, allowing them to roll up a ramp through the rear hatchback right to the driver's seat. The clunky vans that had been the main adaptive choice for years were cheerfully dismissed in favor of the stylish retro look. The push from the disability buying public helped jump-start sales for the Cruiser, rescuing Chrysler from a slump and momentarily baffling automotive editors and experts who had second-guessed the novelty and boldly predicted that it would be a dud. Now, GM, Honda, Ford, Toyota, and Volkswagen are starting to take a closer look at this market segment.

Something similar happened at Nokia, where the company was at first baffled, then delighted by the rush to buy its handsets. The sales jump turned out to be demand from hard of hearing customers who deemed that Nokia's handsets were the most compatible with hearing aids, and recently, the Nokia 6620 handset was the model for TALKS by Cingular Wireless (whereby all the functionality of a screen reader is available in a phone, allowing blind and low-vision customers the equalizing technology so they can access caller ID and their phone directory and check battery status). These companies are the winners, and the valuable prizes are not just plaques on the chairman's wall but profits, and an increasing alliance of brand-loyal customers.

Other companies famously had the community in hand and then fumbled, including Nike, which used cause marketing that featured Casey Martin, a star of the disability rights pantheon, to pump its image after an idiotic ad campaign for Dri-Goat sneakers in *Backpacker Magazine* in October 2000 that was perceived as mocking people with spinal cord injuries and cerebral palsy. Nike repeated the error with Chinese customers, who were lured by the Yao Ming endorsement and turned off by a dumb martial arts campaign that was lambasted in the mainland Chinese press for its cultural insensitivity. Never underestimate the power of the grapevine.

The successes should not come as a surprise. Once the numbers are assembled, finding the market almost looks like shooting fish in a barrel. There are 20.3 million families in the United States that have a member with a disability (out of 69.9 million families), ensuring that a disability-specific marketing campaign actually reaches an astonishingly high four out of every ten consumers nationwide. The demographics are even juicier once they are broken down into the key groups most avidly sought by marketers. For example, 73 percent of people with disabilities are heads of households, and 48 percent are the principal shoppers in their homes (58 percent own their own homes). While 46 percent are married, 77 percent have no children; half of all Americans over sixty-five have a disability, and another six and one half million Americans with disabilities are between three and seventeen years old. In an ad culture that is youth crazy, it is important that the most economically active of the consumers with disabilities is the golden group of eighteen- to twenty-nine-year-olds, 57 percent of whom have jobs and 59 percent of whom eat out regularly (compared to 61 percent of their nondisabled peers), and, moreover, 23 percent of people with disabilities visit a shopping center, department store, or mall once per week (compared to 41 percent of their nondisabled counterparts). The National Captioning Institute showed that 73 percent of Deaf people switched to a brand that had its commercials captioned. A Paralympic Committee survey revealed that 54 percent of all households pay more attention to and patronize businesses that feature people with disabilities in their advertising. When Nabisco hired a well-known Deaf actress and her hard of hearing son for an Oreo cookie commercial, sales within the Deaf community shot through the roof.

The prospects for the disability sector in particular, especially as its members defy the stereotype of the economically disenfranchised person with a disability, are worth far more attention on the part of consumer forecasters. There are prime urban markets involved. Among the top five cities where people with disabilities live are Detroit, Baltimore, and Miami, according to a 2000 study, "Ten Places of 100,000 or More with Highest Percentage of People with Disabilities in the Civilian Noninstitutionalized Population 5 Years Old and Over."

Hitting this niche should not break the marketing budget. For Kmart, it cost nothing—the photo shoot for its historic circular would probably been more costly if it had entailed a bratty child model anyway. The resounding symbolic significance of that ad pays off handsomely to this day. Other win-win marketing stories, benefiting the community and the company, punctuate the pages that follow. Most efforts have been decidedly less spontaneous than the Kmart breakthrough, now formally a component of the company's sales efforts. Similar campaigns worked for Toys "R" Us, Target, and Nordstrom.

Some companies' histories in this area, however, are frankly scandalous. It took a Supreme Court decision on accessibility to force Norwegian Cruise Line to welcome aboard travelers in wheelchairs. The Norwegian Cruise Line decision came after similar Air Carrier Access Act suits against airlines, which also had a deplorable record of accommodation, which is utterly counterintuitive when one considers the upside potential. Yet this was *after* the General Accounting Office reported a 12 percent increase in hospitality revenues just by simply implementing the provisions of the Americans with

Disabilities Act. Princess Cruise Lines figured this out long ago. It says that 12 percent of people with disabilities take cruises, as opposed to 8 percent of the nondisabled public.

Travel and hospitality companies have a long way to go to gain the trust of the disability market, but the trip will be worth it. After all, an estimated 21 million travelers with disabilities spend $13.6 billion a year on travel, according to a phone and online survey by the Chicago-based advocacy group Open Doors and the Travel Industry Association of America. This number excludes the amount spent by family members or aides who often escort travelers with disabilities. Another and more gung ho study, by the Society for Accessible Travel and Hospitality, estimated that people with disabilities spent more than $81 billion on travel in 1995. The bad news from the survey is an index of how far the travel industry still has to come. It noted that 82 percent of people with disabilities had difficulties at airports; 60 percent had problems at the hotel. With the travel market up 50 percent since 2002, the justification for the improvements is more than there. Princess Cruises has had a disability specialist on board for many years, Jan Tuck (chair of the U.S. Access Board), and recently hired a marketing specialist in the field to attract more wheelchair users especially for Caribbean trips.

Follow the Leader

Somewhere between Kmart's lucky shot in the dark and the shotgun wedding of cruise lines and the disability community there should be an informed sales effort among major corporations to target this niche. Marketing departments are always hankering for a way to boost sagging revenues and meet growth objectives set by chief executives who can no longer accept the excuse that the recession is lingering. After all, the boss's compensation is tied to stock performance, and the price-earnings ratios of retail, airline, cruise line, restaurant, casino, and hotel stocks are no longer as stellar as they once were. So disability, at least theoretically, is in the sites as the new minority target. Every industry has its stake in the discovery of the path to this sector. People with disabilities buy just as much toothpaste and ice cream as anybody. They are more likely to reward companies that reach out to them. Cause marketing (appealing to consumers by linking a product or service to a particular good) is a proven way to steal customers from your competition and turn them into loyal return buyers. According to a Cone/Roper Cause-Related Marketing Trends report issued in 1997, three out of four adults say they would be likely to switch to a brand associated with a "good cause." Alongside environmentalism and the eradication of poverty, disability is one of the top three such causes. But how does the smart salesperson capture this little-understood market?

The step-by-step game plan for success starts with assembling solid demographics on the specific disability subgroup that offers the most likely demand. Then the plan follows a pattern. A private-public partnership between the company and a grassroots, usually membership-based, national disability organization delivers not only invaluable coaching on the customers but exposure to its membership. For example, within the last few years, Tari Susan Hartman-Squire's EIN SOF Communications has joined forces with Joseph Craig, a senior vice president with Nielsen Entertainment, to conceive and activate their "Disability Community Market Research Initiative" that was featured in *Fortune Small Business* and *Adweek*. Endorsement and research go hand-in-hand.

Disability-specific focus groups have been recruited—composed of the leadership of such national disability grassroots membership organizations as the National Spinal Cord Injury Association (NSCIA), Self Help for Hard of Hearing People (SHHH), American Council of the Blind (ACB), Telecommunications for the Deaf, and others—and asked for their impressions of products as diverse as cell phones, restaurants, banks, Internet service providers, rental cars, and pharmaceuticals. Armed with input from the disability-specific leaders, trendsetters, key influencers, and opinion makers, the seller can choose to modify a product, or its key marketing or advertising message, or product accessibility, or relationships with the disability community—within the parameters of cost-benefit logic, of course—to tailor the product to the needs of the customer and to develop the most effective messaging. Internal design and marketing teams can use this as a golden opportunity to get up to speed on disability codes (linguistic as well as design) and emerging trends. Then it is time for the hard sell: The unique characteristics of the product can be trumpeted to the community as well as to savvy mainstream consumers. Also, crossover possibilities for multiple uses of accessibility features can be explored. For example, captions designed to facilitate entertainment access for Deaf and hard of hearing TV audiences are now common in noisy environments such as airports, gyms, and sports bars.

Here is how a successful campaign might expand. First, a cause-marketing campaign or strategic alliance with the disability community is conceived and launched. Occasionally, the press picks up on this and reports it as a "trend" story, and retail outlets get interested in the prospects to further illuminate their own image-boosting, disability-friendly efforts. Carefully crafted advertising and promotion finds the buttons to press to attract the community's approval. Then the company's commitment to customers and employees with disabilities itself is woven into the text of the message. The minute the product shows signs of taking off, the campaign turns its success into a "trend" story and pushes the lead companies in the sectors further. "Aha" turns into "I told you so."

Ready for Prime Time

This is all terra incognita for most old-school marketers even in the nearly tapped-out minority field. The closest cousin to disability is the vital "mature" sector as exploited by the campaigns led by the American Association of Retired Persons (AARP) and big pharmaceutical companies. For various reasons that are especially related to sense of identity rather than commonalty of needs, the sophistication of mature marketing has not carried over into the effort to reach the disability demographic. The cornerstone of the disability market segment is self-identification, whereas most aging baby boomers are stuck in the evolving reality of their newly acquired "age-related functional limitation." They have not yet made the psychic leap from "them" to "us" or "you" to "me."

Lack of expertise inside major companies has launched a cottage industry of consultants who guide retailers, manufacturers, banks, and others to the customer with a disability. The best of these scouts is the indomitable Tari Susan Hartman-Squire. She is trilingual (speaks disability, public policy, and corporate strategic-marketing talk), and her guerrilla- and strategic-marketing expertise is complemented by high-level contacts that include government officials, community-based advocates, and corporate executives, as well as a thorough grounding in high-stakes media. Her thriving business, the Los Angeles–based EIN SOF Communications, was founded in 1987. Before that, Hartman-Squire spearheaded the formation of the Screen Actors Guild (SAG) committee of performers with disabilities, which, with other actors with disabilities, pushed hard in Hollywood for casting policies and practices that would include more people with disabilities (instead of dumb actors pretending to play the part—as offensive as white actors in blackface). She and other performers with disabilities including Alan Toy, Les Jankey, Julianna Fjeld (who later won an Emmy for the TV movie *Love Is Never Silent*), and Henry Holden, and the Beverly Hills Barristers' Committee for the Arts, were successful in adding disability (then referred to as "handicapped") into the nondiscrimination and affirmative action clauses of the 1980 Theatrical Collective Bargaining Agreements a full decade before the Americans with Disabilities Act became the law of the land. She discovered the disability field during a bout with a cervical sprain in 1979 that turned out to be an eye-opener when she faced discrimination in the casting process. The experience to this day remains her "true north." Now fluent in American Sign Language as well as the informal "dialects" of every imaginable disability subgroup (she has advised the AP Stylebook editor on evolving disability semantics for over ten years), Hartman-Squire is a consultant whose number tops the speed-dial list of the heads of virtually every national disability organization and select Fortune 500 companies. Even before we get to her corporate strategic smarts, her street credit is impeccable. She has been one of the nation's most prominent and trusted advocacy bridges with the press and business since before the epoch-defining struggle to pass the ADA. Since then she has rolled up her sleeves and worked in Washington, D.C. on regulatory and legislative issues as they percolate through the process of enactment and served as media consultant for a variety of national disability organizations. For two years she chaired the important (and productive) Communications Subcommittee of the former President's Committee on Employment of People with Disabilities.

For all her political effectiveness, these days Hartman-Squire's direct economic impact on the community stems from the influence she wields with business leaders. Her corporate clients have included Cingular Wireless, Bank of America, Macy's West, Microsoft, Hewlett-Packard, and AOL. Among her launches have been Nickelodeon's Pelswick, Mattel/Toys "R" Us release of Share a Smile Becky®, Universal Studios Home Entertainment's "DVS® Enhanced" DVD for the movie Ray, among many others. (DVS stands for Descriptive Video Service, which is narration between the blocks of dialogue so that blind and low-vision audiences can experience scene changes, facial expressions, gestures, etc.). She is also "behind the scenes" adviser on media, strategy, business, and/or government affairs to several companies including Northwest Airlines, Federated Department Stores, and many nonprofits, notably the U.S. Business Leadership Network, the American Council of the Blind, the Academy of Television Arts & Sciences EMMY Magazine, the National Spinal Cord Injury Association, and the Youth to Work Coalition, and has been retained by Career Opportunities for Students with Disabilities (COSD), Mitsubishi Electric America Foundation, Disability Funders Network (DFN), and grassroots disability organizations such as ADAPT, World Institute on Disability, TASH, and the National Association of the Deaf. She functions most effectively when she flips her virtual Rolodex to yoke together partnerships between private and public sectors. The networking takes political skills specific to both the community and the executive suite. Recently, she worked quietly with staffers in helping to bring together a strategic alliance memo between the Small Business Administration and the U.S. Department of Labor's Office of Disability Employment Policy.

Her 1989 award-winning marketing strategy for Miramax's *My Left Foot* launched disability niche marketing as a genre, complete with an A-list screening that debuted audio descriptions for a major motion picture, subtitles, advance reviews by disability rights scholars and historians, and a homemade chocolate left foot for everyone attending. In a marketing milestone achievement, the real line in the sand, Miramax agreed to not show the film in movie theaters that were *not* wheelchair accessible—even before the ADA and its Title III (public accommodations) went into law.

She was in charge of the ultra-effective public relations campaign that put Mattel and Toys "R" Us on the networks and in the headlines for Share a Smile Becky®, and for hiring dozens of babies and kids with disabilities for mainstream and specialty advertising. Inside the movie and television industry she learned all the right moves needed to get people with disabilities into position for their close-up, as the founding executive director of the Media Access Office in 1981. Hartman-Squire's multidisciplinary competence makes her a sharp commentator on the progress (or its lack) of the disability movement not only in business but in politics, entertainment, and the press, and her grasp of the connections among these areas is one of the keys to her understanding of what corporate America needs to do in this area, how to get there, and how it could reap the benefits. "The hallmark of every EIN SOF campaign is a unique and sophisticated blend of guerrilla marketing and traditional PR tactics that all move harmoniously in some way, shape, or form toward increased awareness of public policy disability issues. If a campaign is not anchored in the disability community, nor conceived and executed *with* the disability community, it is token, hollow, self-serving, and disingenuous," she says.[1] Her multiple talents as a consultant allow her to make improvements in many departments inside a company. She is the rare type of consultant who is as welcome in human resources as she is in the customer service call center, external affairs, or corporate communications, and she can hold forth on regulatory issues as volubly as she does on ad campaigns and training videos.

In the executive suite, Hartman-Squire is one of the few pros who has the information and experience to convince decision makers of the dollars-

and-cents rationale behind focusing on the untapped potential of this emerging community. It would be hard to think of a more seasoned bunch of salespeople than the veterans at Macy's West Department Stores (part of the Federated family with its sister Bloomingdale's), where a string of successes with niche markets (Asians, African-Americans, gays, teens) has prevented the calamities that befell many department stores that stubbornly stuck with the straight suburban housewife demographic. When Hartman-Squire arrived at Macy's door, she started to work with the vice president of external affairs, Carol Jackson (who chaired the National Retail Federation's Council on Diversity and really "gets" disability-inclusive diversity). Hartman-Squire was invited to present the business case for "Strategic Marketing WITH the Disability Community" to the Council at its June 2004 meeting, and Jackson immediately saw the potential for her own brand of stores. Macy's was already well on its way with innovations such as "Fast Facts" stuffers inside paycheck envelopes during the month of October (designated National Disability Employment Awareness Month).

Hartman-Squire worked with Macy's the course of nearly a year, by means of a video introduction with the president and CEO, as well as her "Weaving an Accessible Welcome Mat for Employees and Customers with Disabilities" training session for the nine regional HR directors. The Macy's West executives are now committed to building an increased level of awareness up and down the hierarchy of the highly stratified corporation. Eventually the proving ground at Macy's West or any retailer will always be the floor, where marketing campaigns are finished by actual sales to customers. In the western region, where Hartman-Squire worked with northern California executives, annual sales of more than $4 billion are rung up (unfortunately, there is no breakout of how much of this total is accounted for by customers with disabilities). Hartman-Squire notes, "Disability is like the infrared and ultraviolet of the diversity rainbow. We know it is there, but others can't always see it. It is an aspect of diversity that deserves to be illuminated."

The two sexiest examples of Hartman-Squire's marketing genius involve direct applications of her movie and strategic-marketing skills: a major push to involve viewers with disabilities in the release of *My Left Foot* in 1989, and a more recent campaign to encourage them to buy DVS®–Enhanced DVDs of the movie *Ray*. In both cases, she had the right product for the niche (*My Left Foot* is a biopic of a painter with cerebral palsy, while *Ray* is about the blind singer and musical giant Ray Charles), but the marketing of each needed fine-tuning. For *My Left Foot*, EIN SOF Communications pursued the advocacy route. Hartman-Squire arranged for a Capitol Hill opening for a handpicked audience of congressional leaders and advocates, exquisitely timed to coincide with the debate on the ADA, which had already passed the Senate and was stuck in the House by business lobbying. Principles of Universal Design were applied to have the film captioned and audio described for blind and low-vision audiences. WGBH's newly established Descriptive Video Services (DVS®) unit had just launched narrations with PBS's *American Playhouse* a few weeks earlier. This screening was the first application of DVS® for a theatrical film, a technique that years later was applied to the movie *Ray*.

Hartman-Squire organized a direct-mail campaign to get out the audience, reviews by disability studies scholars, most notably one by renowned media expert Paul K. Longmore, Ph.D., called "The Glorious Rage of Christy Brown," and a ton of feature stories that brought the film vastly more media attention than it would otherwise have received. Her advocacy even generated news: Miramax refused to release the film to theaters that were not wheelchair accessible (going well beyond pre-ADA compliance), a first and a stunning example of a major corporation influencing its business partners in regard to wheelchair access. Disability rights activists in major cities surveyed the movie theaters and reported back on levels of accessibility—Miramax then pulled the movie from some inaccessible theaters, much to the dismay of the theater owners, thus giving a hint of the potential commercial power of this market segment.

The move brewed mainstream buzz and community backing, raising awareness of the film in its race to win Oscars (it zoomed past *Born on the 4th of July* in the disability court of public opinion and at the box office), the gold-standard measure of its popularity. *My Left Foot* stood out in the highly critical eyes of the disability community as a rare example of respectful representation, a reputation for sensitivity it still enjoys even as standards have risen, and even though Daniel Day-Lewis, who portrayed Christy Brown, did not have a disability.

If *My Left Foot* was an exercise in adroit public relations, then the *Ray* DVD was a classic case of packaging. Cost effective because primary outreach targeted blind/low-vision leaders with a large-print/Braille postcard and list serve/Web site announcements, the Enhanced DVD directly reached thousands of first-time buyers who can now be firmly counted as Universal Studios Home Entertainment loyalists. It turned out that the clincher was as basic as printing a "ribbon" on the packaging that proclaimed the endorsement conferred by the American Council of the Blind (ACB) "Winner: ACB Media Access Award." The DVS®-Enhanced DVD of *Ray* is priced the same as the "regular" one and was released on the same "street date." In the future, DVS®-Enhanced versions will similarly be added to other DVD products.

Both hits—*My Left Foot* for the grassroots organizing and press, and *Ray* for the use of DVS and sales—underscore the role of effective communication and cost-effective strategic marketing *"with,"* not "at" or "for," the disability community. For *Ray*, Hartman-Squire started by convincing the brass at Universal Studios that a significant group of blind viewers was missing from the DVD audience for the movie, some of whom had enjoyed the DVS version in their neighborhood movie theaters, and that a timely and skillfully executed campaign could bring them around. By pitching the effort directly through an influential grassroots nonprofit organization, the American Council of the Blind, and including the masterful narrations already created by WGBH for the theatrical release, Hartman-Squire had confidence that blind and low-vision audiences would get on board for the launch. More important, they would bring along with them a broader disability demographic, acting in solidarity with and approval of Universal's recognition of the greater disability sector as a viable market segment.

Universal executives, ACB, WGBH, and EIN SOF focused on the movie's release, counting on the same sort of spin generated with the prerelease disability component of the *My Left Foot* campaign created for Miramax in 1989. With *Ray*, Hartman-Squire aimed even higher. Its mainstream appeal guaranteed a safety net for the deeper foray into disability-specific selling. Jamie Foxx was an early favorite during awards season to take home a ton of gold for his portrayal of Ray Charles, eventually garnering an Oscar, a Golden Globe, and a SAG award. With a blockbuster on their hands, the brass at Universal were more likely to be on board for a technical innovation that would make the DVD fully accessible by its regular "street release" date, not as an afterthought. Nothing in Hollywood is ever cheap or simple, especially when it comes to altering content. Just as closed-captioning has long been available to open a film or television program to Deaf and hard of hearing audiences, the descriptive narrations included in a DVS-Enhanced DVD would translate the picture for those who are blind. In this proprietary description method, invented by WGBH-Boston, narrations inserted between chunks of dialogue brief the listener on changes of scene, characters in the frame, costumes (or lack thereof in the sexy bits), facial expressions, gestures, and movements.

Enter the nonprofit players. The marketing system was a collaborative effort, enlisting not only the Hollywood expertise of Hartman-Squire but also a major national advocacy organization, the American Council of the Blind (ACB), and a crackerjack team at public television station WGBH that specializes in accessibility. WGBH's Media Access Group is not a newcomer to this field. It created the first closed-captioning system in 1972 to make *The French Chef* accessible to Deaf viewers. Since then, the Media Access Group has expanded to include services for blind viewers, which began with PBS's *American Playhouse* in January 1990 (just one month before the Capitol Hill screening of *My Left Foot*). The group also has proprietary technology for "Rear Window" captioning in movie theaters run by AMC-Loews, and National Amusements Showcases among others, and has put together descriptive as well as closed captioning for *The Lion King* and the Harry Potter movies, among other headlining projects. Its research arm, the National Center for Accessible Media (NCAM), originated in 1990 with a grant from the Corporation for Public Broadcasting. The dozen or so staffers at NCAM are among the nation's leading minds in devising the technology that provides alternative formats for movies, television, and the Web. Their work, and Universal's backing, has set the standard for future DVD releases. Since the studio already contracted for the asset (descriptions) for the theatrical division, they can easily be adapted to the DVS version at little added expense. Universal filmmakers may have the technical know-how to blow up intergalactic space ships onscreen, but they needed WGBH to show them the way to adapt their films for the blind audience.

Once the *Ray* DVD was ready, it was endorsed by the American Council of the Blind, only the second time a major organization of this kind has given its seal of approval to a product. The "ribbon" around the package proclaimed "DVS® Enhanced; Created for the Original Feature Film; Primarily Intended for Blind and Low Vision Audiences." This is all very well as a gesture, but if only a token number of DVDs are pressed and retired to a warehouse, or handed out at benefit cocktail parties, you might as well add "Is That All There Is?" to the bonus disc. Mass media means major-league distribution. Universal needed commitments from bona fide outlets, and it hit the big time with Wal-Mart Online and Amazon, both of which agreed to carry the original *Ray* and the DVS-Enhanced version, in addition to the ACB store.

Crossover Hits

It does not stop there, however. Any broadcast or entertainment organization ought to be aware of what the Media Access Group brought to Universal and could do for other products or events. ABC television got the message, ensuring that Steven Bochco's *Blind Justice* police show would be video described (although the show got canceled and WGBH didn't do the descriptions, which were done by We See TV, a small business owned by Rick Boggs, who is blind). ABC is using its Secondary Audio Programming (SAP) feature that usually is dedicated to Spanish. Similarly, the ad industry, with its addiction to "convergence," ought to be checking with the caption crew to see what can be done to extend any print or electronic campaign (consider the fact that 73 percent of Deaf people switch to a brand that has its commercials captioned). The ripple effect spreads from there. Captioning is a basic way for patrons in a gym, bar, airport, or other public space to tune in to their news and stock quotes. Hartman-Squire notes, "In addition to audio books, drivers who have DVDs installed in their cars can now enjoy the same movies their kids are watching in the backseat thanks to DVS-enhanced DVDs without taking their eyes from the road. This crossover effect and audience is underexploited and grossly underestimated." A basic tenet of Universal Design (as we see in the chapter on the accessible office) is the rapid growth of popularity among "nondisabled" users of the convenience that an adapted product offers.

Fine Tuning the Message

Striking the right tone with the disability demographic is tricky. Cause marketing is one element of the sales strategy, but this should not be a pity pitch. "Don't go after this market because it's the right thing to do; go after it because you want to make money, and the rest will follow," says Carmen Jones, another of the nation's top disability and marketing consultants. Since 1998 she has advised corporations and organized the largest trade show featuring disability-specific products and services. She is president of the Solutions Marketing Group in Arlington, Virginia, which has developed disability-marketing strategies for clients such as Darden Restaurants, American Express, AOL, and Bank of America. She emphasizes the importance of what she calls "buy-in" from senior execs at the companies so that the training and promotional strategy is top-down.

Much of her exposure comes from organizing the Disability Expo, which annually tours to five major cities and attracts over 100,000 visitors. As with many another minority-based trade fairs, the souk mentality prevails. A smorgasbord of cottage industries and services are surrounded by massive booths sponsored by companies that sell telecom, computer, and mobility devices, durable medical equipment, wheelchair accessories, and so forth, all of them eager to boost their image. Family members and rehab therapists as well as people with disabilities turn out. On the plus side, the potential for business-to-business deal making is high, and for those trying to get a fix on the direction in which the disability marketplace may be moving, the expo offers one-stop shopping. When my magazine started up, we angled for a chance to give it out free at the 1998 expo in New Jersey, but never returned. Why? The flip side of this expo and other ideas of its kind is that they tend to be narrowly confined to disability-specific projects (hearing aid batteries, wheelchair cushions, and other ancillary products). As important as it is to recognize this specialized sector, which certainly represents a chunk of what we call the disability market, there is too great a temptation to face in that direction and turn one's back on the larger interface between consumers with disabilities and the mainstream economy. As a trading zone, it lacks the balance of non-disabled participation.

Learning from Elders

Then there is the senior market, so brilliantly exploited by AARP, a slew of quick-thinking consumer products manufacturers, and a parallel universe of niche consultants. The senior and disability markets actually overlap significantly, since over one-fourth of all disabilities are incurred by those who are sixty-five and older. The rise in boomers (closing in on 75 million and expected to be double that by 2040) is feeding the disability niche, and companies selling any of the vast roster of products that are targeting one niche should be seriously considering the other. Baby boomers, though, are terrified to self-identify with "those" people with disabilities—desperately clutching to the false "us and them" safety net. You have to market to their "functional limitations": Are you needing a larger font on your computer, or increased volume on your cell phone? That is the way to try out the accessibility angle. If anything, this synergy between the two niches should add fuel to the fire for those warming up to the disability idea. The seniors are touted as the richest niche, with $19 trillion in net worth (three-fourths of the nation's wealth) and per capita income 26 percent higher than the national average, which beats the disability crowd even though both come in at an even $1 trillion in spending. Much of the seniors' spending is healthcare related, as with the disability group (74 percent of prescription drugs go to seniors, 51 percent of over-the-counter). Seniors account for 80 percent of all luxury travel (people with disabilities also tend to fly first or business class, and take along companions), 41 percent of purchases of cars, 25 percent of toys. With $7 billion in online purchases last year, they outspent teenaged Web shoppers. There are notable crossover campaigns that blend disability and mature demographics. In 2000 Avis needed less than a year to become the rental car company of choice for people with disabilities after launching a targeted effort in that direction. To complement existing services, Avis introduced a suite of products for customers with disabilities. Avis® Access—a no-cost package of options geared to a range of disabilities—includes a transfer board that eases a driver or passenger from a wheelchair into the car seat, a swivel seat requiring minimal effort to turn or be moved, hand controls that bypass the pedals, a "spinner knob" that enables a full turning radius of the steering wheel by one hand, and panoramic mirrors that are useful for deaf or hard of hearing drivers. As an added financial incentive, Avis waived fees for designated drivers for blind customers.

The program was tested in eighty-one North American locations and was eventually extended from reservations to walk-ins (and roll-ins). Avis ran an extensive print campaign in disability magazines and AARP publications, recognizing that the gadgetry as well as the services would appeal to mature travelers, too. A series of press releases featured rave reviews, including one from Eric Lipp, executive director of the Chicago-based nonprofit Open Doors Organization: "The Avis Access Program is a beacon in the tourism, hospitality and rental car sectors for all companies to learn from and follow." Based on call volumes and anecdotes, Avis figures it saw an increase in its disability business. Michael J. Caron, vice president of product and program development, is pushing hard to expand the program from its grassroots success. "We want to be in front of this, serving needs. I don't think we really anticipated how well accepted this would be," he says with enthusiasm. "We are developing new market tactics to build awareness."[2] Avis is planning to expand beyond the original locations with these services and is moving fast. As Caron advised me, "To make this work, you need to understand and visualize the ever-present barriers for a large percentage of customers."

Focus on the Future

As with so much in the disability movement, it has taken far too long to reach this point. Signs of further progress are in the offing. In a landmark research effort, Nielsen Entertainment's Joseph Craig (the sister companies are famous for their television ratings and box-office grosses) and Hartman-Squire's EIN SOF Communications put together a multipronged project titled "Disability Community Market Research Initiative" that was featured in *Fortune Small Business* and *Adweek*. In this format, a focus group of people with spinal cord injuries (including family members) was interviewed vis-à-vis the individuals' perceptions of products, brands, corporate reputations, and service. The National Spinal Cord Injury Association, which recruited the participants in the study, is joining forces with NRGi and EIN SOF to create the first-ever disability community "White Paper Report," inspired by the NAACP "Report Card" that measures the economic impact of people of color. Much as the National Organization on Disability in 2000 used the Harris Interactive Poll (a landmark influx of data uncovering, among other things, the enticing statistic that four out of ten people with disabilities are online and spend twice the time logged on than their nondisabled counterparts), NSCIA is teaming up with Joseph Craig of Nielsen, the nation's premier market research firm (and with Hartman-Squire of EIN SOF), to pump up the volume of its message and to drill deeper into the consumer lifestyle choices and preferences of this untapped emerging market. By design, Craig and Hartman-Squire started with wheelchair users. Using the typical one-way glass and the precisely articulated battery of questions customized for the participating companies, the Disability Community Market Research Initiative conducted two focus groups, and then in 2005 followed with a hard of hearing group in conjunction with SHHH. The spring of 2006 will yield focus groups with the NSCIA, the American Council of the Blind, SHHH, and Telecommunications for the Deaf. The format of each of the "syndicated" studies was essentially the same. As many as half a dozen companies representing a range of industries including banking, telecommunications, restaurants, Internet service providers, pharmaceuticals, rental cars, and others pooled resources to convene a focus group. One set of questions is formulated to serve the whole syndicate of clients, then the rest of the session is devoted to each individual company's proprietary interests. Only one company per sector participates in any specific focus group. The basic questions are designed—with all the sophistication for which marketing pros are known, and unlike other disability market research heretofore—to measure the factors that drive consumer decisions, to examine what makes the disability community tick, what drives these consumers' lifestyle choices. The Nielsen/EIN SOF team is seeking rich qualitative data with the focus groups (and quantitative proof in the case of telephone and Internet surveys) on the causal relationship between a company's friendly image and visibility in the disability community and its ability to attract customers and workers. If the spinal cord group is any indication, the researchers nailed their thesis. Isn't it odd that it took this long to convene a focus group, though?

Traditionally, cause marketing has concocted a mix of advertising, sponsorships (sporting events are popular, as are conferences, while rubber chicken dinners are passé), and public relations. Craig and Hartman-Squire were after leads on new ways to break through the relatively steady, and low, levels of brand awareness achieved by sticking to the conventional wisdom. Craig and Hartman-Squire explained what they were looking for after the two spinal cord sessions were finished: "What does it take to get your business into the consciousness of the community? What moves the consumer with a disability out of the comfort zone to try a new bank, cell phone, ISP, restaurant, or medication?"

Sector by Sector

A few of the conclusions are broadly applicable to a range of consumer-marketing problems. For the last decade, the temptation was to treat the disability community as one great lumpen mass that moves together toward or away from products—a homogeneous market. The more focus groups that Nielson's Joseph Craig and EIN SOF's Hartman-Squire conduct, the more they realize it is important to break this group of consumers into sectors, by disability and by industry. "You need to understand what makes each component of the community tick. A certain type of ATM works for blind people, but does not benefit customers who use wheelchairs, while Web accessibility is not a factor for wheelchair users but is for the blind community," says Hartman-Squire. In a survey of disability-marketing success stories that recently appeared in *Business Week*, "What Marketers Should Know about People with Disabilities," reporter Kipp Cheng noted, "What's more important than accommodating message delivery is articulating the unique selling propositions of a product or service for a niche market that's very different from the market as a whole." Credibility is fragile in matters of this kind. There are so many examples of misfires that only a few will suffice. Nike, which actually played disability big as a cause-marketing angle with the multimillion-dollar Casey Martin campaign (Martin alone got a million to act as sponsor), had blundered badly less than a year earlier with the Dri-Goat print ads in *Backpacker* and other magazines, yanking the ads after a hailstorm of protest from disability community advocates. Nike compounded the problem by issuing an apology that was perceived by the community as just as patronizing. Nike has never quite recovered from the blunder; Martin's game faded, and those ads were pulled. Nike along with McDonald's has used wheelchair and Paralympic athletes, the stars of the Paralympics (not to be confused with the noncompetitive Special Olympics), to add realism to its mix of endorsements, but the shadow of the Dri-Goat perdures as an object lesson to other callow, not to mention shallow, marketers.

Agenda

- *Communicate your commitment* in labels, advertising, packaging, press campaigns, Web sites.
- *Graft* a disability affinity group of consumers *onto other existing "diversity groups."*
- *Create a customer advisory board or task force* composed to provide guidance, insights, expertise.
- *Explore the crossover demand* of multiple purposes and applications.
- *Know the customer's needs* and comfort level.
- *Enlist the expertise of the disability grassroots nonprofits* (not service providers) and the support of top brass.
- *Avoid patronizing or insulting* language and images.
- *Ensure alternative formats,* such as Braille and large print, for promotional materials and Web sites.

Notes

1. Personal interview, October 2005.
2. Personal interview, November 2005.

Chapter 5

Start Spreading the News

Tips for Public Relations Strategists

From you I get the story.
—Pete Townshend, "Listening to You," *The Who's Tommy*

A ny cynic would wonder, what earthly good does it bring my company to do the right thing and not get the recognition? Public relations strategy is part of building a disability presence. It candidly affirms the ends-driven motivation behind accommodating employees and customers. It also harmonizes with a major theme emerging from the best practices we have examined: the vital importance of communications. Within that rubric, formulating a media plan for businesses large or small that make the commitment to disability is a logical extension of the agenda. It complements the marketing initiative in cost-effective ways that PR managers instantly recognize. It also externally completes the internal project of articulating the company's disability agenda. The salesperson worth his or her commissions knows the added value of good press beyond the ad campaign (and often linked to it, as needy media outlets readily trade editorial for paid pages). Word of mouth as conveyed via blog, Listserv, and specialty press is the eight-hundred-pound gorilla of disability marketing, especially when the community decides to act in unison and get behind a product—or sink it. A few headlines in the mainstream press can sway that second circle of customers who are friends, colleagues, and family. The truly colossal impact on sales is measured when a national TV news outlet picks up the story. This is how Mattel and Toys "R" Us scored with the Share-a-Smile Becky®

(Barbie's companion who uses a wheelchair). By the time CNN had aired its two-minute piece around the world, along with the other five hundred worldwide news hits, the smiles were spread all over Mattel and Toys "R" Us. The doll was sold out in two weeks.

There is an even broader applicability of PR to the disability-forward image. When leading consultants make over a corporation, a high-ranking representative of the press office is always in the room. As one of these consultants, Tari Susan Hartman-Squire, observes, "If you genuinely work with the community and the community knows what you are doing is authentic and not token window dressing, then the community could polish your halo effect." This may be the most daunting wilderness on the business map when it comes to disability literacy. While the time machines in the HR and marketing departments appear to be stuck in 1990, the press office setting is at least a decade behind that watershed epoch. There are two historic reasons why there are so few examples of an adroit media play even from the major companies we have observed. The first is the overall backwardness of the corporations when it comes to the subject of disability. Reticence is natural when one is unsure of the message. But the heavier responsibility lies with the mainstream press itself. As I have extensively shown in a previous book, the media are clueless when it comes to the real disability story. Consigned to "soft news" categories such as human interest, triumph over adversity, or profiles in courage, disability rarely makes it to the business pages at all. When it does, it is inevitably preceded by the perfume of charitable benevolence. Even if publicists delivered the ideal ingredients for a story on a silver platter (which is precisely how many features arrive in our newspapers every day, we now know, thanks to glaring examples of prepackaged news delivered from the White House, among other sources), the press is likely to fumble. For example, the only disability clips of recent vintage from important business publications were announced by department heads such as "medical miracles" or "philanthropy." Late in 2005 the *Wall Street Journal* ran four front-page features on people with disabilities, all profiles that involved medical or human rights issues. Powerful as they were in terms of sociology, and remarkable for their position (left-hand column, above the fold), they were not "business" pieces per se. In March 2006, *Adweek* ran a cover story on disability by Joanne Voight that is considered a milestone. The print highlight of 2004 was, without much question, the cover story by Elaine Pofeldt that *Fortune Small Business* magazine gave to disability and marketing in the May 1, 2005, issue, but it was not the "regular" *Fortune* cover—it was *Fortune Small Business*. A cover story in the real *Fortune* that gives disability the full Time Inc. group (we used to call it "grope") reporting treatment, complete with company profiles and hagiographies of the CEOs as well as trend charts and investment tips, is still waiting for its moment. The last section of this chapter essentially sets up the PR groundwork for participating in it, but even if your company is ready, *Fortune* has to be ready, too. That will take more time (and *Newsweek*).

To my astonishment, the academic publishing machine is oddly just as sparing as the mainstream in its analytic attention to the role of disability in economics, management, consumer trends, or even ethics, with the exception of the economists at Cornell studying labor trends in the Employment and Disability Institute under the aegis of the Industrial Labor Relations Board. In the eyes of the typical manager or small-business owner, this appears to be no great loss, in that few enough of them can wade through the mind-choking jargon of the average journal article. Yet research of this kind often becomes the source for mass media reporting. It is picked up by Wall Street analysts or consultants at such influential firms as Sanford Bernstein, Cone/Roper, and McKinsey and Company. With the exception of legal scholars trying to worm their way around the ADA, there is little action on the grant-supported front. The absence of cutting-edge university- or NGO-sponsored research on disability issues in business has left a gap in such vital areas as statistics, theory, ethics, and the analysis of trends. Stripped of their doctoral dissertation varnish, papers of this kind yield story ideas for the media. Unlike engineering and design journals, where a considerable literature on disability has been available for some time, the academic journals devoted to business have missed out on this topic. This is all the more surprising as disability studies has become hot in the humanities journals.

Journalists alternately neglect and obliquely tiptoe around people with disabilities in positions of business leadership. The awkwardness is reminiscent of the kid-glove treatment women, gays, and African-Americans were afforded until about a decade ago. To offer an idea of how rapidly that has changed, consider the arc of coverage received by two conspicuous figures in the news during 2005: Carly Fiorina, the former CEO of Hewlett-Packard, and Martha Stewart. During their ascendancy, the press was in its "you-go-girl" mode, cheering on the executive-suite achievements of any CEO in a skirt. It was among other things an overt way in the eighties and nineties to demonstrate the commitment to corporate diversity at Time Inc. or Advance Publications, as well as a sop for advertisers who sponsored advertorials on HR policies that promoted women. Just toss the troublesome minority a cover once in a while and shut them up. If you are lucky you gain niche readership. But the press moves rapidly, and the appetite for novelty is too massive for rehashes to satisfy. By the time the dish had turned sour—

Fiorina was ousted by her board even while Stewart's ankle was chafing in its parole bracelet—the business media had matured. They were ready to treat both Fiorina and Stewart as regular guys and essentially slam them as they would any other fallen idol. For those of us who had worked in the press for some time and recognized the rarity of a journalist eating his or her own words, it was particularly amusing to mark the turnaround of specific correspondents who had hyped the two of them on the way up. The press revels in its power to make and unmake business stars. With Stewart the media still seem to be taking this puppeteer power to its limit by reviving her career with the tenebrous suggestion that they could eventually turn against her again, like sportswriters who give a drug abuser who pitches well a third or fourth chance. What finally mattered in the case of Fiorina, who was terminally squashed, was not that she was a woman but that she was fair game as a failure.

This is a good thing. The straightforward application of the regular journalistic rules, especially the baseline one about everybody being a potential target of a hit piece, is an implicit recognition that women have arrived. They can be superheroes just as they can be crooks, tyrants, or losers. No such plateau has been reached by business figures with disabilities. If they make it to the page at all, they get the rubber-glove treatment as saintly heroes who, as it always goes, overcame by grace of their own courage and the paternalistic heart of companies willing to take a chance on them. Two of the poster boys, founders of multibillion-dollar empires, happened to share the same disability, dyslexia. Charles Schwab "came out" as a dyslexic in the eighties and is often held up by the community, and his company publicists, as an example of how far a person with a disability can go in the entrepreneurial world. More of a cowboy, and much further out there in terms of disability, is Kinko's founder Paul Orfalea. After he retired from the $2-billion-a-year company he started in 1970, he penned his best-selling autobiography, provocatively titled *Copy That: Lessons from a Hyperactive Dyslexic Who Turned a Bright Idea into One of America's Best Companies.*[1] Although Orfalea is funny and candid about his disability (he refused to write any business correspondence and could not sit still through meetings), he retains his saintly aura of being beyond reproach both as an "inspiring" story of small-business ownership and as a person with a disability. The closest thing we have to Martha Stewart is the vile Larry Flynt, a litigious pornographer who gets a bye from the press not because he is a media tycoon but because he is a paraplegic. That awkward politeness, by contrast with the bared fangs Stewart drew, is one indication of how unprepared the media is for disability. Business press coverage is far more likely to focus on "heroic"

CEOs and middle- or lower-level employees happily plugging away at jobs they were "lucky" to get than to try to unfold the dark and light layers of a story like Flynt's.

Just as workers with disabilities are not quite recognized as subjects for media, on the other side of the microphone the press is struggling to find competent reporting talent to cover them. The best-informed and most widely read business journalist out there is former *Business Week* columnist John Williams, who covers assistive technology but has written with immense insight about marketing, advertising, finance, and a range of other issues. Williams on assistive technology is the gold standard for how disability can effectively make it to the pages of mainstream journalism without the usual patronization and pathos. Like many journalists, he is a true polymath. He is one of a number of prominent Washington-based journalists with disabilities (he stutters). As long as the sources are there, he can get up to speed on the story. As he observes, "The most important aspects of writing a story are knowing the issues and players and how they interrelate. I know the issues, players, and their relationships. My fascination in writing about disability centers on quality-of-life issues regarding access to education, health, transportation, jobs, housing, the community, civil rights, assistive technology products, and independent living."[2]

Pitching the Upbeat Profile

One press office strategy is to accept this insulting state of affairs and go after that pity piece as a surefire "hit" that makes the company look benevolent. Good news is hard to come by, after all. If the company hires and promotes people with disabilities, then the most direct way to take credit is by spotlighting a success story within the ranks. For the mainstream consumer or shareholder who does not know any better, the piece affirms the positive image of the company. A plug of this kind has a dollars-and-cents effect that more than justifies the energy and resources expended on getting the coverage. If the happy stories of self-sufficient Wal-Mart and Microsoft employees could all be told seriatim, the companies' reputations would steadily rise. So would the stock prices and, one hopes, the standing (and sitting) of workers with disability in the eyes of public perception, even though the sappy and patronizing tone of these stories gets eyes rolling in the community. It seems the least that a press office can do.

The best way for a publicist to orchestrate coverage of a company's employment or marketing outreach to the community is undoubtedly through offering a detailed look at the job performed by a person with a disability. The step-by-step development of the story is relatively straightforward and routine for anyone who has been in public relations, although the initial stage can be complicated by the now-familiar question of self-identification and privacy. Some companies have a go-to spokesperson on disability who is trotted out to represent them whenever the call comes in. For instance, journalists who seek a disability quote from IBM get bumped to Jim Sinocchi, mentioned in the previous chapter. Luckily he is a flak as well as the company's leading expert on disability culture inside Big Blue, so it is hard to imagine anyone better qualified to present the company line, the disability primer for unsophisticated journalists, or the advanced quotes for the disability-specific press, while avoiding the harrowing moments of candor that corporate PR managers dread. Similarly, reporters who call GM have for years been referred to Paul Ulrich, manager of the Paragon Project for adaptive mobility products. This has the whiff of tokenism, but on the pragmatic side it solves a number of problems, beginning with the self-identification aspect. And it gives me the opportunity to suggest that a person with a disability be included in the press office corps itself. Just as he or she would make a convincing public face (it works in marketing), the press officer with a disability offers up-front proof of the company's disability consciousness. As we turn later in this chapter to ways to deflate the critical investigative piece, he or she is also a first line of defense.

Rounding up a previously unknown person with a disability to handle a media query is not that simple. The routine response to interview requests has to be modified in the disability case. It is not unheard-of for a press officer to send out an all points bulletin on a Friday afternoon at four thirty begging for anybody who answers to a certain description to come forward and answer a journalist's query. This sort of thing happens all the time in the press offices of major companies. They prepare "available for interview" lists and bullet points to be ready. It is not always *CBS Sixty Minutes* on the horn. A small-town paper calls with a query for a local source at work on a high-profile project; a gay news blog appeals for a gay source; a television producer wants an on-camera quote from a black marketing manager. Press officers keep lists of potential sources that can be offered to the journalist according not only to expertise but also to identity. Step one is adding disability as a category to that list of interview candidates, the company's ambassadors and spokespeople.

The next challenge is ensuring that both the journalist and the source are on the same page. The press officer has to be as ready to educate the journalist in disability culture as in the corporate culture. Similarly, the source has to be coached not only on toeing the party line but on how the company expects him or her to keep the journalist on message about the way it abides by the dos and don'ts of disability. I have known plenty of line managers in major companies who could talk the talk when it came to their corporate policies but were completely unsure regarding the up-to-date rules of disability etiquette and semantics, largely because, although some were people with disabilities, they did not consider themselves to be in the community but certainly thought of themselves as being part of the corporate culture. There is no need to get hard-assed about this and call it denial (as some advocates do). It is a choice that clearly reflects the reality of the times, which rewards company loyalty above disability advocacy.

Returning to the job of the press officer, one of the best arguments for a minicourse in the language and protocol of disability culture is this dual responsibility for cutting off the gaffes, linguistic as well as attitudinal, that would mar the reception of the piece among readers in the disability community. Those readers are the smell test. Tripping over "wheelchair-bound" or getting snagged in one of the old clichés is not just a problem for the ignorant writer but a missed opportunity for the company to score real points with the reader or viewer who matters. Serving the disability agenda by respecting the code is one side of the story. The other is representing the company's disability platform as established by the marketing or recruiting effort. That will be the essential content of the story. Even in the case of a "good news" piece, the press office has to proceed with caution. The bigger the corporation, the more paranoid it always seems to be regarding the message that it sends out. The problem is coaching the insider with a disability who has been tapped as a source on the talking points for the article from the point of view of the press office. Ostensibly the story the company wants told seems pretty obvious: Company X is a great place to work for somebody like me, or is doing its utmost to reach out to the customer and prospective employee with a disability. The bosses get it. Depending on the publication and the circumstances, this message can be delivered straight or shown in more subtle ways that permit the reader to put together the conclusion that the company is doing the right thing. One of the classic story forms is the "day in the life" piece, for which a journalist accompanies the profile subject through a typical day as orchestrated by the press corps. As a journalist who has done this dozens of times, my first bit of advice is to avoid the mistake of having a press officer accompany the writer and the subject. This is all the more important in the case of a person with a disability, as any such shadowing makes it look like a caregiver has to be around. Controlling the message by interrupting an extended interview with the party line may be an efficient way to avoid a slip of the tongue that reveals more than was planned, but it ruins the authenticity of voice and experience that the journalist seeks.

Instead, press officers ought to learn in the case of a disability profile to suspend their usual suspicions and *trust* both their own source and the journalist. Although journalists are not obliged to promise that an article is going to be positive, and have been known to dangle that prospect in exchange for access to leads for a hit piece, a savvy PR person has sufficient radar to sort the potential puff piece from the hit piece. Most disability profiles are still likely to be favorable, and when the press office shows sufficient confidence in its own source to let him or her handle the reporter one on one, it sends a strong first message about the confidence the company shows in its own staffer. (The PR staffer can always circle back with the source and then the journalist under the guise of "fact-checking" to help smooth over potential glitches.)

For a disability-savvy reporter, a confident and trusting PR stance can buy a bit of indulgence if the company is less than splendid in certain disability areas. In 1999, I profiled Wendell Garrett, one of the most fascinating people in the auction business, an expert in American antique furniture at Sotheby's and a rising star on the TV hit *Antiques Roadshow*. The piece was set up by my sister Robin, who was a senior press officer for Sotheby's at the time in what was one of the most nervous, controlling PR departments in New York (justifiably, it turns out, as Sotheby's was covering up a tale of corporate malfeasance that exploded in the press a few years later). As it was her brother and a disability magazine—simpatico from the start— my sister managed to relax enough to let me have Garrett to myself for one of the most delightful and informative days I have ever spent as a business journalist. She also knew Garrett could handle an interview on his own. Not only was he becoming one of the company's media stars through the television exposure, but he was the editor of *Antiques* magazine for forty years. He knew the drill. It all began inauspiciously, however, as I wound my way through a rabbit warren of offices to find Garrett holed up in his splendidly cluttered office, more like a professor's library than corporate digs. As a responsible disability journalist with his own set of eyes, I could have taken a potshot at the company for inaccessible architecture and ruined my sister's day. Instead, the piece was not about Sotheby's at all. It was a raving paean to a world-renowned expert who loved the job he did so well. Sotheby's could take peripheral credit for giving him a place to hang his hat. If the press office had known to push this opening further, it might have urged Garrett to insert an aside on how the auction house had accommodated his needs or was reaching out to the community, but I suspect there was little to offer in that way (the company certainly hadn't made his life easier on the job, judging by the office layout). My story ran under the slug "People on the Move," a front-of-the-book, two-page section that celebrated achievers like Garrett. Among the high-powered figures we put in that position were singer Gloria Estefan, Oklahoma City bombing prosecutor Joseph Hartzler, and White House attorney Charles Ruff.

From the corporate standpoint a profile, especially in the mainstream press, has a great deal to offer. It is an engaging way of using an "objective" point of view to demonstrate that the company is hiring, accommodating, and advancing its workers with disabilities. Break this down in terms of the elements of the story. The on-the-job setting offers a descriptive vehicle for spotlighting the company's efforts to build an accessible and disability-friendly workplace. A bit of coaching from the press officer can ensure that the less obvious features are not missed by the reporter—preparation for the story might include a brief list of the accommodations in place. The narrative of the career path, from recruitment through mentoring and promotions, is an ideal way to get the diversity story out and demonstrate the company's follow-through on promises made to the community vis-à-vis human resources policies. An essential element in this for the journalist is a clear timeline by which the movement of the employee through the system can be tracked, with particulars on how promotions came about. Although it is unusual for compensation to be spelled out in a piece about midlevel employees (the figures for the big shots at the director level of publicly traded companies are easily found in the Securities and Exchange Commission documents they are required to publish), for stories that the company does want to use to demonstrate its commitment to disability within diversity it might not be a bad idea to give a salary range as well as mention bonuses and perks.

Quotations of the main subject are the meat of the article, opportunities for an audience with disabilities to hear directly from one of their own that the company is including them in its policies. Standard fare in a business profile is a set of quotes as well from superiors or peers, usually rave reviews of the subject. Most journalists use these in longer articles to add to the mix of voices. In the case of the disability profile, the danger of this from the point of view of making the company look up to date is the all-too-likely possibility that the boss puts his or her foot in it by using archaic language or saying something patronizing along the lines of "for a guy in a wheelchair, Wendell sure does get the job done." The subliminal message of a profile that allows the subject himself or herself to speak without these condescending choral remarks is that the autonomous success of this person is endorsed rather than given by the company. Although it is usually company policy to have one of the top brass weigh in for stories of this kind, the potential advantages of not doing so might give the press officer pause to consider making an exception.

The problem with scoring one of these profiles of a success story on the job is that they still usually wind up perpetuating the status quo. Just as major studio biopics that win Oscars for sugarcoating life with a disability end up doing more harm than good, the feel-good business profile is too often a placebo. Here's a sobering thought: nobody seriously reads this sort of filler, anyway. Frontline decision makers have little patience, because soft journalism is no substitute for the news-you-can-use meat of a paper, magazine, or program. As the speed of commerce accelerates, it is harder than ever for print journalism, especially, to deliver the kind of reporting that affects significant moves such as purchasing, stock picking, capital investing, hiring and firing, and other gritty actions. Magazines and TV investment programs are already in danger of becoming mere entertainment, losing their role in the loop of business decision making that matters. An executive I once covered for *Fortune* scornfully told me the magazine was his weekend bathroom reading. This is all the more true for innocuous little feel-good pieces. Nobody at rival Oracle ever lost sleep over a nice story about a programmer at Microsoft who got a terrific mouse and good parking. Investigative journalism and news reporting is far different. A story that breaks news about the risk of class-action lawsuits will cause heads to roll, but we will get to the PR defense against hit pieces later in this chapter.

Product Placement

Press offices use releases and background materials to directly pump the marketing efforts behind a product or service. The news disseminated through such materials is tailored to the various media that cover an industry. The trade press receives a kit heavy on specifications, while overseas publications get the version based on availability to customers online, for example. At the very least corporate publicists ought to start adding the specialized disability media to any contact list for a product launch. An edited version of the press kit makes clear the disability-specific news peg (slang for the *new* fact or development on which a story is hung). General releases do not usually answer the primary question about whether a disability audience would care about and be able to act on the news. Throughout the release, editorial changes may be necessary anyway to avoid insulting readers with disabilities, but I would argue this kind of stylistic revamping is necessary for all the copy that a press office turns out.

Certain companies that have danced with the disability community on HR and marketing programs have mastered the steps. The texts and images in the media kits and television B roll (the prepared videos that publicists offer to news outlets to save them time and money) use people-first language, stay clear of the "wheelchair-bound" type of goofs, avoid clichés, and do not career into either the "medical miracle" or "freak" errors. In addition to the regular suspects (Microsoft, IBM, General Motors, Bank of America, Cingular Wireless), one of the most sophisticated media offices in corporate America when it comes to disability is found in Motorola headquarters in Schaumburg, Illinois. The company has plenty of product to move in the disability market. It also has, among its sixty-eight thousand employees, a core of managers with disabilities who work from inside to ensure that the company appears disability-forward. As with service provider and partner Cingular Wireless, whose success in this sector we consider in the coming chapter, Motorola wisely invested in accessibility features more than a decade ago and is reaping the profits today. The multimillion-dollar press and ad campaign conducted in 2004 was given the title "Seamless Mobility" (apt enough for our purposes, given the number of wheelchair users in the disability market). "The end of there is here. And here is a great place to be," reads the koanesque copy. The accent is on linking and synching the computer and TV at home, the phone in your pocket or in the car, the networked devices in the office. Just as the overall "liquid" service this message promises would be a godsend to executives on the move, or teenagers who cannot bear to be out of touch, it is a clear winner for people with disabilities who similarly crave "easy living" through advanced technology. One of the strengths of Motorola's recent presentations to Wall Street analysts is the compelling argument that as Homeland Security spends billions on emergency-management infrastructure, telecommunications is already experiencing a major windfall in the way of procurement contracts. I predict the next phase of the federal procurement cycle, although Motorola government affairs experts probably already have called it as well, is likely to put together public and private sectors in a new way. Since the notification and evacuation of people with disabilities is now a hot-button issue in Washington policy circles, the company's ability to position itself as the premier provider of the equipment that deaf, blind, and other users with disabilities will use to get the word on disasters such as a terrorist attack or hurricane could bring even more profits.

The media offices of Motorola and other major publicly held corporations have a dual function. They handle both press queries and shareholder services, including presentations to analysts and pension funds. The materials used for both purposes are often derived from one another, as press releases are pilfered for PowerPoint presentations. In this cut-and-paste world, why draft new copy? Once the experts provide the accessibility information that is often originally destined for the owner's manual, it finds multiple uses in press releases, sales brochures, Web downloads, and presentations. A single phrase ("speech input and output features for users with vision disabilities") migrates through several incarnations.

Who writes this stuff? Motorola insiders with disabilities are the company's secret weapons. The new expert is Scott Kelley, but Nancy Valley has served as manager of the company's Disability Access Program for more than a decade. This required her to wear many hats. On the development side, she pushed for integrating "accessible" product features into the cell phone line (which generates $17 billion a year in sales). She also directed sales and consumer relations with disability organizations worldwide. In house, she created the company's training programs on disability awareness and inclusion and was used by the media office as company spokesperson on access and disability issues. She initiated the alternate format program that provides manuals and other product literature in Braille, large print, and audio versions. Motorola has earned points through nonprofit community work. In 1999, Valley conceived the Text to Protect Program—a national service, using donated Motorola text pagers, that allows deaf women and those with speech impediments who are at risk from domestic violence to call for emergency assistance. She has won all kinds of honors for this immensely important achievement, including the Personal Communication Industry Association Distinguished Corporate Citizen Award (2000); The Los Angeles Commission on Assaults Against Women Honoree Deaf and Disabled Services (2001); and the Award for Innovation in Disability Service, Deaf Women Against Violence (2001). Valley represents Motorola at the super-advanced MIT Media Lab in Cambridge, where some of the greatest high-tech innovations for disability have been invented.

Another ambassador for Motorola is Kevin Foster, a senior manager in HR who deals with diversity and compliance issues, when he is not out recruiting at conferences and picking up awards for the chairman's office. A thirteen-year veteran who has handled a wide range of disability-related duties, from organizational development to equal employment opportunity compliance, employee relations, training, research design, statistics, database management, and the development of measurement tools and systems,

Foster lost 90 percent of his sight to a congenital illness. He earned his master's in industrial organizational psychology as well as a bachelor's in psychology from California State University in Sacramento, and is an avid skier who once competed in the Paralympics as captain of the U.S. team. Among his accomplishments, he launched and led the Arizona Business Leadership Network. Funny and assured in front of audience, he is a superb choice for the road shows that keep Motorola and its disability efforts in front of college seniors, HR and legal conferences or seminars, and the press, whom he handles with aplomb. His repertoire of anecdotes as well as his own presence are proof enough of the company's commitment. He often recounts the story of a deaf colleague he helped out of a rut, who explained through an American Sign Language (ASL) interpreter that he was frustrated in his position and isolation. The employee's request for accommodation got Foster going, and eventually the frustrated man was promoted to a far better spot in preventive maintenance, where he thrived. "He challenged the comfort zone for the management team around him, and while he had been great at his former job, he really excelled at his new one," Foster observes. The story has autobiographical relevance. As he says, "I had an overwhelming reluctance to ask for accommodations initially. I was concerned about the cost. I was concerned about rocking the boat."

Foster is a presence in the community, sitting on the board of directors for the American Foundation for the Blind's National Employment Center, on the planning committee for COSD, and heading the Arizona Business Leadership Network while sitting on the countrywide U.S. Business Leadership Network steering committee. He delivers the giant Motorola checks to such business-centered organizations as Career Opportunities for Students with Disabilities (and hosted its 2004 conference at headquarters in Illinois) and the National Business & Disability Council on Long Island. He has been there to garner Motorola's many awards, including the 2002 Distinguished Corporate Citizen Award from Horizons for the Blind, the 2001 Appreciation Award for Innovative Technology Use and Assistance for Deaf Women from Deaf Women Against Violence, the 2001 Award for Initiatives for the Introduction of Wireless Technology to the Disability Community from the Personal Communications Industry Association, and the 1999 SHHH Access Award from Self Help for Hard of Hearing People. To its great credit, Motorola realizes that the catalogue of accessibility features and the long list of these awards are its ticket to great press hits and community good will, and the company plays it shamelessly. Several of the handsets in the "Seamless Mobility" line are specifically touted for their accessibility, including the A840 phone, which has the gizmos (camera, global data downloads, video playback) but also has speech input and output features that the press materials and online advertising identify as "for users with vision disabilities." The CDMA (Code Division Multiple Access, one of the two main types of digital wireless communication platforms, the other being GSM for Global System for Mobile Communications) also sports a camera and fancy ring tones. It is especially good for blind users because it offers advanced speech recognition. Some of the "hands-free" features that drivers in many localities are required by law to have in the car are also important for users with mobility restrictions. The hottest items at Motorola, at least at the moment when this is written, are the ROKR music phone and the Ojo personal videophone. The ROKR was the brainchild of Motorola CEO Ed Zander and Steve Jobs, whose smoking iPod is the source of the one hundred tunes the phone can hold. The most anticipated gadget of 2005, the ROKR was held up by intellectual property complications for months and even then had a rocky debut. The usually implacable Jobs, whose product launches never go awry, had trouble onstage at the San Francisco event when it was unveiled. As Cingular Wireless also found, one of the most efficient ways to cut through government red tape is to brandish the accessibility advantages of a new gadget, and Motorola did just that. The ROKR is far more disability-friendly than the iPod (the "rhythm lights" that interact with the ring tone and the vibration features are popular with deaf users, who would seem to be the last audience for the product but who enjoy the captioned music videos). The Ojo uses broadband to send live video at thirty frames per second, which is equivalent in smoothness to television. It sits up vertically on a desk or table and, with hands-free speech input capability, will be ideal for deaf users who either use ASL or read lips, for people with mobility limitations, for families who want to see a relative who has a disability, and many others. When Foster showed up at the Career Opportunities for Students with Disabilities conference in the summer of 2005, he brought along a couple of Ojos to be raffled as door prizes. Motorola attends dozens of disability-related conferences and trade shows every year, including the Abilities Expo, the SHHH technology expositions, and similar conferences for organizations for blind and low-vision consumers.

The company's immense menu of Web materials splits disability off into a gateway of its own that has been expertly designed to be user-friendly for people with disabilities. Its welcome page offers a preview of the effort the company is making to reach phone users with disabilities, who are linked with the mature market: "Motorola is making a difference in people's lives by opening up the world of telecommunications—enabling more people to enjoy the great benefits and opportunities. Motorola has accomplished this through a commitment to providing quality products and services to all of our customers—including mature customers and those with disabilities. We create new products which will meet the needs of the widest range of users and at the same time make our products easier and fun to use by everyone." The Web links divide again into accessibility features for deaf and hard of hearing users, and make it clear that product manuals are offered, free, in alternate formats including Braille, large print (at 18 point font), and audio. As Valley set it up, the team of blind/low-vision users who rewrote the manuals made sure they were less "display dependent," which is a simple but great idea for all press office materials, including PowerPoint presentations. Like the icon-driven world of Web design, graphic design for product manuals tends to rely heavily on schematic diagrams, which are completely lost on blind users. Most of the best press materials for people with disabilities are text driven. In the case of Motorola manuals and Web copy, this means there are written directions that enable users to navigate a product's keypad and menus by using either fingers or voice, with audible feedback. Put simply, it works. The strong press and accolades that Motorola receives for these initiatives are earned. As the saying goes, "It ain't braggin' if you done it."

Building the Think Piece

Product launches generate news coverage and consumer-directed reviews. Promotions and honors bring profiles. The longer, more involved stories, called features, that publicists crave deal with trends and issues. The ideal article on business and disability that does a company the most good in the community and with the public is a feature that positively presents the cultural transformation into a disability-friendly company. By linking this inside story with an industry trend in marketing or HR, you come up with what journalists call a "think piece" that advances the business rationale for the policy and then examines how well it is working in terms of market share, hiring statistics, stock price, or other performance indicators. Given the tight competition in such areas as diversity or cause marketing among industry leaders, it is a wonder that more of these articles have not been published. Assembling the elements for a journalist is an interesting test of a press office's progress. It requires not only sources who are qualified and important enough in the company to show its commitment to promoting people with disabilities, but policy documents and—here comes the tough part, apparently, if current research is any indication—producing the numbers to show that the policy is getting results. Editors of business publications and programs demand numbers from their reporters. A paragraph without a dollar figure or percentage lacks the basic facts the business reader is entitled to expect. Much as I admire the disability advocates inside many corporations, at this writing their main shortcoming is an almost universal lack of solid numbers to offer a journalist like me. For a decade, the press has asked the same set of questions of acknowledged leaders such as IBM, Microsoft, Bank of America, and others: How many self-identified employees with disabilities do you have? What percent of the workforce has a disability? What sales figures can you provide for the disability market you reach? These are easy numbers to crunch for women, blacks, Latinos, and other minorities, but, except at IBM, they are nowhere to be found for disability, and that limits the possibilities of the story for serious business publications.

The prominence of features gives them the depth and gravitas that publicists hope to find in the coverage of their company when it comes to an issue as complex as disability. A "think piece" usually takes the research talents and experience of a beat reporter who has some history in the industry and with the company, who can place the ideas in the context of the progress they represent and compare this progress with what goes on at the competition. Business publications have beat editors and reporters who spend all their time on telecoms, cars, oil, Wall Street, politics, and other specific corners of the world of commerce. The stories they file are usually news pieces and profiles, including corporate profiles that examine the ups and downs of major companies. A "think piece" takes this to another level, and disability is just the peg for a more expansive, broad-brush treatment. Publicists can deliver quite a bit of the content in cases of this kind, leading the journalist to the story and providing a significant chunk of the argument if it is supported well. Since it would look fishy if all the sources in the story were connected to the company, it is essential to have spokespeople from grassroots disability organizations, NGOs, or service nonprofits willing to back the thesis. One of the best all-purpose repositories of this kind of information and thinking is the U.S. Business Leadership Network (USBLN), whose massive contribution to disability rights in corporate America is examined at length in the next chapter. The USBLN and its committees not only keep tabs on trends; they set them, and they work closely enough with the corporations' representatives (Kevin Foster, mentioned above, being one of them) to steer reporters their way as well. In-house materials for a think piece are more plentiful than some publicists realize, and are posted on the Web at www.usbln.org. At the tech, telecom, and car companies in particular, researchers prepare "white papers" on ideas or issues in their fields, many of which are already available on the company Web sites. These are among the best documentary mines for a reporter's early digging. Just as a beat reporter maintains clip files of articles that would feed the factual requirements of a longish think piece (usually two thousand words or more, up to about fifteen thousand at the very longest), a publicist should have files ready on such subjects as accessibility, diversity, and disability hiring, accommodations in the workplace, and regulatory compliance. All these are topics ripe for the picking for a writer who wants to file a great disability feature.

Damage Control

Life in the press office is not a day in, day out caravan of cozy profiles, robust earnings reports, and public adulation. Publicists aren't called flaks for nothing. Much of the routine is spent in siege mentality, preparing for or fighting back against investigative "hit" pieces that threaten the company's reputation (and with it, sales, stock prices, risk of lawsuits, and punishment at the hands of regulators). As always, disability issues have traditionally taken a low priority on the list of hot-button issues. The general inattention and inability of the press is largely to be thanked for that. That does not mean there are not a hundred hit pieces out there right now ready to be launched by capable investigative reporters.

Most major companies are wide open to negative press on their lack of effort on the disability front. The premise of this study is the appalling unemployment-underemployment situation of people with disabilities. Advocacy journalists have traditionally focused their blame for the macroeconomics of this disaster on government policies and "society." The private sector has so far escaped the type of scrutiny, especially from the specialized disability press, that it faced from other minority journalists. There is no reason for that immunity to last. At any moment, their weak employment records and spotty marketing leave Fortune 500 companies vulnerable to the charge they don't do enough. An alert reporter on the HR beat could turn up inconsistencies in the written diversity policies on a Web site, and could pose uncomfortable questions regarding how many workers are on board with disabilities or how many EEOC or Department of Justice complaints have been filed. Any undercover consumer reporter could cream some major retailers on the appalling way they treat their customers with disabilities. The story list is long, and it is a time-honored tradition in the media to reward a juicy hit piece far more lavishly than unctuous puff pieces. Let's tighten up the defenses and consider what Trojan horses might be out there.

The news stories that hurt the most will be triggered by discrimination or accessibility complaints. The paper trails of class-action or individual suits against major corporations are gold mines for investigative reporters, who could expose patterns of legally and morally reprehensible behavior at a number of companies. Without naming names here, there certainly is a long list of big, fat targets in these two areas for a journalist steeped in the ADA and Section 508 rules to pick off. Not having hired enough people with disabilities, and underemploying the ones who have been hired, most companies are liable for criticism. (Personally, I am eager to see a strong tech reporter expose corporate Web sites for their inaccessibility, but as I watch the computer sections of the *New York Times* and other publications shrink from sight, I realize the prospects for a lethal hit piece along these lines are becoming more remote with every passing month.) When offensives are launched, the reflex actions of press offices are often predictable. One tactic that a press office often reverts to, in conjunction with the legal department, is suppressing such stories through various types of gagging devices, including nondisclosure clauses and the ubiquitous "no comment" answer during litigation. But as long as the plaintiffs are available for interviews, usually through their lawyers, and advocates are ready to back them in public, the stories can go on.

For the press office that decides to step up to the plate and take a swing, there are two ways to whiff that many companies continually and foolishly attempt. The first strike is the argument that the company supports a number of disability-related nonprofits to the tune of thousands of charitable dollars. Let's call this the "I gave at the office" mistake. Plenty of companies take a nice juicy write-off to buy a page in the dinner programs for charitable events and send enough flunkies in black tie to fill a front-row table at galas for medical research at the Ritz each year. Admirable as their philanthropy may be, not all of these companies are doing the right thing in a business sense. Many journalists with disability-specific publications, not to mention marketing consultants, have had their serious inquiries referred to the foundation arms of major corporations, as though the only possible reason someone might be calling on disability matters would be to ask for a handout. The notion that charitable giving might buy off the media watchdogs and stave off negative press is insulting and beside the point. It is even losing much of its luster in court, if the legal travails of AT&T are any indication. My advice: Hold your bat steady and don't swing at this one.

Another common strategy is to offer up a counterexample of a happy camper from inside to defend the company. For those in the community, this is the "Some of my best friends are disabled" fallacy, and it places the spokesperson in a lousy position. In light of the lawsuit, he or she just looks like an Uncle Tom. Save this cut for the most desperate situations.

Despite my reservations as a journalist and a disability advocate hoping to see companies under pressure change enough that they earn the right to contradict charges of discrimination, allow me to offer an alternative strategy. It strikes me that there is one fairly obvious line of defense, offered by the law itself: Play the old "don't ask, don't tell" card. Let's suppose that the public affairs department is pressed for details on the company's track record of hiring and advancing people with disabilities. The spokesperson can answer that disability, in accord with the ADA and company policy, is a private matter. Employees are not asked to disclose medical information of that kind, and the company respects their right to work without interfering in that area. Given the prevalence of invisible disabilities and the statistical probabilities, it is even within the realm of possibility (particularly from a desperate flak's perspective) to imply that as much as one-fifth of the workforce "probably" does have a disability, simply because that is the going rate for the population as a whole. The journalist has no way to confirm the figure as it applies to the company, so it is unlikely to make it into print. The 20-percent solution does muddy the waters somewhat if the point of the hit piece is that, in a company that employs thousands of workers, those with disabilities are nowhere to be found. Then it is time for plan B. Mention any mitigating facts that can be assembled, particularly as applicable to the company today (rather than corporate history, which is likely to be spotty anyway pre-ADA). Point out your company's existing in-house affinity groups, its disability representatives on diversity committees, its advisory boards or recruiting teams, its policy briefs or marketing efforts. Rapidly search your press releases for the key term "disability" and bury the journalist in paper that somehow indicates the company is consistently conscious of its employees and customers with disabilities. Scour the legal and HR files for accommodation records and use any and all examples to show that the company responds to its employees with disabilities. If you are lucky, all this will deflect further pressure and forestall the worst of assertions—that the company deliberately or carelessly discriminates. At the least, it becomes part of the "fair comment" built into any balanced reportage. You will never get the press to just go away. Hopefully, when the media hounds return, they will be ready to ponder that "think piece" on disability you have been waiting to pitch.

Agenda

- *Edit your copy* for media kits and presentations to ensure people-first language.
- *Top the release or press materials with the disability angle* for the specialty press.
- *Position the articles* in metro, news, and business, not in health or lifestyle.
- *Have a lineup ready of trusted in-house sources with disabilities* who can represent the company.
- *Pitch the people or products,* not the disability.
- *Make your copy clear and consistent on disability and accessibility,* from manuals through media kits and presentations.
- *Avoid using philanthropy to deflect discrimination accusations* in the case of hit pieces.
- *Build a disability history or story platform* to show the legacy within the company and community.

Notes

1. Paul Orfalea and Ann Marsh, *Copy That: Lessons from a Hyperactive Dyslexic Who Turned a Bright Idea into One of America's Best Companies* (New York: Workman, 2005).
2. Personal interview, November 2005.

Chapter 6

Diversity by Design

Perfecting the Accessible Workplace

How do you think he does it?
—Pete Townshend, "Pinball Wizard," *The Who's Tommy*

The clock is a couple of ticks away from nine on a Monday morning in midtown. As Gordie rolls from the elevator toward his office, wireless sensors alerted when he swiped his ID adjust the temperature, lighting, and airflow to his preferred settings. His computer boots up and unlocks sealed personal folders on his desktop, and the report he left to be tweaked on Friday evening is onscreen just as he turns the corner. A panel hung on ceiling tracks silently slides back, and he swoops in one easy curve to his desk. Simultaneously, a "buddy list" of his team colleagues is alerted that Gordie has arrived, and one of three colored overhead lights (blue, red, and green) let those walking by know that he is in, but not ready for visitors. A flat-panel message board on the wall flickers to life and displays the day's agenda and announcements. If a journalist or corporate spy from a rival happens to be in the hallway and the message board is showing sensitive or proprietary information, the visitor's ID will trigger a screen saver. In this day and age of "hoteling," Gordie's space is shared, and the keyboard and file cabinets automatically readjust to his wheelchair height. The "smart" technology with which the office is wired means that sensors in his chair and desk communicate throughout the day with controls on ambient noise and lighting so that he is not distracted. The computer and phone are voice activated, so he can be across the office and still activate them. Every inch of the space is ergonomically fitted to his range of mobility. The PowerPoint based on that report will be ready for the team's eyes in an hour or so. When it is time for the first meeting of the day, it is not hard to predict whose office the team will choose as their gathering place. They always end in the one with all the cool gadgets, including the voice-activated "Everywhere Display" projection system that turns the whole room into a giant whiteboard.

Welcome to BlueSpace, an amazing office of the near future put together in a joint venture that combines the wizardry of IBM's Pervasive Computing Division and Steelcase, the office furniture giant. Gordie may be fiction, but the prototype of BlueSpace is fact, already part of the Steelcase road show and getting the awestruck looks of longing that concept cars receive at the auto shows. It is the office that adjusts to the user rather than vice versa. Most of its sharpest ideas are straight out of the repertoire of Universal Design and assistive technology, the business-driven, barrier-breaking design disciplines that address the needs of people with disabilities. "When you empower people to make choices that enhance their work style and work process, you open the door for increased effectiveness and a more satisfied worker," explains Mark Greiner, vice president of Steelcase's cutting-edge design team.

Every company needs architecture that enhances efficiency, collegiality, morale, and even thinking. BlueSpace offers the beginning of an answer to the question, What would be the ideal conditions for the trading zone in which customers and colleagues, with and without disabilities, could thrive? The locus has to be more than just permeable to both cultures; it must also be welcoming and conducive to productivity. For the nondisabled, it should not seem alien, a "ward" in which the lack of a disability is as conspicuous as the accommodations. From the disability side, it has to be überaccessible. As important, the trading zone must be geared to the users' needs without calling undue attention to them. Even if business offers no such thing as a "level playing field" in the broader sense of that overused expression, the trading zone as embodied in design must give this utopian concept a local approximation. It is not an easy assignment for a company's diversity architect or its literal architect, either.

There is good news on this front. One of the most exciting and encouraging developments is the immense progress that has been made in office architecture and design, which may be the one area in which we are genuinely ready to be open for business for people with disabilities. What wows first-time visitors to the ultraconvenient workplace is the ingenuity. The two words to describe it ought to be "that's awesome" and not "ridiculously expensive." Even the most advanced computer peripherals are now in that second-generation stage where the costs have dropped significantly from the pioneer days, so that we do not have to unravel the business argument for disability inclusion on the basis of the cost of accommodations, as recalcitrant lobbyists attempted to claim when they tried to block the ADA. In the pages that follow, we will visit many of the paradigmatic accessible working places of today, where the spectra of physical and cognitive limitations are so adroitly sidestepped by design elements that you may wonder if this is science fiction or fact.

The physically accessible workplace is judged on the basis of the environment created. Just as lawyers have taught us what "hostile environment" means on a behavioral level, architects have their own scale of disability-friendliness. According to the criteria set by Titles I and III of the ADA and OSHA, barriers to entry have been reduced, and certain standard features are in place. This is just the minimum grade. An advanced approach goes many steps further toward the creation of a facilitating environment, vanquishing the frustrations that are surprisingly still prevalent even when corporations are in compliance with the law. The most sophisticated ideas in Universal Design (UD), the philosophy that has guided architectural approaches to disability for three decades, are no longer merely functional hardware (grab bars, ramps, other apparatuses that make an office or home look like a hospital). There are not enough pages in this book to fully convey the social and commercial importance of Universal Design, a philosophy launched by a remarkable innovator named Ronald L. Mace in the seventies. Mace, who passed away in June 1998, was a wheelchair user who had polio in childhood. An immense presence in the history of the disability rights movement, Mace graduated with a degree in design from North Caroline State University in 1966. He left conventional architecture after four frustrating years to launch a new type of practice. He founded the Center for Accessible Housing at North Caroline State University, still a hotbed of the newest new thing in UD, and created environments that would not just suit other wheelchair users but would allow people with a range of disabilities to be self-sufficient at home. That was not the only drafting he did. An architect-advocate, he became involved in establishing the first building code for accessibility in the nation. It became mandatory in North Carolina in 1973 and served as the model for other state legislation. Mace's activism and designs fit hand and glove with the contemporary civil rights breakthrough of independent living, and paved the way to workplace access issues raised by the ADA. He broke new ground in residential design, pioneering the brilliant notion of "aging in place" or creating solutions for the future problems posed by physical limitations. In his most famous speech, to an international conference on Universal Design just ten days before he died, he offered a rallying cry that is remarkably business-centric:

> Universal design *broadly defines the user*. It's a consumer market driven issue. Its focus is not specifically on people with disabilities, but all *people*. It actually assumes the idea that everybody has a disability and I feel strongly that that's the case. We all become disabled as we age and lose ability, whether we want to admit it or not. It is negative in our society to say "I am disabled" or "I am old." We tend to discount people who are less than what we popularly consider to be "normal." To be "normal" is to be perfect, capable, competent, and independent. Unfortunately, designers in our society also mistakenly assume that everyone fits this definition of "normal." This just is not the case.[1]

Mace was probably as instrumental in the history of disability rights, as thinker and doer, as any political figure. His influence on contemporary architecture is also more pervasive than his name. You are more familiar with his work than you realize. Every time you breathe a sigh of relief that you have a lever instead of a doorknob when you are trying to get in the door with two heavy bags of groceries, thank Ron Mace for a hardware solution to a problem that affects more than just quadriplegics. Power garage door openers, showers without sills or steps, television remotes, and pagers are all part of his legacy. He taught the world of architecture that the time had passed when a home or office could be mass-produced to fit the "average" young, able-bodied, six-foot-tall male, with light switches too high, electrical outlets too low, and everything else out of reach.

Universal Design is more than just a manifesto for architects. Its principles can be used as a guide to thinking about the way you interact with your employees and customers. It has reached a discreet stage in its maturity that introduces subtle aids to mobility or supplements to the senses that do not call attention to themselves. In the same way, human resources programs that parade their minority candidates, especially in-house, have long since given way to more respectful, quieter processes of integration. The paragon is not just a "barrier-free environment" but one that hides its accessibility features, making it more comfortable for both the person with a disability and the person without. For architects, this is license to make the building beautiful as well as functional; for corporate leaders it is a challenge to make the entire company productive on the basis of equality of expectations as well as conditions. Architecture that screams "accessibility" is for a hospital or nursing home, not the office. In the same way, a diversity program that blares continually the good news about all it does for minorities is bothersome and embarrassing beyond a certain point. The beauty of this analogy is the symmetric way it addresses the other (nondisabled) side of the company. For those entering the trading zone, the invisibility of the disability-friendly design is also a matter of importance. Because it will be decades if ever before a wheelchair, hearing aid, or cane does not set off at least a mild sense of alarm in the minds of coworkers or customers, the corporate environment is better off concealing the ramp, literally and metaphorically. The more ostentatious the accommodation, the more apprehensive it is bound to make both parties. A similar wave of consideration for the comfort level of the user has swept the manufacturers of the assistive technology for the thousands of students (11 percent of the population) with disabilities covered by the Individuals with Disabilities Education Act (IDEA). They can be self-conscious about what the other kids think of their listening devices, visual aids, mouse trackers, screen readers, and text pagers. Whatever is conspicuously different is uncool, unless it is itself cool. My favorite story along these lines is a speech-recognition and reading program (made by Lernout and Hauspie for students who are blind or have dyslexia) that swapped the voice of Britney Spears for the weird mechanical voice. When the student does not want any attention, he or she can use headphones or earphones.

Architecture is not just a metaphor for business strategy—it is the embodiment of corporate ideology. Impediments to progress are physical and attitudinal, and the persistence of the physical generally testifies to the stubborn half-life of the attitudinal. When Universal Design dawned on the consciousness of the architecture community, the universality of its benefits for disabled and nondisabled was its great selling point. Later it became clear that as a tool for inclusion it could reduce the isolation and segregation that was holding back the careers of so many people with disabilities. A lavish corporate headquarters that is best approached in a wheelchair from the subterranean garage is gaining one effect at the expense of alienating anyone attentive to the needs of the wheelchair user. In many cases, the patience and acquiescent habit of this constituency (at least, those who are drawing a salary as opposed to political activists) are relied on to avoid confrontation. "They're used to it, and besides, we're in compliance," is one way this problem is shrugged aside—I have heard those very words in a chairman's office in New York. On my way to work each day I pass both the elegant Forty-second Street entrance to the Chrysler Building and the sparkling new corner entry to the headquarters of PriceWaterhouseCoopers, the once-great accounting firm. On the massive glass doors of both buildings is that telltale "handicap" icon with an arrow directing the wheelchair user a few hundred

feet around the corner to the push-button-door access. The Chrysler Building predated the ADA by seven decades; the accounting firm's new building, designed by Skidmore, Owings and Merrill, was completed just a few
months ago. Both are technically ADA OK, but they send the same wrong
message. The ADA is no longer the benchmark of accessibility, nor should
it be a satisfactory indication of the disability-ready office environment in
the broader cultural sense. For example, most of the offices and hotels that
are compliant are set up for right-handed people to transfer from wheelchairs or use the hardware. This is an arcane detail, perhaps, but indicative
of the negligence that persists. Meanwhile, Universal Design has pushed
well beyond the ADA's clumsy mechanics and brings with it the designed
diversity of the disability-friendly corporation.

One of the most charming and vocal proponents of Universal Design
has been George Covington, former special assistant for disability to the
vice president of the United States and cochair of the Universal Design Task
Force of the former President's Committee on Employment of People with
Disabilities. His book, *Access by Design,* is a classic in the field. Covington
was an adviser and frequent contributor to my magazine not only on design
but on business and political issues as well. Whenever our graphic design
went awry, he would blast me on contrast and font size and their relation
to legibility. He was also the greatest comedian with a disability I've ever
known, capable of reducing a stressed-out newsroom to fits of hysterical
laughter with his Dan Quayle stories. As Covington taught me:

> Most of the elements in our society that define us as "the disabled" are caused by
> poor design. If I cannot find a building's address because the numbers are tiny or ar-
> tistically hidden, I am "visually impaired." If a friend of mine in a wheelchair blocks
> the narrow aisle in a grocery store or cannot get onto a sidewalk because there is no
> curb cut, my friend is "mobility impaired." In the past, designers have failed to real-
> ize that when a disability meets a barrier, it creates a handicap. A landscape archi-
> tect, a designer of furniture, or a computer engineer is each a designer, no matter
> what their titles. A person who creates a bank or credit-card statement that can't be
> read or understood by millions is a designer. There is not a single aspect of our daily
> lives that is not affected by designers. Too often those creations throw up barriers
> that result in our being labeled "the disabled." The object of Universal Design is to
> create a building or a product that can be used by the widest range of individuals pos-
> sible. When it can be used independently by both someone who is eight years old and
> one who is eighty, then it hits the essence of Universal Design. By designing for as
> broad a market as possible, it is no longer "special," setting a certain consumer apart
> from everyone else. Universal Design at its best is seamless, almost invisible.[2]

Laying the Foundation

The fundamentals of office accessibility as spelled out in Sections 504 and 508 of the Rehabilitation Act, IDEA (Individuals with Disabilities Education Act), Fair Housing, and Title III of the ADA are little changed in the past decade. They break down according to type of disability and compose a punch list that should already be old hat to buildings and grounds supervisors from ADA training sessions. Many small businesses, exempt from the law, may be unfamiliar with the code, which applies to new building construction or alterations (many problems are grandfathered). In assessing your company's facilities, take a copy of the building floor plans and a tape measure to check the dimensions against these standards. Essentially, for wheelchair users the rules are as follows:

- At least one entry to the building should not require stairs and should be stable, firm, and slip resistant.
- The slope of a ramp must be no greater than 1 inch of increase in height for every 12 inches of length (1:12).
- Curb cuts must exist at drives, parking, and drop-offs.
- Parking spaces 8 feet wide with a 5-foot access aisle should constitute one of every twenty-five total spaces in a lot (and closest to the entrance, with a curb cut if necessary to gain access to the building).
- Ramps longer than 6 feet must have railings *on both sides* between 34 and 38 inches high.
- Can the alternate accessible entrance be used independently?
- Door handles must be no higher than 48 inches and operable with a closed fist.
- There must be a clear pathway throughout the building that is 36 inches wide (the law says 32 inches at doorways).
- Rugs or mats must be secured to the floor (important also for people who are blind).
- A 60-inch clear radius or T-shaped space must be available in hallways for turning around.
- Desk, workstations, and countertops should be between 28 and 34 inches from the floor (including sinks), with knee spaces 27 inches high, 30 inches wide, and 19 inches from the bottom to the floor.
- Materials or objects, including fire alarms, water fountains, or public phones should be within reach, no higher than 48 inches, 54 inches when approached from the side, no lower than 15 inches from the front, 9 from the side, with clear space of 30 by 48 inches in front of them.
- There must be ramps, lifts, or elevators to all levels.
- No obstructions such as trash cans are allowed in the restroom path of travel.

For blind or low-vision office users, the starting point is also that same, essential clear pathway. The stereotypical image of a blind coworker is one who uses a cane (first painted white in 1921 by an English artist, James Briggs, to be more visible against a black road—two red stripes mean the user is deaf-blind) or a service dog. Offices should be ready for him or her, but they should also accommodate the range of other vision disabilities. People with macular degeneration or other conditions that permit some vision are troubled by glare, so a glass atrium or skylight can often be a problem, and the control of light is important. Similarly, burned-out bulbs or badly lit areas of an office should be addressed. The basic list of details includes the following.

- No objects (signs, plants) hanging overhead should be lower than 80 inches from the floor.
- Objects to be detected by a cane must be within 27 inches of the ground.
- No shelves or objects should protrude more than 4 inches from walls or stand higher than 27 inches from the floor.
- There must be clear paths along handrails, and no objects such as plants or ashtrays in unexpected places.
- Signage and materials posted on bulletin boards should have their center line 60 inches from the floor and have tactile, raised characters, pictograms, easily readable fonts (Arial or Helvetica), large fonts (at least 14 point), or Braille, or be available in alternative formats such as on disk for screen readers, audio cassette, digital audio files, CD, or voice mail.
- Elevators should have visible and audible door opening/closing and floor indicators (one tone = up, two tones = down).

The list for deaf or hard of hearing users focuses on the ways in which essential communications features are made accessible. Beyond the building code requirement to have visual fire alarms, the standard features include:

- Phones must be Telephone Device for the Deaf (TDD) or teletypewriter (TTY) not only in offices but in public areas and conference rooms.
- Phones must be hearing-aid compatible, adapted with volume control, and if there are four or more public phones in the building, one must have TTY or TDD, and the location of the text telephone identified by accessible signage.
- Written or text-pager versions of announcements and recorded information, or a separate number the deaf person can call, must be available.

In addition to these three staple areas, there are other considerations to bear in mind. Many people who are postpolio or living with MS, MD, or arthritis have stamina issues. As one of them once explained to me while we were evaluating a college campus for its accessibility, it makes a massive difference to have chairs or benches in areas, for instance, where lines form or along the route from one part of an office complex to another. If it were my business, I would have a sign at the copier or other places where people wait explaining that people with stamina issues should move to the head of the line. People with allergies and multiple chemical sensitivities (also known as environmental illness) need windows that open, enforced no-smoking policies, and colleagues who take it easy on the cologne or perfume. One of the breakthrough areas in disability design will also be a distraction-free environment for those with attention deficit hyperactivity disorder (ADHD) or attention deficit disorder (ADD), similar in its choreographed stratagems to the attempts at behavior modification and even therapy that architects have applied to designing safe and stimulating, but enclosed, environments for people with Alzheimer's in extended care residences. The visual clutter that wreaks its peripheral havoc on our already mutilated attention spans, and is often a warning of bad design run amok, has its aural equivalent in the din of many work spaces. People often underestimate how important sound is to orientation. When the painter David Hockney was going deaf, he told me in an interview that his sense of perspective was utterly changed along with his ability to orient himself in unfamiliar surroundings without the radar-like echo of his own movement. The great architectural spaces have their acoustic as well as visual ingenuity.

Finding the Way

To borrow one of the most elegant and philosophically noteworthy principles of interior office planning, it is time that business incorporated "wayfinding" into its disability thinking. The term was introduced by architect Kevin Lynch in 1960 in the book *The Image of the City,* and rapidly made its way into the UD movement because of what it promised to architects planning for blind users in particular.[3] It emphasizes spatial "legibility" and ease of movement. Some of the ideas remind me of the legendary flow of a Frank Lloyd Wright interior, the way it transmits light and sound as well as people from room to room. In the built environment this means the comprehensive deployment of materials, technology, light and sound, form, and texture to guide, for example, a blind colleague along the corridors and offices of the building. There is a fascinating range of ideas and devices that come into play when wayfinding is achieved. While there are gee-whiz infrared systems for delivering aural directions to headphones, creating something like a museum Acoustiguide to a building, some of the means of wayfinding are cleverly low-tech as well. One of the most ingenious I ever experienced was the use of four inlaid stone markers in a diamond shape set in the wooden floor at junctures where halls or doors meet to indicate turns to a blind user of a cane at the Manhattan headquarters of Visions, a nonprofit service agency for blind people in a nineteenth-century former paper warehouse. With twenty-six professionals and 1,500 clients per year, most using canes, the third-floor offices had significant traffic problems for architect Frankie J. Campione (of Manhattan-based Create) to solve. The 11,000-square-foot project was completed in 1998, at a cost of $250,000. Every moment taps an idea. Tactile guides that can be discerned with a cane, such as the stones, are incorporated into the floor and walls. The office partitions are low, to keep light flowing from the glare-protected windows and to permit staffers to spot clients as they stroll by. The ebullient executive director, Nancy D. Miller, scouted more than two dozen other recent buildings that offered services to blind clients before convening the advisory panels that worked with Campione. As she comments, "We had a lot to work with in terms of raw space, and when the staff submitted its wish list, there was the feeling we could do anything. We steered clear of grab bars on the walls or anything giving a hint of an institution—and people here find their way very nicely, thank you."[4]

Wayfinding can also be high-tech. Concealed Braille or digitally encoded transmitters under a "trailing rail" along corridors and stairs tip the user off to how many steps are left to the next level. Even a description of what can be seen through a window can be added. Signage is a multimedia affair, in some of the best offices translated into five different forms. There are visual icons in high contrast, such as a stick-figure man for a lavatory set in a blue triangle. A tactile ledge, angled at 45 degrees because Braille users find vertical signs uncomfortable, displays the message in both raised lettering and Braille. At the bottom of the ledge, three little infrared bulbs light up as a receiver is passed under them that transmit recordings for the blind/low-vision person with diabetes or other conditions that affect the tactile sense and make it difficult to read Braille. Talking or audible signs powered by transmitters, installed in ceilings and at key points throughout the building, reassuringly tell you where you are, using global positioning programs that meld assistive technology with the architecture. All this relies on an ensemble of signals built into the plan to lead the colleague or visitor seamlessly from one area to another safely, pleasantly, inconspicuously. From entry to an office or the watercooler and eventually the exit, the wayfinding system eliminates point-by-point the obstructions that make the physical world an obstacle course. The best wayfinding is invisible to the untrained eye—the tiles in the floor are decorative as far as most people can tell, the Braille is concealed below the handrail. You can be in the trading zone without even knowing it.

As with many Universal Design features, wayfinding benefits all users, even those who are not plugged in to its high-tech side. In an airport, travelers in a hurry to make their connections will naturally benefit from corridors and entrances that use colors and textures to orient them and, with rolling luggage, will take full advantage of curb cuts and ramps. Inside an office building, the same efficiency is enjoyed when deadlines loom and harried staffers get to the office on the other side of their floor without a hassle. Thirty minutes spent wandering the halls trying to locate the copier are thirty minutes lost. Wayfinding, which also places plants, furniture, and even art as landmarks through a building, leads us back out of the labyrinth of standardized cubicles under uniform fluorescent lights. This is the metaphor cleverly invoked by Barry M. Katz, a professor of humanities and design at the California College of the Arts and a consultant to Steelcase. As Katz writes in an amusing and thoughtful article published by the company whose name, ironically enough, is synonymous with the grid of cubicles that creates an office maze: "People in the modern age, having mastered the mass-production of objects, turned next to the mass-production of spaces, and the result is that we are more often lost than found . . . But transposed onto the modern workplace, one thing is clear: standardized spaces encourage standardized behavior, regulation-size ideas and modular thinking. If nothing more than the force of habit guides you to your desk, nothing more is likely to guide what you do when you get there. Happily, the modern-day Theseus has many ways to rescue the sense of place from the sense of space—some proven, some under active research by cognitive psychologists, anthropologists and even designers."[5]

The high contrast between the colors on the edge of one step and on the beginning of a flat surface, essential safety features for those with low vision, are also handy for the messenger on the run. A common misconception holds that blind people do not need much light, but low vision and most disabilities are better accommodated by a brightly lit building—another way in which all users are better off. Deaf and hard of hearing people, for instance, also benefit from better lighting, since they often need to lip-read. Much of the architectural thinking spurred by wayfinding moved past signage to such areas as tactile communication. The epitome will always be Braille of course, but this also takes the form of knurled doorknobs, textured floors and walls, "rumble strips" at landings and escalators. Then there are the interactive audio-tactile maps used in lobbies and entrances. The purpose is to establish what architects refer to as "shorelines" and "trails" along the well-traveled routes that visitors with disabilities might take, allowing them to navigate as well as the everyday regulars in the building who have memorized the plan.

The best examples of wayfinding are buildings where traffic flow and the ease of locating essential points of interest are superior to the bunching and bumping of an unplanned space. If the analogy holds, then the corporation that pays attention to wayfinding for its employees with disabilities is likely to see a dividend for all employees. Making career choices and changes possible for one constituency opens possibilities for others, so that the flexibility and receptivity of management to a move by any employee is the type of support that all receive, not just the workers with disabilities. The zeitgeist of wayfinding is ideally suited to the creation of a disability-friendly organization. It is not simply a matter of getting in the front door. Once inside, it is important that a person with a disability moves through a planned environment that offers choice and guidance along as many routes as any other colleague might pursue. The old ADA-style concentration on entrances, bathrooms, and fire exits (more and more a priority at companies and in the eyes of policymakers who are concerned about disaster management) is more suited to a visitor than a colleague, who deserves unrestricted access to the company's nooks and crannies. For this reason, disability policies that have focused on hiring and firing are inadequate. They smack of the fear of litigation and the paranoia of ADA compliance, negative forces that can go only so far in the creation of a disability-friendly environment. By contrast, wayfinding offers an aggressive welcome, a come-on to the curious individual rather than a checklist of answers for the inspector. It must be integrated, a design strategy that uses every element from floors to walls, lighting, acoustics, and electronics to make guidance a part of ambiance. In business terms, this is tantamount to a multipronged organizational approach, calling in the forces not only of human resources (the most obvious element, akin to the ramp) but management (opening doors and offering the signposts), marketing (the bargaining table), finance (structuring pay and benefits in an equitable way), and perhaps most obviously information technology (the interface between virtual and real design for many workers with disabilities, at least half of whom rely heavily on computers, 28 percent of which are equipped with assistive technology). Corporate wayfinding should lead as subtly and easily to the marketing department as it does to operations or management. The route must be equipped to accommodate the disability, but it should not be marked at each turn as specific to the disability, like the "designated" wheelchair seat on the bus. Nothing is more retro, or damaging, than the assumption that people with disabilities must be relegated to a desk job, out of sight.

In the architectural sense, this cannot be unplanned. Wayfinding, like signage, has to be in place *avant la lettre,* and gaps or miscues undermine the effectiveness of the whole. The cross-organizational approach to accessibility has at least two benefits. It ensures the cooperative input of leadership and expertise from all corners of the corporation, so that wayfinding leads to any area. It also compels the entire organization to learn about disability, to give the specific needs of a large minority of colleagues its attention, and to consider the community as a vibrant presence in its midst as well as a client base. In the guidelines offered by the U.S. Business Leadership Network, there is this chestnut: "Disability perspectives enable all employees to contribute their full work potential to corporate success."

Wayfinding in a corporate diversity sense involves more than hiring, which is only the initial point of access. It devises a map for movement through a career, including training, unexpected diversions, the occasional retracing of one's steps, and the investigation of byways. Many who are recruited stay on track, in sales, accountancy, or information technology. Others see opportunity in a different area from the one for which they were recruited. As the architect at his drafting table anticipates the movement of the office user through the lobby to the floor where he or she works, the diversity designer foresees and builds wayfinding into the organizational structure. Making a large multinational organization, or even a midsize business, *open* to the aspirations of minorities has long been the goal of diversity planners. Rhetorical references to discrimination, from "ghetto" to "glass ceiling," draw heavily on metaphors of closure. By contrast, an open organization connotes mobility, both upward and lateral. The whole tempo of work and career can be affected. Once oriented, the person with a disability advances not only with ease but with speed from one stage to the next, in the confidence of constantly knowing where he or she is and what to expect at each turn. In place of obstacles there are signposts, in an environment that leads on rather than pushes back. Meanwhile, colleagues and outsiders are barely aware that these measures are in place, or unknowingly benefit from them because the open floor plan (or organizational plan) is a dynamic improvement for all. The trading zone becomes an inviting area of empowerment, the win-win site, instead of a penalty box where one is out of the game for a compulsory period of time.

As in the built environment, the crucial tests of wayfinding in an open office are the transitions: turns, steps (up or down), doorways, and angles. Any change from one level to another requires mediation, and any change in course needs advance preparation. This sounds like a question for human resources, but that is relegating it to the obvious. Corporations and policy-makers have focused for so long on the bare difference between inside and outside, employment and unemployment, that the inner navigation of a career has become an afterthought. Once the person with a disability is hired, the diversity effort all too often fades or turns to the next candidate. The new colleague is "placed" and left to his or her devices. Many people with disabilities who quit or are fired remain convinced that their lack of success involved a lack of involvement, training, or sensitivity toward them on the part of management or of their nondisabled colleagues, who also play a part in perpetuating the corporate culture that is embracing or rejecting of disability. They lost their way.

Guided by the User-Expert

Every field has its superstar. For Universal Design, the woman to see is Valerie Fletcher, executive director of Adaptive Environments, a remarkable nonprofit design cooperative started in 1978 based in Cambridge, Massachusetts. Fletcher is to office design what Tari Susan Hartman-Squire is to marketing or Ted Childs to HR—front-runner, innovator, compelling communicator, and committed professional-advocate. While her direct impact on a business space would involve the consulting work that is part of Adaptive Environment's brief, she is also an educator and the champion of a cause. As was true of her former colleague Ron Mace, there is a public-private duality to her job, which emphasizes architecture as a "social art." In addition to offices she is involved in public transit, affordable housing, and urban planning, acting as principal investigator for the New England ADA and Accessible Information Technology Center, a National Institute on Disability and Rehabilitation Research (NIDRR)-funded project. Interestingly, in light of the way disability consciousness moves from the physical to the mental, she is the former deputy commissioner of the Massachusetts Department of Mental Health, where she handled a budget of $70 million to be invested in a landmark community-planning process. You can detect her master's in ethics in public policy from Harvard in the way she frames her approach to what she calls "human-centered design": "I work and think through a lens of Universal Design. Fundamental to that is a conviction that disability is contextual. Functional limitation is factual and measurable.

Disability occurs in the interface between the individual and the built, communication, and information environment as well as the attitudes of others. One is more or less disabled in relation to the environment."[6]

One of the lessons she offers businesses that need a primer on Universal Design is to make sure they pay attention to some of the less obvious needs posed by the spectrum of abilities, including cognitive disabilities. On her desk now is a research project that will be a boon to corporations. Having devised the best available checklist for office accessibility, she is working on a complementary tool that measures an individual's performance in the intersection with the built, communication, and information environments. Going beyond ADA standards, which are too narrow in terms of the populations they target, the performance yardstick uses the World Health Organization's way of identifying "barriers" and "facilitators" that create the contextual experience. She is already putting the idea to use. The way disability is defined and understood has also changed in the last decade. Disability was once conceptualized as a way to characterize a particular set of largely stable limitations. Now the World Health Organization (WHO) has moved toward a new international classification system that emphasizes functional status. The new system is not just about people with traditionally acknowledged disabilities but about all people. It assumes there is a continuum of degrees of ability and acknowledges that many disabilities are not apparent but based on chronic health conditions—like arthritis, heart disease, back problems—that have an impact on function. The WHO recognizes ability as a contextual variable, dynamic over time and in relation to circumstances. Increasingly, it is also acknowledged that the prevalence of disability corresponds to economic status.

Another vital and provocative idea to come out of Adaptive Environments is a concept I have been exploiting throughout this book outside the scope of architecture: the value of the "user-expert." The term was coined by Adaptive Environment's cofounder and Fletcher's predecessor as executive director, Elaine Ostroff, now a consultant to the organization. In her words, "User-expert describes the role of ordinary people with valuable life experiences who could inform the design process. Children and adults with disabilities and older people have expertise about design that is mostly overlooked by people designing for an imagined norm. As the population becomes more diverse in age and ability, notions of majority norms have less relevance." I have already suggested that user-experts be drafted to sit on advisory committees in the context of marketing and HR, but it is particularly their input on the design side that is essential. Many of the accessibility alterations that companies embark on when a building is already in use are far more expensive ex post facto than equally effective ideas that are included in the blueprints. Having the user-expert at the table is not just a gesture toward equality and collegiality but a way to put policy and practice together to enhance the benefits for all who use the building—to get results *and* to save money. Think of the millions that companies lavish on research into "usability" to support their product designs. People with disabilities are the ultimate "usability" focus group.

The Tools are the Rules

Many of the top design firms that target offices are among the best practitioners of Universal Design. Knoll and Steelcase are the front-runners in the workstations and office systems with which we are most familiar. Both have reconfigured their basic units to make file cabinets, storage spaces, desk areas, and conference rooms far more accessible not only to wheelchair users but to mature workers with vision or mobility limitations. When ergonomics hit the office design world in the eighties, it inspired a complete revision of the standard chairs and desks. Millions of dollars and years of research later, leading designers have added armrests, adjusted seat heights, fiddled with the lighting and dimensions to adapt what used to be rigid and frankly dehumanizing standard-issue cubicles to the needs of people with disabilities, and in turn made them easier for all workers.

What could be more central to an office than the copy machine? In 1998, a group of Pitney-Bowes researchers in Connecticut took a hard look at the highly successful office copier they had only recently issued, with its LED display for the user to set the number of copies, darkness, collating, and all that. They were getting complaints from users with low vision that the buttons and commands had to be memorized because they were too tough to read. So they turned to an inventor, Dr. Khosrow "Caesar" Eghtesadi, who is a wizard at adapting and developing accessible products. A member of the team that drafted the original Section 508 requirements, he specializes in speech recognition, biomedical engineering, and industrial design solutions for blind users, often in conjunction with the American Foundation for the Blind. His company, TechforAll, is based in Alexandria, Virginia, and works with medical technology supply companies as well as Cisco, Adobe, and others. Pitney-Bowes used his design to build the world's first Universal Access Copier System, completely Section 508–compliant, which was released in 1999 and revised in subsequent years. It shot out twenty-three pages per minute, as did the other machines, but it was equipped with speech recognition technology, an extralarge touch-screen interface, Braille labeling, even a lower and angled display for wheelchair users. The key to the copier was the controls. The voice activation and the keypad gave users a choice of how to operate the system. Without even touching the copier, the operator could adjust settings, and the copier would talk back to confirm them. The same choices could be made from the large touch-screen color monitor, easily reached from a wheelchair. The copier control and the feeder were located at desk height as well. Pitney-Bowes took a successful product and improved it for everyone in the office by making it state-of-the-art accessible. With current models at $23,000 a pop, these copiers are not the cheapest pieces of equipment around, but their popularity has proven a point among office managers.

Computers

Covering assistive technology and computers would take a whole book of its own, and I am not the author for it. My major disability is my chronic tendency to crash and burn the hard drive of every computer I use. I may even be a little wary of the abuse of computers in another way—they tend to be the default position of planners and strategists who think the Internet or computerized gadgets can solve every problem for us. The colossal failure of corporate Web sites to be accessible for customers, job applicants and employees with disabilities is a design and business scandal of such epic proportions that it is beyond the scope of this chapter. I attacked the media's role in this catastrophe in an earlier study, but the legal and business implications would require yet another book to fully uncover. So many of the strategies offered by designers and architects to accessibility problems involve high-tech gadgetry that we cannot leave it out of the repertoire. Anyway, it is always intriguing to sneak a peek into the inner workings of a major technology corporation's research and development labs and see what is next on the agenda. After years of effort on behalf of computer scientists in one of the top laboratories in the world, the Microsoft Accessible Technology Group division at company headquarters in Redmond, Washington, had produced a handful of new features and products, including the assistive technology goodies that come in the revised Windows software package. Like Universal Studios Home Entertainment and its collaboration with nonprofit ACB and WGBH, Microsoft in 1988 turned to a major nonprofit design lab, the Trace Research and Development Center at the University of Wisconsin at Madison, to devise accessibility features for Windows. The first full-time accessibility position at Microsoft was created in 1992, and products followed soon after. By 1997 the staff had grown to forty and the Accessible Technology Group, which is the driving force behind making Windows state-of-the-art ready for deaf and blind users, was launched. This is big business for Microsoft. On the company's Web site, visitors with disabilities find a vast array of assistive technology products from a number of vendors who partner with the software giant in the Microsoft Assistive Technology Vendor Program (MATvp). These vendors get enhanced technical support and increased access to Microsoft technology codes to help integrate innovative products with the company's leading platforms. More than seventy assistive technology vendors have already joined MATvp.

The accessibility project team delivered a succinct message to add to Bill Gates's stump speech on "digital inclusion." Accessible computing is focused on two cardinal principles: flexibility and customization. This distillation of a wide and complex array of problems offers us an easily remembered pair of ideas that apply not only to computer design but to management. Whether a company is as vast as Microsoft or as small in scale as a mom-and-pop shop, the bywords "flexibility" and "customization" apply to the all-important question of maximizing the productivity of the workforce, particularly in the areas of scheduling and time management. The lab discoveries gleaned from Microsoft's engineers offer an approach to disability in the workplace that has already proven effective at the computer workstation.

Right from the start, critics are bound to take issue with what sounds like a relaxation of standards and lowering of expectations. As is often the case in diversity thinking, flexibility and customization appear counterproductive on first impression, because they seem to present concessions to inability rather than disability. Nothing could be further from the reality, which is one of the reasons the source for these ideas is crucial. Customization and specialization, in computer design as in human resources, enhance rather than hinder the power of the computer or worker. Off-the-shelf hardware loaded with a basic software package constitutes, at this point in the history of the personal computer, a commodity that long ago reached the one-size-fits-all state into which most other household appliances fall. When a Microsoft engineer begins tinkering, the customization offers an upgrade that improves performance for everyone, above and beyond those with disabilities. In managerial terms, this removes the job from one category—that of yet another midlevel functionary in a cubicle—and places it in another. The unique capabilities of the worker, along with the particular needs, are used to tailor the job.

Does this connote "special" yet again? In a major corporation, where the rank and file move according to a precisely regimented mass rhythm, flexibility and customization sound like deviations from the "normal" order, threats to discipline and morale and possible sources of resentment.

But where the rubber meets the road—accommodation—is where the daily needs of a new hire or an employee returning with a new disability are either met by the company or, as is too often the case, ignored on the pretense of ignorance. The way in which a company provides accommodation is the most reliable measure of the degree to which it has embraced disability as a component of its diversity program. In the comparatively enlightened situation at Microsoft, as we have seen in the HR chapter, new hires are given the opportunity "right away" to stipulate needs they may have. Not surprisingly, landing a job at Microsoft ensures a person with a disability a goody bag of technological toys, from the wide range of accessibility features already built into Microsoft software to state-of-the-art screen readers, magnifiers, Braille printers, scanners, touch-sensitive boards, voice recognition software, PDAs, alternative input devices, FM and infrared amplification systems, voice mail transcription, captioning services, pagers, sign language or oral interpreters, voice mail transcription services, and mobility specialists. That's already a jump start. What I find more impressive, however, is the interdepartmental team of "accomodators" who turn up on behalf of the new hire. An internal committee is immediately on call to make sure these requests are met. Its members are drawn from the human resources, benefits, legal, ergonomics, and facilities departments as well as, naturally, the diversity division. This is not an ad hoc "welcome wagon." The interdepartmental committee, consisting of as many as a dozen managers, convenes monthly. Only part of its brief involves assistive technology, despite the high-tech orientation of the company.

A number of in-house stories show the lengths to which Microsoft is willing to go to accommodate staffers with disabilities. One of the successes has been that of Ted Hart, development lead for the Natural Language Group, who is deaf and who schedules an interpreter to be in the office on Monday and Wednesday mornings when his meetings are concentrated but at other times relies on e-mail and a package of software solutions the company devised. When his interpreter is not around, he can use a service called RapidText, which provides CART (Computer Activated Captioning in Realtime) when he hooks up to a meeting via Microsoft's NetMeeting. Neither lipreading nor a cochlear implant have been a great help to Hart, who became deaf at thirteen. He leans heavily on e-mail, text messaging, Instant Messaging, and his text telephone to communicate. He realized that sound without accompanying visual representation was becoming a more and more important part of the computer-to-human interaction, much to his frustration (although it has meant progress for speech recognition). Hart and Bill Graham, managing editor of Microsoft's Encarta encyclopedia project, are both deaf, and between them they have ensured that Encarta includes closed-captioning for sound presentations. It is also interesting to note that Hart's sign interpreter, Bernie Taylor, has taught a number of his coworkers some of the basics of sign language so they can communicate with Hart in the hallways and in meetings without an interpreter.

Microsoft is not the only company that drives accessibility through technology. It helped get Tony Norris back to work at Sears. Norris uses a wheelchair because surgery to remove a tumor wrapped around his spinal cord resulted in paralysis. In 1987 he finished rehab and got a call from his former supervisor at Sears, where he had worked for eighteen years as a systems specialist in the Chicago headquarters. The company wanted to know what it would take to get him back on the job. It turned out that the Dragon was the answer. The Dragon NaturallySpeaking speech recognition system is a no-touch wonder that lets Norris, who never used a computer before 1988, not only surf the Internet and send e-mail but use the phone, Power-Point, and other applications. He recently celebrated the thirty-seventh anniversary of his first day at Sears. This is a retail giant that has $40 billion in sales and three thousand stores and knows how important it is to have Norris and other employees like him inside the building. As Sears publicist Jan Drummond says, "It's simply a smart thing to do. Whether you accommodate someone already in your employ or you accommodate a new hire, it adds an element of loyalty. And it's good for the morale of a company to see an employer running on all cylinders, working on all phases of diversity, including disability."

While we are on the subject of computers, we cannot leave out Big Blue. Well before concocting the BlueSpace scenario with which we began this chapter, IBM and disability crossed paths for the first time. In fact, the company was founded by a person with a disability. In 1873, Herman Hollerith, a student with a cognitive processing disability, started jumping out of his schoolroom's second-story window to avoid spelling lessons. In 1886 he devised a punch-card system to record, transport, and tabulate information, the earliest computer. By 1896 he had founded the Tabulating Machine Company, which in 1924 was renamed, you guessed it, International Business Machines. We have already seen how proud the company is of its record in human resources management and hiring when it comes to workers with disabilities. Naturally enough, its workers with disabilities get some pretty cool tools to play with when they arrive. Voice activation, screen enlargers, hookups between mobile devices and their desktop are all state-of-the-art. IBM developed the Half Kwerty keyboard, which is still favored by amputees and people who struggle with the old-style version. Its tablet computers are used by deaf workers to type in commands and open documents remotely, and the improvements IBM has made in handwriting recognition as well as speech recognition exemplify the tolerance for error (i.e., inexact or variable input) that is one of Valerie Fletcher's main points as she analyzes what it means to have a range of abilities. The user-friendly tolerance of these products becomes all the more advanced as IBM uses its algorithms to anticipate "errors."

In the following scenario from the accessibility reports IBM publishes, the direction in which its accessibility solutions are moving is clear. The scenario follows the hypothetical case of Clair, a manager at a software company.

Today

Clair is a lead program manager at a large software company. Clair has a learning disability that targets her reading and writing skills including organization and reference skills. The computer is an essential tool that helps her capture her thoughts "in the moment" and to organize them at a later time.

Tomorrow

Clair has found that now that she can actually "talk" to her computer without having to remember specific commands; she is even more productive than before. As a team manager, she schedules many meetings each week and sends out status reports. She talks to her computer to schedule the meetings and then tells her computer when she wants to start writing status reports. Clair can write her status reports in her own handwriting. Although Clair is a very fast typist, she prefers to first write her thoughts down on paper. She now is more efficient because the thoughts she writes in her own handwriting on her tablet computer are transitioned to text by the computer. Because the computer understands what Clair tells it to do, she finds that she no longer needs to call her company's help desk.

Because Clair's new computer manages her documents for her, she no longer has to keep track of how her reports and research data are actually stored or organized. Her memory and intuition are geared toward time and task, and having all her documents and files presented this way works great for her. She can quickly and easily find the exact report she is looking for.

The prospects for accommodating multiple disabilities, and multiple cultures as well (through language translation programs), make the possibilities both more complex and more exciting. Access becomes less a niche and more pervasive in corporate culture, just as computers themselves have. They are part of the master plan. Giving the trading zone its physical realization is the company's outward sign of commitment. The accessible workplace in our time, equipped with the latest in assistive technology, is one of the most advanced environments for business thinking and practice, a place of supreme productivity and creativity when it's built to work right from the start.

Agenda

- *Let user-experts guide designers* to both problems and solutions.
- *Audit the workplace for design shortcomings* based on a range of disabilities.
- *Tinker with technology.* Not all solutions come off the shelf. There is no cookie-cutter solution.
- *Solicit cost-effective suggestions* from customers and visitors with disabilities.
- *Automate everything possible* with voice activation and smart technology.

Notes

1. Ron Mace, "The Evolution of Universal Design," excerpt of a presentation made at Designing for the 21st Century: An International Conference on Universal Design, June 19, 1998. Title and text edited by Jan Reagan for publication, August 1998.
2. Personal interview, January 1999.
3. Kevin Lynch, *The Image of the City* (Cambridge, Mass: MIT Press, 1960).
4. Personal interview, March 1999.
5. Barry M. Katz, "A[maze]ing Space," 360, Steelcase Research, October 2003, pp. 2–3.
6. Personal interview, November 2005.

Chapter 7

Culture Club

Managing for Productive Change

The camp with a difference!
—Pete Townshend, "Tommy's Holiday Camp," *The Who's Tommy*

My friend and mentor Patrick stood in the pasture and eyed the stately, homogeneous line of forty-foot pines that marked the property line. He looked worried. "The trouble with a monoculture," he began, "is that it is so susceptible." He was talking trees, but I inadvertently found myself thinking of the stereotypical image of the old IBM, with its legions of executives filing into Armonk headquarters in their regimental blue suits, white shirts, red ties. Their uniform was the emblem of all that seemed cohesive and impregnable about IBM during its heyday in the sixties, before rigor mortis set in and IBM forfeited its mighty predominance. The object lesson is now a parable of the innovate-or-die reality of industry. Big Blue was nearly driven from the field it had created by more vigorous competition from Apple, Microsoft, Sun, and, later, Dell. Even though diversity programs began to pull inner-city college graduates into IBM's maw, the mainstreaming effects of that company-first zeitgeist were strong enough to strip them of the remnants of any other culture. They were true blue first, and black or brown a distant second. There is nothing diabolical or wickedly imperialist about this rather natural process. Organizations large and small tend inexorably to revert to monocultures unless a deliberate hand plants a different cultivar. By self-selection, like-minded individuals club together, hiring their own clones to serve a common end or perform in a mutually recognizable style. Linguists could demonstrate the reversion just by study-ing its reflection in the institutional, boilerplate language of convergence and team spirit: "Everybody on the same page . . . didn't you get the memo?" Yet teamwork at its most complex (and interesting) level is achieved by a dy-namic coordination of differing talents, a healthy hybridization that spreads the experiential gene pool and gains vitality from the strongest traits drawn from varied origins. Disability culture needs to be recognized as a robust strain in that broadened mix.

Far more than demonstrating the "do-gooder" mentality, the competitive advantage of diversity has long been its most viable rationale. Disability is the next genetic "line" of corporate biodiversity, which otherwise has reached a late stage in its growth. After two decades, the initial excitement of racial and gender-based diversity has become boring and familiar. The early seedling sprang quickly from civil rights legislation (specifically, the Civil Rights Act of 1964) and bloomed in the double-digit employment-rate gains of African-Americans by the 1970s. Within a decade, women, Latinos, and Asians branched off and flourished. The growth slowed, partly because of bailouts to start up small businesses and retention problems at major corporations. In 1985, African-Americans made up 12.1 percent of the na-tion's workforce and 4.6 percent of managerial jobs, and in 2003 (the most recent statistics available), the figures were 13.8 percent of the workforce and 6.5 percent of management. Asians, growing in percentage terms too rapidly, had to be pruned from affirmative action programs, and quotas that were once set for recruiting became quotas on hiring, especially as immi-gration issues spoiled a few bunches. Diversity management careened through themes, from race relations in the seventies to sexual orientation and disability the next decade and a focus on language issues, to genera-tional differences in the nineties, and to religious and cultural differences as well as work-life balance, issues that have been the trend since 2000.

Even after all that, though, 69.9 percent of today's American workforce, and a whopping 84.5 percent of top management, remain white. We are nowhere near as diverse as we pretend to be. Geopolitics has played its part, clouding the visa prospects of mainland Chinese because of trade wars, Indi-ans and Mexicans during the recessionary panic over outsourcing, and, most dramatically, Muslims after September 11, 2001. But globalization should have made diversity more obviously desirable from both a sales and a man-agement perspective, because companies are selling to foreign markets and hiring internationally. Executives a decade ago might have thought a training session in Asian or Hispanic culture in the middle of Ohio would be weird, but now they know they could be posted to Beijing or Guatemala tomorrow.

Diversity is artificial, anyway. As in the garden, it takes an adroit hand to create the right combinations. The choice of adding disability to the mix stimulates and revitalizes the company culture in ways that strategic planners and managers are only beginning to enumerate. If you accept the notion that there is a "disability culture" that provides its own perspective on the experience of work as well as on your customer base, then importing that fresh point of view broadens the intercultural repertoire of the company. It has been successful with other niche groups. Older-vine stock was grafted onto the plant when advocates pushed the cause of "mature" workers, as advocates at the American Association of Retired Persons (AARP) call them. Gray became the new black. Promising the fruit of a major consumer base, and successfully downplaying the physical limitations attendant upon old age, the mature movement offered the model for a parallel disability graft. Now driven by the angst-ridden buckling of retirement plans, beginning with Social Security but not ending there, as larcenous corporations raid the 401k coffers for executive compensation, bailouts, and other inexcusable misappropriations, the mature worker movement has lost some of its vigor. Insofar as a number of chronic conditions are age-related, the overlap between disability and seniors is literal. The seniors took root more rapidly, I suppose, because hiring managers figure they are somehow mentally more capable than people with disabilities. This is a throwback to that stubborn association of physical conditions, such as cerebral palsy, with mental ones. Many people with physical disabilities a generation ago were clapped into institutions. I might interject that at my own small business the younger staffers were particularly insistent on distancing themselves from those who had incurred their disability through aging. This was particularly true of a twentysomething deaf reporter who regarded herself as vastly more disabled, culturally, than an old hard of hearing person. But the strategy of AARP deserves emulation, particularly for enlisting in-house corporate support. Those companies who are starting out, however, are better off exercising caution before officially binding together people with disabilities and seniors, as neither seems entirely comfortable with the other at the office.

Birds of a Feather

Making room for a spectrum of subcultures inside a complex organization is a hallmark of flexibility and a point of pride for many sophisticated major companies. Before we launch into an exploration of disability cultural affinity groups, however, we have to consider the fact that not everyone is on board with the disability culture idea. For one thing, there are deep divisions inside the overall demographic, as we have noted, particularly along lines of cleavage formed by physical and mental conditions, or the independent, often militant streak of the Deaf community and AIDS groups. Valerie Fletcher of Adaptive Environments admonished me as I was pulling this book to its close: "I think it is critically important to communicate that disability culture attracts only a small percentage of the spectrum. The majority of folks simply don't embrace the identity. It has real value but remains largely a white and middle-class choice and pervasively fails to attract large segments of people with acquired disability. Employers cannot serve the population if they don't understand this."[1] Fletcher is a veteran of the disability culture wars and a highly regarded authority, as we have seen in the previous chapter, on the accessible workplace. She is not the first to alert me to the distinction between those who grew up with a disability and those who incurred theirs later, another plane of division in the demographic. Even after adopting precautions about the too-convenient generalities of a community or culture when no such unanimity exists, I opt to follow the path taken by disability studies and stick with the cultural rubric, mainly because "culture" leads business planners away from the rut of "condition." It is a starting point for identification, and it is time to see how it can take its rightful place in the multicultural organization.

The inculcation of a minority culture into a corporate one is not without precedent. One of the most intriguing, and perhaps surprising (given the party politics), models for this comes from the rapid growth of overt religious expression in the workplace. Tracking the growth of the Christian evangelical movement in such large corporations as Microsoft, American Express, Coors, Intel, the fitness chain called Curves, and even the Centers for Disease Control (a federal agency), a recent article titled "Faith at Work" in the *New York Times Magazine* suggests that the marketplace was once more becoming a center of religious interaction where, particularly, Christian evangelical pastors were finding ways to combine expressions of faith with the secular pursuit of gain. The article traces the formation of company-sponsored, formal (with bylaws and objectives) "affinity groups" to the spate of discrimination suits that hit big companies in the nineties, including a particularly ugly $192 million racial discrimination suit against Coca-Cola. Alongside prayer groups for evangelical Christians, the article also spotlights other niche organizations such as the Intel Muslim Employee Group, which gets space at headquarters and a modest $2,300-a-year budget. As Russell Shorto writes, "One of the movement's objectives is to give Christians an opportunity to 'out' themselves on the job, to let them express who they are, freely and without feeling persecuted. Few would argue with such a goal: it suits an open society. And if it increases productivity and keeps CEOs from turning into reptiles, all the better. Then again, the idea of corporations dominated by a particular religious faith has a hint of oppressiveness, a 'Taliban Inc.' aspect." [2]

The use of "outing" in that passage caught my eye. It sorts well with the challenge of self-identification of people with disabilities in corporations such as Microsoft, which has three such affinity groups for people with disabilities (blind, deaf, and ADD/ADHD, the largest). The on-campus presence of a club, particularly one that has the blessing of the boss, is bound to make workers feel more confident about gathering and expressing what once was considered private. Most of the *Times* story is about a small bank in Otsego, Minnesota, that enjoyed a tremendous growth in business (deposits up from $5 million to $75 million) after it broadcast its pastoral mission as part of the "faith-at-work" movement, a sort of anti-Enron where the bank president would continually drop to his knees and pray with customers. Just as this book emphasizes the business case for building disability consciousness, it is obvious that such faith-friendly banks and other industries are motivated at least in part by profits. Look at the way the box-office success of *The Passion of the Christ* spawned copycat maneuvers in Hollywood. The producer Peter Lalonde, himself a Christian, timed his sale of the movie rights for *Left Behind: World at War* to Sony perfectly, just as *The Passion of the Christ* passed the $370 million mark in receipts thanks to faith-based grassroots' marketing. When his movie was released in November 2005, he complained about the puny $1.2 million marketing budget and drew attention to the continuing difficulty of surmounting cultural barriers: "It has been a battle . . . Everybody sees this marketplace, but there's a barrier to entry, which is a cultural barrier." [3]

We should not push the evangelical aspect of this tactic too far. It probably sounds a little too wacky for many in the business community to handle, especially in a small-business context. The disability community is also sick of the pseudo association with spirituality. The inimitable George Covington, whose design ideas we visited in the previous chapter, steered my magazine clear of stories about the spiritual powers of people with disabilities, noting that it was just an old myth and perpetuated a stereotype. But what is intriguing about the participation of Microsoft, American Express, and small businesses in the faith-at-work movement is not the religious aspect per se. The surprising thing is the way in which the affiliation balances one set of cultural values in counterpoint with others, where the profit motive and company loyalty might be construed as cultural values. It is also a matter of competing rights: "Freedom of religious expression trumps many other rights," notes Shorto, with evident apprehension.[4] (His article was the third in a year-long string of long, nervous investigative pieces in the *Times* about the rapid growth of evangelical Christian power in such areas as business, politics, education, and the media, suggesting a journalistic crusade). By recasting Pentecostal fervor as a component of corporate diversity, the HR officers at these companies were restoring rights that had long been squelched or politely ignored. If the cultural label makes this palatable, then disability advocates and the corporate diversity officers who have been scratching their heads over how to satisfy the demands of the disability community should try it. In tandem with the cause-marketing potential (see chapter 3) that the story of the little Minnesota bank suggests, the redefinition of disability as a cultural phenomenon rather than a medical or (although the advocates may not like this) a political one makes way for a far more sophisticated diversity model than any of the previous ones. On the one hand, the cultural approach gives diversity more appeal as the expression of a private matter. Just as gay culture as an expression of pride or values is far easier for nongay coworkers to accept than intimate sexual details, so too the characteristics of disability culture would be less morbid and uncomfortable than the medical particulars.

One group that has learned the empowerment of cultural representation, if not in the business world then certainly in politics and society, is the Deaf community, which for decades has vigorously prosecuted its independence, complete with linguistic ramparts, sharply defined group identity, loyalty, and, arguably, a shade more intolerance for outsiders than might be good for it. Some of the dynamism of the Deaf movement derives from one of the same strategic sources of power that the evangelicals enjoy (including, we are told, the Muslims), and that is a penchant for organization. This alone requires a leap of faith on the part of management. On the face of it, a monthly lunchtime meeting in a bland conference room halfway through the typical workweek scarcely appears subversive or ambitious. Advocacy groups, by contrast, do have their edge. They go to bat for members who have been denied promotion or let go, and they have that adversarial stance that unions, which are the extramural version, traditionally assume. Along those lines, the original, in-house support groups for staffers with disabilities were formed to vent complaints and make suggestions to management, often for accommodations. It was that old model of neediness and caregiving. But the presence of a "regular" association as an affirmation of a cultural identity, a beachhead inside a corporate culture, is different. Just to extend the religious analogy further, what freaks out many people when they learn about the evangelical meetings is the prospect of proselytizing and of using the company as a platform for making converts. It would be easy to dismiss this anxiety in the case of disability—after all, who would voluntarily incur a disability? But this is not a matter of becoming disabled—it is a matter of affiliation. Just as friends, family, and interested academics in particular sought inclusion in such movements as gay pride, feminism, or black power, it would not be unhealthy for a disability group to become a vehicle of acculturation, education, and, ultimately, understanding. The online sites and blogs of disability affinity groups, especially at high-tech firms such as Microsoft, are visited by many nondisabled employees who have family members or friends with disabilities and are interested in the recommendations or discussions. (For privacy purposes the site users are not monitored, but they often make themselves known to the moderator and other participants). The drop-ins are curious to know what they should know, or what they can do, to assist colleagues. Just as "corporate chaplains" assume the leadership role and minister to the pastoral needs of the company, a disability group leader could be the point person and reference guide not only for those with disabilities but for those seeking to understand.

The perception of a cohesive group, proud of its affiliation and coordinated in its advocacy efforts on behalf of its own inside the corporation, offers comfort to those seeking the company of others with disabilities and engenders collegial recognition, as well as respect. In place of the isolated individual viewed with curiosity, and often pity, the group presents the image of a vital source of ideas, resources, and strength. The dynamics of internal communications and relations are always tricky territory for managers, and of course the self-identification quandary rears its ugly head yet again. One of the most famously successful of disability employment programs is found at the Goddard Space Flight Center of NASA, located in Greenbelt, Maryland. It offers some of the plum internships for students and is a perennial presence at recruiting events, making it one of the outstanding recruiters of science graduates with disabilities. A handbook written by Michael J. Hartman, Disability Program Manager at Goddard, was first published in 1994 by Goddard's Equal Opportunity Programs Office and updated regularly for every employee at Goddard. It was originally developed as an etiquette guide for the inauguration of President Jimmy Carter in 1977. Right in its title and throughout its pages you find an emphasis on communication. "When in doubt, ask" is a byword of *People with and without Disabilities: Interacting and Communicating,* which is the most sensible disability training manual I have ever seen (the full text is available online: www.eeo.gsfc.nasa.gov/disability/publications.html.

Membership in a disability cultural affinity group would seem to be synonymous with self-identification, but there are delicate exceptions. A well-publicized, emphatically authorized (by the powers that be) group offers an easy way to encourage self-identification. That in turn ripples through the rest of the company as news of a functioning, purpose-driven element on board. By contrast, I think there is always something staged about training videos and events, the typical avenues for disseminating disability etiquette or raising awareness inside the company. The one-off sacrifice of a day or afternoon to an obligatory session implies the marginal importance of the group. Try instead a visible, even popular, committee that melds individual concerns with company strategic planning, commands attention, and sends the message that the culture represented has a business as well as social rationale. It would be pushing the truth to pretend the affinity group constitutes the management version of the trading zone we have been marking out in previous chapters. This is more like the locker room. It is in the arena, the door can be left open or kept closed depending on the sensitivity of the conversation inside, and we emerge from it to more publicly enter the trading zone where the game is played for real stakes.

Two analysts of workplace issues in a social context have recently advanced original theories, one of them directly focused on disability, that managers could use to frame the productivity aspect of this cultural question. Both address one of the most striking puzzles of disability in the workplace: *under*employment. Waste is a notorious structural flaw of multinational giants. Each of us who has had corporate experience probably recalls the downtime that temporarily signified underemployment in our career. People with disabilities, often stuck in menial or mindless jobs that barely challenge their real abilities, know this as a full-time quandary. Lisa Belkin is a *New York Times* columnist who addresses the balance between personal and company priorities in a weekly piece called "Life's Work" that the *Times* runs on the first page of its Sunday jobs section. She based one of her best articles on a fascinating, surprising study conducted by the Hidden Brain Drain Task Force, with funding from Unilever, General Electric, and Time Warner. The study proposes an innovative "360-degree" résumé incorporating life and work experience that adds credit for achievements and skills developed outside the workplace. From the task force study, she focuses on African-American women who were community leaders but undervalued at work, where only a fraction of their potential was tapped by their managers. Using the yardsticks of community service and leadership, the report found that African-American women outperformed white men by a vast margin. For example, 25 percent of them were active leaders in their religious communities (compared with 16 percent of white men), 41 percent were involved in social outreach efforts (32 percent for white men), and 25 percent played the role of mentors (compared to 14 percent of white men). As Belkin philosophically observes,

> Few of us ever bring our true selves to work. We bring adapted and arranged versions, edited to fit the job. Our dress tends to reflect the rules of the workplace, written and not. We don't talk of our families nearly as often as we think about them. Our hobbies, our problems and our health are subjects generally left at home. We are someone else in the office: a flattened, incomplete, wan but professional version of ourselves. The result, possibly, is workplace harmony, but at a cost. If we are not bringing our true selves to work, a recent study suggests, and if we are judging one another by superficial constructs rather than three-dimensional connections, then we are cheating the workplace and ourselves. "A 360-degree look at a worker's life would uncover all sorts of leadership energies and potential that remain unseen because no one is asking and no one is telling," says Sylvia Ann Hewlett, president of the Center for Work-Life Policy, an organization that studies obstacles to professional women and members of minority groups.[5]

Along these lines, one of the most renowned historians of disability and labor, Ruth O'Brien, advances a novel thesis in her recent book *Bodies in Revolt: Gender, Disability and an Alternative Ethic of Care*.[6] She suggests that the ADA, which she views as the most revolutionary labor and civil rights law in American history, has the potential to turn employers into caregivers, instilling a new ethic of needs-based accommodation that promotes the individuality of the worker through the enhancement of his or her human capital. Accommodation refines the corporate ethic for all employees, creating an equilibrium between care and profits. Within the company, workers with disability turn into agents of resistance ("bodies in revolt") that buck the standardization of Taylorism and other prevailing corporate ideologies. She writes, "If able-bodied workers could either overcome misconceptions they have about disability or the resentment they harbor against employees who receive accommodations, they could join forces with persons with disabilities. The ADA's employment provisions could give disabled persons a more universal notion of the organic mind and body. These provisions could help American workers, giving them protections where the civil rights and labor laws have fallen short."[7] O'Brien draws on the writings of Michel Foucault and other darlings of academic theory and is probably too iconoclastic for most corporate chiefs to digest. However, her optimism, originality, and confidence in the power of workers with disabilities to cause such a transformation is inspiring. In an e-mail about how shocked she has been by the strong reception (both positive and negative) the book met in its first months on the shelves, she admitted "this is really an extension of my rather idealistic days."[8] The clarity of O'Brien's earlier work on the ADA and workplace power structures is felt in this quotation from the introduction to an earlier book, *Crippled Justice:* "Disabled people derive power from alternative means of performing the ordinary and the extraordinary tasks of everyday life, because what circumscribes disabled people from completing these tasks the 'normal' way gives them special insight. The forethought and creativity required to develop the alternative means to accomplish the tasks provides disabled people with the capacity to help themselves and, sometimes, others."[9]

Every one of the top companies named in the appendix to this book has some sort of affinity group, advisory committee, or other regularly convened in-house body to address disability issues across departments, no matter how geographically spread out. The news of their vitality is a card the companies play in marketing, public relations, and recruiting, but the benefits exceed the bragging rights. These groups are potential agents of transformation. Although affinity groups that play strategically significant roles remain largely a frontier phenomenon, the experience of the more seasoned veterans in the area reveals the stages through which a company can progress. The disability culture's presence can rapidly grow from nothing to the initial affinity group meeting, to the working group on accommodations, to the advisory council on external as well as internal efforts (product development to customer service, marketing and public relations), and finally to the strategic planning panel that lets top management know how disability fits into the battle plan. While the initial stages might be nothing more than gripe sessions, the focus gradually shifts from problems in the office to solutions to ideas that can represent the company outside the building. Let's pay a call on Cingular Wireless, which has been in this game for half a decade, and see how far along its disability consciousness has evolved.

The nation's largest cellular network has more than 64,000 employees and over 55.8 million subscribers. It recognized disability as a formal part of diversity from its inception in 2000, when it was formed as a single entity out of the chaotic telecom soup of the Baby Bells following the breakup of AT&T and regrouping during the merger mania of the nineties. That was also the year Cingular burst upon the disability scene with a highly acclaimed ad starring an artist with cerebral palsy named Dan Keplinger, whose nickname, King Gimp, is indication enough of the disability-forward tone of the spot. It ran during the Super Bowl—you can't get more external than that!—and won national acclaim from advocacy as well as ad groups. Cingular is on the speed-dial list of disability activists, having cleaned up in the awards department and supported advocacy and research efforts of Hearing Loss Association of America, Telecommunication for the Deaf, American Foundation for the Blind, and the National Spinal Cord Injury Association. Some awards mean more than others. The company was honored by the U.S. Department of Labor in 2003 as the winner of the "New Freedom Initiative Award" for its innovative management of employees with disabilities—the award even mentions productivity, quite a step forward. The company earned that one through a tightly woven mesh of management, marketing, and human resources initiatives. Our focus will be the creation of an active employee affinity group as well as continuing empowerment of the Wireless Access Task Force for the development of products and services. Every year Cingular goes all out to host Disability Mentoring Day events, participates in the Youth to Work Coalition, and served the first two terms of the FCC's Disability and Consumer Advisory Committee. All employees complete a Web-based training course on disability. The company assembled a national call center team dedicated to customers with disabilities that receives more specialized training on disability-related issues. It sweetened the deal with exemptions on monthly service charges for VoiceDial, its voice activated dialing feature. Cingular wields its procurement influence positively, checking to make sure the local vendors' stores are fully accessible through the offices of its real estate department.

The extra effort is paying off nicely. We have already seen how disability smarts was a significant factor in the company's ability to receive approval for the merger with AT&T Wireless. There is no breakout figure available for how many of its 55 million and counting customers might be people with disabilities, but it is a sure bet that the steady growth of the disability call center is keeping pace with trends in aging. It is more than invoking a metaphor to point out that the secret of Cingular's success with the community is communication through networking. The company talks a great game, and uses its web of partners well. The phrasing of its internal as well as external policies is worth imitation. Here is how the company Website outlines its management strategy:

> Cingular has taken a unique interdisciplinary approach through its disability-inclusive diversity policy to support full inclusion, employment, and career advancement opportunities for people with disabilities. Cingular worked to dispel myths about disabilities through innovative advertising, education and community outreach; developed tools to improve communication; encouraged employment and career advancement opportunities through collaborative efforts including dynamic

public/private partnerships; created a disability friendly environment and mentoring opportunities; and leveraged the full benefit of employing people with disabilities to better address the needs of its customers and communities. The most public example has been the memorable 2000 Super Bowl ad that featured a critically acclaimed artist with a disability. Internally, Cingular seeks to ensure that people with disabilities are aware of company-wide opportunities. Job announcements are posted with Career Builder and jobacccess.org, which targets the disability community. All employees are required to complete Web-based training on disability, and the company has developed disability etiquette training materials for managers. Recruiters at the National Call Center are made aware of the importance of developing relationships with local disability organizations.

This is a team effort, but there is an ambassador who ought to be singled out as an example of disability-forward management. Susan Mazrui is Director of Federal Regulatory Affairs for Cingular and also facilitates its Wireless Access Task force. Mazrui, who is blind, was with Pacific Bell for five years before moving into Cingular at its inception. Her career trajectory is interesting—she started in marketing and then switched into the regulatory area, so she has been based in Washington, D.C., for six years. Her own experience with accommodation at the company, such as requesting a Braille embosser or other technology, is completely lacking in drama. "It's not a big deal. I think we all have the expectation that accessibility will be provided, and it is," she notes in a matter-of-fact voice. "The accessibility tools you get are just productivity tools. It's nothing special. It's just what you need as an employee."[10] Along those lines, she admits that affinity groups are far more lively and active in companies where there are complaints, which is far from the case at Cingular. "The contacts I have made in the affinity group have been more social than employment-related, because things are going well. It is different in a corporate culture that does not accept. If you feel at a social level you are not accepted, that you are excluded, then you are. If you are asked if you can navigate the hallway, then you're not getting the job. That's not our situation here," she says.[11]

The action is in the task force, which meets twice a year but handles questions and problems that need faster turnaround by e-mail on a regular basis. They are an all-star team with pan-disability qualifications. Not surprisingly, a few of the members specialize in the needs of hard of hearing customers, including Larry Eng, a professional audiologist as well as advocate Claude Stout, executive director of Telecommunication for the Deaf, Inc., Dale E. Young, a representative of Hearing-Impaired Professionals, and John Darby, the executive director emeritus of the Hearing Society of

Northern California. The mature market is covered by Clyde Hostetter of AARP. There are members such as Roger Peterson, vice-chair of the Technology Committee of the California Council of the Blind, and Bernice Kandarian, first vice president, Council of Citizens with Low Vision International. Because mobility disabilities are a significant constituency, some members use wheelchairs including Sandra G. Bartlett, an adviser to the Fair Housing Administration, Carmen Jones of Solutions Marketing Group, and Greg Smith, one of the best-known journalists with a disability and founding host of *On-a-Roll*, the nationally syndicated radio talk show. Others are advocates for independent living, such as Patricia Yeager, former executive director of the California Foundation for Independent Living, and Jackie Brand, president of the Independent Living Network and founder of the Alliance for Technology Access. This multitalented panel of experts focuses on improving Cingular's products and services, so the agenda is often a technical and market-driven one. It is tough for Mazrui to quantify the group's impact on sales, as opposed to corporate reputation (which has soared in the disability community), because not every buyer is ready to self-identify. "Most people won't say they bought the phone or application because it's accessible. They say they buy it because it's cool and they can use it," she explains. You have to admire Mazrui's candor as well as that user-expertise we have elsewhere extolled in this study. She is proud of the fact that the company does not try to buy the thumbs-up from the task force with a few perks:

> We have a reputation that goes beyond just making us look good. We have developed a sense of trust. These task force folks are tough. They don't just say yes for a free meal. That helps our reputation in the disability community and with regulatory bodies. If it can be done we try to do it. And if it can't, we call for the changes. We had people in the community saying they wanted to support us not because they thought we were going to give them money. They felt the way we were pushing the industry would make the world more accessible.

Success draws imitators, but Cingular's technical lead is, well, singular. The vibrating alerts for deaf users and the "talking phone" features that let blind users know the battery is low or let them screen calls were imitated six months after the fact by competitors, an eternity in that industry. The company has already taken the pole position in age-proofing its services (with keypad numbers that are easy to see, for example, and multimodal output that rings, buzzes, or vibrates). All this works just as well for the hurried executive, the construction foreman, and the senior, for whom it is more than a convenience. The strategy from there is basic: "Take that paradigm and expand it," says Mazrui.

The ripple effect spreads fast. As with race or religion, disability insiders at corporations have achieved an historically informed return to the marketplace as a site not only for exchange, but for change. Maybe they were helped by the current political climate and the swift economic returns that could keep any idea afloat in a cost-benefit context, but the turnaround from unspoken, shadowy minority to proud, up-front profit center is dramatic. If one of the first steps is to exploit the corporate willingness to recognize cultural affinity groups in the context of diversity programming, then this is the way to go. People with disabilities have tried so many avenues. The political and legal battles were fought two decades ago, with notable if limited success. Social change in a class-conscious world is always going to be tied to economic mobility, and here is a brilliant opportunity to use business as an agent of change in two senses—economically and socially. That is why Ruth O'Brien's call to arms in *Bodies in Revolt* is so timely, even if it overstates the political proportions of the change.

The structure of an affinity group is perhaps easier to mandate than the content. While it has always been clear what Christian or Muslim groups would do with their time—there is a central text on the table after all—what would be the focal point of a disability-based cultural association at a major company? The easy answer in places like Cingular, Microsoft, or IBM is shoptalk about assistive technology or disability-specific gadgets being used or developed. There is room, however, for a more ambitious agenda. The current definitions of disability culture have been proposed by the academy, as well as, to a lesser degree, political advocates. These historically important articulations of a nascent social and political movement have been immensely influential, but they have also been, as so much inside universities tends to be, heavily theoretical rather than useful. There is room for a pragmatic and up-to-date version of disability culture, and there is no reason why it should not be as likely to come from within the business world as from the academy, the media, or a political think tank. The experience of building a career, collaborating with individuals with and without disabilities, finding a place for disability at work or finding ways to "lose" disability at the job—all are means to an end, shaping a work-inflected sense of disability culture. Just as women, particularly, have helped raise the awareness of work-life balance, with a persistence and eloquence that has affected their male colleagues and society as a whole, a similar examination of the work-disability equilibrium is possible. The trading zone provides a level base on which these scales can balance.

My own experience inside advocacy groups serving other minorities has been that strategic planning and networking dominate the conversation. The most formidable example of this I ever saw in action was the National Association of Women Business Owners (NAWBO), which was a lobbying group that leveraged its business power for regulatory and political gain. The grassroots efficacy of NAWBO was beautiful. Small, carefully "curated" meetings of women who are entrepreneurs gather over wine and cheese in the evenings, or at luncheons, and setting aside speeches or rhetoric get down to the brass tacks of ensuring access to capital, partnering on buying supplies, sharing sales contacts or other useful inside information—activities that had long been the privilege of old boys' clubs. I never knew one member of NAWBO, which has 8,000 members, whose business did not profit from participating in the group. Feminism was implicit, so the agenda was cutting a path to success through networking and a willingness to actively intervene on each other's behalf. This is what the disability community needs inside the business world. One of the most interesting umbrella organizations similar to NAWBO is the Washington-based U.S. Business Leadership Network, which we briefly considered in chapter 3. With its national scope and emphasis on hiring, this nonprofit, with 5,000 companies enrolled, represents the elite cadre of disability-conscious managers. Backed by the U.S. Chamber of Commerce and such major corporations as SunTrust, Medtronic, and Qualcomm, its meetings via forty-three chapters in thirty-two states are dedicated to reviewing best practices and sharing job leads. The Web site, usbln.com, has resources for employers and job seekers, and the networking capabilities of the all-volunteer administration (headed by SunTrust's Katherine McRary) are formidable. Conference calls, meetings, and events fill a yearlong calendar that pulls in a fantastic cross section of exactly what any network needs most: decision makers and people who get things done. Some are executives at major corporations (the list is heavy on big banks, perhaps because of the leadership), but federal and state bureau of labor officials, vocational rehabilitation administrators, college counselors and job placement officers, as well as many of the most business-savvy disability NGOs participate. The good work of the USBLN is the great white hope of advocates who have chosen the economic route to empowerment for people with disabilities.

Out On a Limb

The best practices and ingenious ideas of American companies that have filled these pages are all worthy of emulation, but I have saved two anomalous stories, both from firsthand observation, for the end. Not only do they strain credibility, but they push the envelope of management guidelines to its limits. In part, it is their sheer improbability I hope to invoke, as well as the lessons they offer in the universality of many of the principles the leading American advocate-executives have developed. The first is from mainland China, one of the least likely places one would expect to find workers with disabilities treated well. Far from the sleek glass skyscrapers of Shanghai or joint venture hangars of Guangzhou that symbolize the ballyhooed Chinese economic miracle, a modest tool shop in the dusty northern town of Baoding, in the economic and political backwater of Hebei province, makes its decidedly minor contribution to the nation's double-digit GDP growth even as it makes far greater strides in the progress of workers with disabilities. Turning out a dozen power transformers a day, virtually handmade in slavish imitation of a General Electric seventies-era model that was long ago stripped and meticulously measured for duplication, the Baoding Electric Transformer Enterprise is never going to make it to *Business Week* magazine's list of the world's most virtuous companies.

China is still a country where birth defects, blindness, and especially mental illness are scrupulously hidden by both the family and the state. For all the tolerance shown by Buddhist societies, the social correlation between disability and dishonor, the notion that malfeasance in an earlier phase of a family history manifests itself in later physical misfortune, brands the stigma far deeper. The best estimate of the number of people with disabilities in China is around 300 million, a total sufficient to constitute by itself the third-largest nation in the world (after China itself and India). As in the United States, a staggeringly high 75 percent of these people with disabilities remain unemployed even as the rest of the country becomes the sweatshop to the entire world, opening factories at a rate not seen since the industrial revolution in England. Even in a nation that led all others in adding jobs over the last decade, to the tune of 9 million new private-sector jobs a year, people with disabilities have not participated in the growth.

Bucking this trend, however, is the little Baoding transformer factory, where more than two-thirds of the two hundred on staff are people with disabilities, most of them deaf. They are not the beneficiaries of philanthropic largess—the elaborate nonprofit disability world of the United States is completely unknown in China. Nor is their employment a shining example of public policy, as the national and local administrations sport a miserable record of neglect in disability matters. This is a for-profit enterprise, one of the first of its kind nationwide, and an especially bold venture in this highly conservative (socially and politically) region. The astonishing success of the factory and its unique diversity effort is attributable to the vision of one individual, a fifty-year-old entrepreneur named Men Zhen Wen. The soft-spoken, highly educated son of an acclaimed doctor, he became a pioneer of both disability rights and private industry in the late 1980s.

Not only did the resourceful Men manage to launch a successful private enterprise, against all odds, but by bringing in disability he defied all the social and business conventions, including powerful superstitions that play a weirdly prominent role in corporate strategies even in sophisticated Hong Kong. His career in business had begun when he was assigned, after a stint in the army, to manage a state-owned factory. He took the initiative to open its doors to deaf patients at what amounted to a nursing home where they sat around doing nothing, just as nearly all of China's people with disabilities spend their days. "It was a total waste of people and their time," he told me.[11] He instituted a pay scale (not exactly equivalent to that of the nondisabled workers in comparable jobs, it ought to be disclosed) that vastly improved their living conditions and became known in the local disability community as an advocate. He also gained a reputation as a shrewd manager. When Deng Xiao Ping was surprisingly restored to power in the 1980s, Men saw his chance to set up a privately managed, state-owned enterprise, one of the hybrid ventures that Deng praised when he gave the nod to "capitalism with Chinese characteristics." Timing is everything in a Communist developing economy where the political wind can shift without warning. In the wake of one of the cryptic endorsements of free enterprise from Beijing, Men took his own leap. He decided to create a new, semi-independent division of the state-owned factory with an initial staff of only twenty, most of them deaf, that exclusively made electric transformers. Borrowing 20,000 yuan (about $2,000) from the central Bank of China, within only a couple of years he had paid back his loan and built a business that was worth an estimated ten times the seed capital, and soon twenty times that. The payroll soared to two hundred people, 60 percent of them people with disabilities. The Baoding city government began to supply, from its vocational schools and hospitals for people with disabilities, a new stream of trained workers who otherwise were finding it difficult to be placed in jobs. It was a time when new enterprises were actually turning down government assignees, arguing that they had higher standards of productivity and skills than the state-owned industries. A jarring hierarchical split between new enterprises and traditional communes emerged not only in places like Guangzhou or Shanghai, where American outsourcing fueled the boom, but even in provincial economies like Baoding's. Men's determination to use workers with disabilities in a private enterprise bridged the gap, even in a modest way. In return for taking on the unwanted workers, the local authorities waived his tax bill, and he gained unspoken immunity from a number of regulatory hassles. He was honored as a major benefactor of people with disabilities in the town. The government steered a few contracts his way, a practice that steadily declined, however, in the late nineties, when domestic demand for elective power was on the rise but competition crowded his field.

It helped to have the government on his side, but Men faced a number of challenges at the outset. Even without the disability twist, the going was by no means easy in those early days. Any wealthy entrepreneur was viewed with a lingering suspicion that was often fed by jealousy, and trouble in the form of corrupt bureaucrats looking for bribes or jobs for their lazy sons was a constant worry for Men. In Baoding, former Red Guards from the Cultural Revolution hold high political offices. To keep up his rapport with the local government, a steady stream of officials had to be buttered up—as American businesses have to endlessly entertain clients, the Chinese have to attend to *hou mir,* "back door," relationships with the government just to keep their own doors open. At the conclusion of one long banquet, during which a dozen toasts to a local politico had taken their toll on Men's usual tact, he turned to his sister-in-law, an expatriate visiting from New York, and confided, "This is not me. I hate all of this, but I must keep doing it to keep the factory going."

Meanwhile, back at the plant, productivity was off the charts, and profits were mounting because capital and labor costs, even by Chinese standards, were low. This is not a plant in which assistive technology or fancy software smooth the way for workers with disabilities. It is decidedly low-tech. Men's close-knit team simply recognized a work environment that could transform a "disability" into an advantage. In the factory, deaf workers had an edge over other workers who might be bothered by all the noise and find it hard to communicate. Signing and gesturing to one another under the din of heavy machinery, the deaf workers paired up to pull copper wire from long spools and wrap it tightly to make the coils at the heart of the generators, a cheap way to knock off the GE models (nobody is calling Men a saint when it comes to international patent laws).

No lawyers or union representatives are around to threaten ADA-style lawsuits, as there is nothing approaching the ADA in China, despite the presence of one high-profile, internationally known disability advocate. Deng Pu Fang, the son of Deng Xiao Ping, has been a wheelchair user since he was pushed from a sixth-floor window by Red Guards during interrogation while the insanity of the Cultural Revolution raged. He is a fixture on the global disability conference circuit, including appearances at the Para-lympics. While his father was the little emperor, he served as China's am-bassador to the outside world at a time when anything in the way of positive spin on human rights was important to the nation's image (and economy). A younger celebrity who has started to take on this role as well is Cang Lan, the petite gymnast who sustained a spinal cord injury during the Goodwill Games in Atlanta in 1999. Between Deng Pu Fang and Cang Lan, the recog-nition of China in global disability circles far exceeds the actual measure of progress the country has made in disability rights.

That is why Men's efforts seem all the more heroic. The harsh conditions (power outages are a major hindrance, some of them planned if not an-nounced by the government when coal supplies run low) and minimal safety would scarcely qualify his shop floor for "model" status anywhere in the world. By regional standards, the factory is about average for conditions of light and air, safety, and other measures that Americans best know in OSHA terms. In China, such health and safety standards in the workplace have certainly improved since the eighties, when Men started his operation, but remain far from exemplary, as recent reports by human rights organi-zations, including one in which I am involved (the International Center for Corporate Accountability) have shown. I doubt Men's factory would pass an ICCA audit of safety conditions. Despite the severity of the conditions, how-ever, Men's accomplishment in his remote corner of the global economy remains significant. Amid the dust and gloom, the screeching flywheels (probably not so offensive to this team of workers as to the touring re-porter), and the dangerous welding torches, there is a vitality that is impos-sible to measure except in the broad smiles, the swift movement, and the absence of torpor one often finds in factories of this kind. Men and his gre-garious personal assistant, a young woman with a charismatic warmth that is often expressed in hugs among the many women working in the factory, or long handshakes and earnest conversations about family and health with the men, are greeted almost as long-absent friends when they make the rounds.

The individual behind this audacious and, fortunately, highly successful experiment in aggressive disability hiring is an unlikely oligarch. His pri-vate life is shaped by an old-fashioned demonstrativeness when it comes to filial piety, a throwback to the old China that is hardly in keeping with the lifestyle of the new generation of *da quan* (mogul or "big shot"). Men's driver drops him monthly at the tree-lined circle before a mausoleum not far from the factory. Alone or with family members, he walks a long corri-dor to a section where the urns of distinguished "friends of the state" are interred and removes a small rectangular cedar casket carrying his father's ashes. Repairing to the garden outside, he lights incense, offers prayers, and bows three times. Men's father was the private physician to one of the most powerful figures in China, Party Secretary Xi Guang, a close associate of Mao Ze Dong and Premier Zhou En Lai. Men was expected by his family to become a doctor himself, but just when he ought to have gone to medical school, the Cultural Revolution shut the universities, and he ended up in the People's Liberation Army. Yet he is vastly better educated and more classically sophisticated than the typical soldier. With a sure tenor voice, he performs entire scenes from traditional Beijing operas and has a ready store of Confucian proverbs or Tang dynasty poetry excerpts to suit any occasion. His luxurious four-bedroom apartment, where he lives with his wife and spoiled son, heir to the business, has the obligatory oversized television and other ostentatious electronics, but it is also graced with outstanding examples of calligraphy and painting, and a fine library. His office is a long, dim room on the second floor overlooking the main courtyard of the small campus of buildings he has created. That is where I received my most memorable lesson in the management of people with disabilities. Men is fond of an old Chinese saying that comes in handy as a toast at banquets as well as a note of harmony in the small, daily negotiations that take the sting of discrimination out of working in this most hierarchical of the world's societies, Communism notwithstanding. The whole operation is beautifully run on the principle of *yi jia ren*—"one big happy family."

If the smiling Chinese deaf-workers scissoring the dusty shop air with their sign language are an unforgettable example of disability at work in an ensemble, then the incredible Dexter Benjamin is a paragon of the solo version. There should always be room in an organization, corporate or entrepreneurial, for anomaly. The most astonishing, and in many ways instructive, such unlikelihood in my experience was Dexter, who was the exclusive bike messenger of *WE* magazine in its heyday and a legend in that highly selective, wild and crazy guild of road warriors, the New York bike messenger community. Dexter was an above-the-knee amputee who did not use a prosthesis. He rode a beat-up racing bike fitted with one pedal, and either hopped or used crutches to finish each job from curbside to the receptionist's desk. His best moments were reserved for the road, where he darted in and out between taxis and buses, zipping to daylight at thirty-eight miles an hour (he was fond of showing me the top speed he clocked, which he saved on his portable speedometer each day). I never met anyone who witnessed Dexter's slalom through traffic who didn't use the word "awesome" to describe him.

The story of how Dexter became our full-time messenger is an unusual recruiting tale. I was running the magazine out of our Soho offices, when Soho was still an artsy downtown neighborhood in Manhattan. My publisher had twice spotted what he thought was a one-legged bike messenger uptown on Park Avenue, but given his propensity to down three quick tumblers of Scotch to open a business lunch the sightings lacked credence. As other messengers dropped off vital packages of photos from the Associated Press in Rockefeller Center or disks from our designers in the West Village, I would debrief them on the existence of the one-legged bike messenger. If you will excuse the irresistible allusion to Moby Dick, several claimed to have actually seen or met Dexter, but they warned me it would be tough to track him down as he was not affiliated with any of the major "stables" that pool assignments. One suggested that, like most freelancers, Dexter was a genuine maverick, and left it at that. The mystery built for months as reports filtered to us of Dexter sightings in midtown and in the financial district. Our office lay between, and one day as I was out for a stroll along Broadway, taking a break from editing a travel feature, I spotted the apparition that turned heads wherever he went—a huge, helmeted figure in blue and black Lycra pumping furiously with his left leg and glaring into the driver's-side windows of taxis and New Jersey SUVs as he beat them downtown. Journalistic instincts triumphing over those of self-preservation, I jumped into the fluvial onslaught of the traffic and blocked his path as he cut right to get around cars at a light. He screeched to a halt and delivered a barrage of off-color epithets in his broad Trinidadian accent. I had broken up a run in midafternoon, that crucial time zone when the flurry of pickups reaches its peak, so his rage (about which I was only just beginning to learn) was more than understandable. Quick as I could, I gave him my business card and assured him that I wanted to hire him for a minimum of a dozen runs a week (at $17 a run), although it shortly became far more. This was no time for an interview, obviously.

A free spirit, Dexter did not call me right away. His girlfriend and erstwhile business manager Beverley, who by day worked at a jazz recording label and was herself a singer, finally gave the office a call, and we set up an account. Dexter's worth to my business far exceeded his virtuosity as a bike messenger, although our whole staff never ceased to marvel at the way he would speed away from our door and start zigging and zagging to daylight along Broadway. We featured his chiseled good looks and mighty muscles in a fashion shoot for exercise wear shot at a trendy gym, where Dexter captured the admiration of the photographer as well as a camera crew from Pax television by jumping rope, lifting weights, and shadow boxing (he had been a welterweight in Trinidad and retained his boxer's instincts for quick, darting attacks). One of the most beloved radio personalities in New York, John Montone, did a series of interviews with Dexter for the morning drive-time show on 1010 WINS, the city's main news station. A documentary filmmaker began tailing Dexter (at least as well as he could—he was utterly unable to keep up on a bike and had to use a van). I used a big picture of Dexter holding his bike over his head on Fifth Avenue as the opener for our annual survey of work and disability—defiant as it was triumphant, it offered the visual fanfare we wanted to sound as the anthem of the issue.

At this point, it would be tempting to allegorize Dexter Benjamin, yet I don't want to reduce him, or any of the success stories in this book, to a rolling symbol. For one thing, Dexter was emphatically not a card-carrying member of the disability rights movement. The cultural or political significance of what he did was not on his mind. The look of consternation he gave me when I offered my business card was easily explained—Dexter could not read, and it had been Beverley who picked up on the legend: "*WE,* a lifestyle magazine for people with disabilities, their families and friends." He did not need an affinity group, and the extent of his accommodations was the way he rigged his bike to be pumped by one pedal. I set up as much business as I could for him over the next couple of years, even letting him do superfluous runs to Wall Street with our business plan. On one of those, when his assignment was to hand-deliver an envelope to Stephen Hammerman, a big shot at Merrill Lynch and a major disability philanthropist who was on our board, Dexter had been stopped by security and lost his cool. He punched a hole in a Sheetrock wall in anger, and Mr. Hammerman called me to have a word with him. I explained that it was our fault for insisting that the envelope be placed in his hands. Here was a guy who would literally go through walls for us. In between, when he wasn't freelancing for others, he started hanging around our offices, sipping diet soda from the chairman's refrigerator, glancing over our shoulders at the pictures on screen, practicing his reading skills (he entered a literacy program), and becoming part of the family. He did not theorize or debate the disability issues. He told us about the long bike races he went on during weekends on Long Island, busman's holidays, or told stories about growing up in Trinidad. One day he had seen a truck driver lose control on a steep slope, at the bottom of which a young girl was on the road. He lunged to get her out of the way, and the truck caught his right leg. He had never been able to find the right prosthesis, so he hopped or used an old pair of crutches.

Dexter, for me, is the embodiment of a particularly strong if obviously eccentric approach to work by people with disabilities. Rather than call it a tale of hubris, we should characterize the Dexter scenario as an act of defiance. By taking on a job that most would consider impossible, he flew in the teeth of his limitations and performed an awesome turning of the tables. It reminds me of, for example, the Polish-born Joseph Conrad becoming a master of English prose style, or the NBA basketball star Spud Webb driving to the basket against men who were literally two feet taller than he was. More than just inspiring us (that old cliché), these improbable instances of beating the odds offer an invaluable sense of the complete inapplicability of job requirements to certain driven individuals who refuse to be constrained by society or science, by business conventions or the expectations of those around them. We all loved the way Dexter sized up the worst possible job for an above-the-knee amputee and went right at it every day. Only a Dexter can pull this off, which he did in a spectacular fashion that opens a perspective on disability and employment where the refutation of limits in the selection of one's métier adds edge to the motivation and in fact ensures success because the Dexters of this world, rare as they are, refuse to take no for an answer.

They can't be the rule; they must be exceptions. It would do no good for a corporation to program the impossible, and it sounds dangerous to propose that businesses ought to be built on such an outrageous flouting of prudence and common sense. Moreover, within the context of current disability theory a serious set of reservations also lurks. Dexter could easily be labeled a "supercrip" in current parlance, rather like another amputee who was a part of my magazine, Tom Whittaker, who made it to the summit of Mount Everest on a prosthetic leg, or Jim Abbott, a major-league baseball pitcher with one hand. There is concern among many advocates that these "supercrips" represent one awe-inducing extreme of the pendulum's swing from the archetype of the "sad crip," who draws pity. Frustrated that these two extremes dominate public perception of the community, disability experts are scornful of the "supercrip." They are wary of the celebrity status of many Paralympian athletes, whose enormous feats of physical strength distort the reality of day-to-day life with disabilities.

I agree that the "supercrips" play an ambiguous role in the perception of the community, partly because it is worrisome to think of them lulling the nondisabled into a false sense that disability cannot be so tough after all if such prodigious feats are possible. Clearly one of the chief concerns of a manager in a situation where a Dexter emerges is ensuring that his flamboyance, inevitably attention getting, does not alienate the other members of the team who have disabilities, so the caveats of the disability scholars regarding "supercrips" are worth noting in a business context. Managing

Dexter was no picnic at times. But I also think it is vital for corporations to support the Dexters of the world, to give them their niche in an organization. It may not be time for blind baseball umpires or deaf judges on *American Idol* (or maybe it is, since visual attraction scores points and musical talent is so lacking), but I am eager to include in this overview of management and disability a place for the utterly improbable and, to invoke an Anglicism, the "bloody-minded" aspirant to a job that is, as the English might also say, "unsuitable." There must always be a place for the person with a disability who simply does not acknowledge the reality of conventional boundaries, who can go against the grain and by doing so, as Dexter did, build the hard muscles and quick reflexes that any contrarian possesses. Like the long-acknowledged significance of "thinking outside the box," such an approach to one's job stretches business thinking.

For the manager or coworker, this kind of defiant yet focused approach to a job creates a set of circumstances that induces productivity all around the company. It heightens the esprit de corps one feels in the trading zone. In our newsroom, in addition to Dexter with his soda in the corner, we had a reporter who was deaf and writers who were blind. The prevailing wisdom in the media business had it that the use of the telephone in about 60 percent of a reporter's interviews would make it next to impossible for the deaf woman to do her job, and that 100 percent of journalists have to see what is on a computer screen. But it was too late to invoke this logic once we put the team together, so I simply had to sit down with all of them and wonder how we were going to make it possible to get a magazine out. We installed relay phones and voice-activated software. We also created an atmosphere of quiet trust, a company that was one big affinity group of user-experts. Coworkers who defy the prevailing wisdom often prefer not to be constantly remarked upon. Nor do they need pep talks. Their drive to succeed need not be supplied from outside, because it is so clearly internal, even personal. The tolerance they require is the freedom of the soloist, a respectful latitude that any star demands. It would have been a mistake to parade the ones on my staff as "miracles," because that would have made them into freaks, and being a freak is distracting. In return, they gave me a great magazine on time, every time. We never missed a print deadline, and we made money.

A moment of self-consciousness in Broadway traffic could have cost Dexter his life. He may be captivating the eyes of bystanders all the way from one end of Manhattan to the other, but he needs to keep his eyes on the road. The business world is not a Hallmark made-for-television movie about some poor little kid who becomes the centerpiece of a coach's locker-room pep talk about how, if Jimmy can do it, anybody can. Here is one of the great unspoken and unquantifiable benefits of working side by side with a Dexter, or almost any person with a disability: just the presence is enough to jog the conscience and stir the admiration of others—to inspire, if I must use that term so problematic in the community—with and without disabilities. There is no need to dramatize when a one-legged bike messenger covers forty city blocks in ten minutes flat. Everyone in the room sucks it up and gives more in response.

As problematic as the notion is in this day and age of corporate conservatism, there is an element of brinksmanship to having a Dexter around, a measure of risk that I think a good manager ought to be ready to take on to reap the rewards of having such a person on the team. The initial shock over the whole unlikelihood of the arrangement soon gives way to proud inclusion. In my own case, even after a couple of years seeing Dexter almost daily, I never entirely got over a sense of wonder, but that translated itself into motivation. The Dexter effect is like that. From customers to coworkers, it shakes up the tendency to see a job as just a job, because in certain cases it can be an act of heroism. We just don't say it.

The sheer improbability of Dexter becoming a bike messenger is one way to take the buzzword "difference" to its extreme. He dramatically stood out among bike messengers for his disability and among people with disabilities for his audacity. It is a stretch to call his eccentricity a mark of genius—one of the best excuses for fostering difference in a corporation is the creative capital it can generate—but by radically stretching the sense of possibility not only of our awestruck contacts but of our cynical staff as well, he appealed to the imagination even as he beat the competition hollow on the road. It was empowerment in its most raw form. Dexter was one of those people with disabilities who were "out there," living the life, fighting the stereotypes as well as the mind-numbing repetition of same old, same old, and earning a buck or two as the messengers of an oncoming wave in business, the new face of disability.

Agenda

- *Promote the growth of affinity groups* dedicated to disability culture.
- *Build teams* based on complementary rather than homogeneous strengths.
- *Apply a 360-degree perspective* to leadership skills.
- *Use constant communications* to sync disability and corporate cultures.
- *Include the recommendations of disability task forces* in company strategy and policy.
- *Play the long shot* now and then on matching disability and job requirements.

Notes

1. Personal interview, November 2005.
2. Russell Shorto, "Faith at Work," *New York Times Magazine*, October 31, 2004, p. 43.
3. Sharon Waxman, "Sony Effort to Reach Christians Is Disputed," *New York Times*, November 1, 2005, section E, p. 1.
4. Shorto, "Faith at Work," p. 47.
5. Lisa Belkin, "The Person Behind the Office Image," Life's Work, *New York Times*, November 6, 2005, Jobs section, p. 1.
6. Ruth O'Brien, *Bodies in Revolt: Gender, Disability and an Alternative Ethic of Care* (New York: Routledge, 2005).
7. Ruth O'Brien, *Bodies in Revolt*, p. 116.
8. E-mail to author, November 2005.
9. Ruth O'Brien, *Crippled Justice: The History of Modern Disability Policy in the Workplace* (Chicago: University of Chicago Press, 2001), p. 2.
10. Personal interview, August 2005.
11. Personal interview, August 2005.

The Top 50 U.S. Disability-Forward Companies

Consulting with experts in the disability field, the author ranked these companies according to their performance in three areas: (1) aggressively recruiting, training, and promoting people with disabilities, (2) investing in assistive technology and accessible workplaces, and (3) recognizing the power of customers with disabilities.

1. IBM
A Big Blue-sized marketing effort in assistive technology is matched by a decades-old tradition of weaving disability and corporate cultures through recruiting (diversity chief Ted Childs aggressively accents disability) and accommodation.

2. Microsoft
Chairman Bill Gates supports national initiatives, including the USBLG, while his HR managers under Mylene Padolina effectively recruit students with disabilities (as early as high school) as interns and new hires. The in-house affinity groups and brilliant accessible technology team make it the dream office for accessibility.

3. SunTrust
This major bank's disability policy has reached an advanced level of cultural integration, including employee and customer awareness, even as its call centers and products attract strong numbers of recruits and new clients.

4. Cingular Wireless
The in-house winner for its savvy niche marketing and outstanding HR policies, this telecom giant invests its dynamic affinity groups with the strategic power to integrate disability into corporate culture.

5. Bank of America
A strong advocate and supporter of the Business Leadership Network, the bank is also notable for its full-blown ad campaign for customers with disabilities.

6. Booz Allen Hamilton
The consulting firm is a perennial award winner for campus recruitment, college internships, and a record of promoting from within. Its Disabilities Task Force and Disabilities Program Manager are used by the NBDC as a best practices model.

7. Procter & Gamble
Under chief diversity officer Deb Dagit, the masters of marketing boast an outstanding recruiting record and benefits program, making them a prize employer for managers with disabilities.

8. JPMorgan Chase
With the acquisition of Bank One, which has enjoyed a hugely successful marketing effort of its redesigned and highly accessible facilities, the fast-growing investment giant strengthens its effort. More important, they get the cultural rationale behind including disability in diversity and apply it to both hiring and marketing.

9. Merck
The pharmaceutical giant uses sponsorships and participation in advocacy efforts to build an image in the disability community, establishing a solid symmetry in its outreach to consumers and recruits.

10. Wells Fargo
A pioneer in accommodation, the bank is also way out front in marketing, with the first accessible ATM (now up to 4,800 state-of-the-art machines with assistive technology) and an award-winning accessible Web site.

11. Motorola
A major presence in college recruiting and advocacy, the leading maker of cool cell phones recognized early in the game the advantages of multiple applications of accessible and usable technology in product design.

12. Nordstrom
The retailer captured its place in disability business history through its high-visibility advertising campaigns have used cause marketing since 1987. More recently, it has made strides on the HR and management fronts.

13. Manpower
The world's biggest employer, a past winner of New Freedom Initiative Award, keeps thousands of workers with disabilities on its rolls, with benefits.

14. UPS
Worldwide shipper wields its purchasing power as an influential force through its Supplier Diversity Program as well as its hiring might through such programs as the Marriott Foundation's Bridges, state vocational services, and non-profit agencies (particularly serving deaf workers).

15. Merrill Lynch
Thanks to the dynamic in-house advocate Chris Fossel, the affinity group and recruiting efforts post significant hiring numbers in combination with targeted retail efforts, a record of success particularly in the Deaf community.

16. Lockheed Martin
The massive defense contractor is a powerhouse in diversity, emphasizing disability in its HR training and garnering perennial awards and high marks from *Careers and the disABLED* magazine.

17. Federated Department Stores
The rookie of the year in 2006 for its employee training and comprehensive marketing efforts is ensuring that its Macy's sales force is up to speed on disability culture.

18. General Electric
As a design innovator of accessible consumer home products, including a highly profitable kitchen, GE is also a leader in reaching the disability market, especially after taking the extra step to make its Web portal completely accessible.

19. Wal-Mart
The new addition of Deidre Davis to the executive ranks as their first director of ADA services is considered a major move by advocates, gaining community points for a company that has already scored high for hiring people with developmental disabilities as well as seniors (225,000 of them).

20. Sears
A solid track record at Sears on accommodation and HR joins a highly regarded disability marketing effort, established over a decade ago, at Kmart to make one of the most balanced examples among retailers of disability awareness.

21. Charles Schwab
Disability awareness starts at the top—the founder and chairman, whose name is on the door, has dyslexia.

22. Medtronic
The world leader in medical technology is a growing presence in the Business Leadership Network, thanks to Karen Quammem, which named it Employer of the Year for 2005 in part for its cultural affinity network.

23. TJX
The nation's top clothes retailer is the source of hundreds of jobs for workers with disabilities through the nationwide Resource Partnership and uses its strong supplier diversity policy to wield wider influence.

24. Blue Cross
This massive healthcare network is a classic example of the medical industry hiring from its core market. It hosted the 2003 COSD conference.

25. General Motors
The carmaker is miles ahead of domestic rivals on accessible design, customer service (including TTY for OnStar) and marketing to drivers with disabilities.

26. United Technologies
Not surprisingly, a major supplier of disability products, including Otis elevators, is also a major employer.

27. Black and Decker
This important holdover from the old industrial economy is an outstanding example of accommodation in an era when too many jobs for people with disabilities are in the service sector.

28. Starbucks
Conspicuously eager to be perceived as a corporate good citizen, the coffee chain literally lowered the bar for wheelchair users on both sides, working and sipping, making it a recent but caffeinated entrant into the recruiting and marketing games.

29. Pitney-Bowes
A copier with multiple access features was a major coup in universal design enabled by disability-forward strategists who spotted a great niche.

30. Johnson & Johnson
The all-round diversity champion does not leave disability out of the mix with its Return to Wellness integrated disability management program that supports employees returning to work on flex-time.

31. Marriott
The hotelier is a pioneer through its foundation program called Bridges ("from school to work"), now in its 17th year, a major force in supported employment that

has racked up over 7,800 placements with 1,500 employers. Caveat: Considered by some advocates to be "old school" for its emphasis on low-skill positions.

32. Boeing
"Forever New Frontiers" is the company motto, and disability is one of those frontiers-including supplier incentives for vendors with disabilities (notably, those incurred in military service). The company scored big diversity points with the appointment of James A. Bell as CEO.

33. 3M
A top-ranking technology company with an outstanding example of an in-house employee resource group (the DisabilityAdvisory Network) and a model HR and benefits policy (Total Disability Management program) that is especially strong in the area of developmental disabilities.

34. American Express
A major employer of people with disabilities, they just appointed EVP Kevin L. Cox, noted disability expert, to a high-ranking strategic HR spot.

35. Northwest Airlines
This is a turn-around tale: The one-time target of traveler's complaints has launched recruiting, workplace accommodation, advocacy, and marketing efforts with their innovative Customer Advisory Board that redeem old offenses.

36. ConAgra
The food giant has nurtured disability awareness as a cultural component of its award-winning Valuing Diversity Initiative.

37. Qualcomm
The Department of Labor recently recognized the telecom supplier as a leader in the employment of veterans with disabilities.

38. Wachovia
A bank with one of the best HR training records in the nation, including an extensive disability segment, coupled with outstanding customer outreach and notable disability benefit plans for small businesses.

39. MacDonald's
With its huge presence in supported employment and philanthropy, which some say is "old school," the burger chain creates thousands of jobs annually.

40. Honeywell
This founding member of the (now defunct) Able to Work consortium has a great track record on turning its assistive tech innovations into employee perks.

41. Mattel
The toymaker made history with Share-a-Smile Becky, Barbie's wheelchair-using friend, and remains disability-forward in its marketing and philanthropy.

42. Chrysler
The automaker's annual design awards promote accessibility, a standout feature of its own models (such as the PT Cruiser, one of the best cars for wheelchair users).

43. Universal Studios Home Entertainment
The studio garnered rave reviews on progress for disability in the media with the simultaneous release of *Ray* in DVD and enhanced DVS format.

44. Hewlett-Packard
For years a dominant player in recruiting people with disabilities, as well as accessible technology, HP is a past winner of the New Freedom Initiative Award.

45. Avis
The rental agency tries harder with Avis Access® services, accessibility, and marketing initiatives aimed at travelers with disabilities.

46. ExxonMobil
The gas giant is a strong supporter of advocacy and recruiting groups, including COSD, as well as nonprofit service organizations.

47. Caterpillar
The huge equipment manufacturer is an assistive technology leader and towering philanthropic force for its support of the Special Olympics.

48. Colgate-Palmolive
A steady supporter of Just One Break and other employment initiatives, Colgate also plays a strong marketing role as an advertiser in disability publications.

49. Ford
An automaker that is going all-out to be regarded as a good corporate citizen, Ford puts user-experts to work designing cars that offer mobility to consumers with disabilities. A recent conference on the issue was titled "Not Just Talk."

50. MGM
Recognizing the tremendous market among people with disabilities for casinos and resorts, this entertainment company is pouring resources into accessibility.

Resources

Employment

Career Opportunities for Students with Disabilities
University of Tennessee
100 Dunford Hall
Knoxville, TN 37996–4010
www.cosdonline.org
Voice: (865) 974-7148
Fax: (865) 974-6497
Executive Director: Alan D. Muir
E-mail: amuir@tennessee.edu

Abilitylinks
26W 171 Roosevelt Road
Wheaton, IL 60187
Tel: (630) 462-4082
Fax: (630) 462-5570
www.abilitylinks.org
Information and Referral Counselor:
Janice Duvall
E-mail: jduvall@abilitylinks.org

Just One Break (JOB)
120 Wall Street
New York, NY 10005
Tel: (212) 785-7300
Fax: (212) 785-4513
TTY: (212) 785-4515
www.justonebreak.com
Director: Susan Odiseos
E-mail: jobs@justonebreak.com

National Association of Colleges and Employers (NACE)
62 Highland Ave.
Bethlehem, PA 18017
Tel: (800) 544-5272 or
(610) 868-1421
Fax: (610) 868-0208
www.naceweb.org
Executive director:
Marilyn Mackes
E-mail: mmackes@naceweb.org

National Business and Disability
Council
201 I.U. Willets Road
Albertson, NY 11507
Tel: (516) 465-1515
Fax: (516) 465-3730
www.nbdc.com
President: Edmund Cortez

U.S. Equal Employment Opportunity
Commission
Department of Labor
Office of Disability Employment Policy
(ODEP)
200 Constitution Ave. N.W.
Suite S-1303
Washington, DC 20210
Tel: (866) 633-7365
TTY: (877) 889-5627
Fax: (202) 693-7888
www.dol.gov/odep
Assistant Secretary: W. Roy Grizzard, Jr.
E-mail: grizzard.roy@dol.gov

Job Accommodation Network (JAN)
U.S. Department of Labor
Frances Perkins Building
200 Constitution Avenue, NW
Washington, DC 20210
Tel: (866) 633-7365 or
(800) 526-7234
Fax: (202) 693-7888
TTY: (877) 889-5627
www.jan.wvu.edu
Project director: D. J. Hendricks
E-mail: jan@jan.wvu.edu

Strategy

EINSOF Communications
Tel: (310) 472-5954
www.einsofcommunications.com
President: Tari Susan Hartman-Squire
E-mail: tari@
einsofcommunications.com

United States Business Leadership
Network
SunTrust Bank
919 East Main St.
Richmond, VA 23216
Director: Katherine McCary
Tel: (804) 343-9575
Fax: (804) 782-7975
E-mail:
katherine.mccary@suntrust.com
www.usbln.com

Office and Web Site Design
and Architecture

Adaptive Environmnents
374 Congress Street
Suite 301
Boston, MA 02210
www.AdaptiveEnvironments.org
Tel and TTY: (617) 695-1225
Fax: (617) 482-8099
Director: Valerie Fletcher
E-mail: info@
AdaptiveEnvironments.org

Center for Universal Design
NC State University
College of Design
Campus Box 7701
Raleigh, NC 27695
www.cud@ncsu.edu
Tel: (919) 515-3082 or
    (800) 647-6777
Fax: 919-515-8951
Senior Project Manager:
    Richard C. Duncan
E-mail: cud@ncsu.edu

Center for Applied Special Technology (CAST)
40 Harvard Mills Square
Wakefield, MA 01880–3233
Tel: (781) 245-2212
TTY: (781) 245-9320
Fax: (781) 245-5212
www.cast.org
President and Chief Executive Officer:
    Ada Sullivan
E-mail: cast@cast.org

The Americans With Disabilities Act of 1990

S.933

One Hundred First Congress of the United States of America
AT THE SECOND SESSION
Begun and held at the City of Washington on Tuesday, the twenty-third day of January, one thousand nine hundred and ninety.

An Act to establish a clear and comprehensive prohibition of discrimination on the basis of disability.

Be it enacted by the Senate and House of Representatives of the United States of America in Congress assembled,

SECTION 1. SHORT TITLE; TABLE OF CONTENTS.

(a) Short Title.—This Act may be cited as the "Americans with Disabilities Act of 1990".

(b) Table of Contents.—The table of contents is as follows:
Sec. 1. Short title; table of contents.
Sec. 2. Findings and purposes.
Sec. 3. Definitions.

*From the U.S. Department of Labor, Employment Standards, Administration, Office of Federal Contract Compliance Program, http://www.dol.gov/esa/regs/statutes/ofccp/ada.htm.

TITLE I—EMPLOYMENT

TITLE II—PUBLIC SERVICES

SUBTITLE A—PROHIBITION AGAINST DISCRIMINATION AND OTHER GENERALLY APPLICABLE PROVISIONS

SUBTITLE B—ACTIONS APPLICABLE TO PUBLIC TRANSPORTATION PROVIDED BY PUBLIC ENTITIES CONSIDERED DISCRIMINATORY

PART I—PUBLIC TRANSPORTATION OTHER THAN BY AIRCRAFT OR CERTAIN RAIL OPERATIONS

PART II—PUBLIC TRANSPORTATION BY INTERCITY AND COMMUTER RAIL

TITLE III—PUBLIC ACCOMMODATIONS AND SERVICES OPERATED BY PRIVATE ENTITIES

TITLE IV—TELECOMMUNICATIONS

TITLE V—MISCELLANEOUS PROVISIONS

SEC. 2. FINDINGS AND PURPOSES.

(a) Findings.—The Congress finds that—

(1) some 43,000,000 Americans have one or more physical or mental disabilities, and this number is increasing as the population as a whole is growing older;

(2) historically, society has tended to isolate and segregate individuals with disabilities, and, despite some improvements, such forms of discrimination against individuals with disabilities continue to be a serious and pervasive social problem;

(3) discrimination against individuals with disabilities persists in such critical areas as employment, housing, public accommodations, education, transportation, communication, recreation, institutionalization, health services, voting, and access to public services;

(4) unlike individuals who have experienced discrimination on the basis of race, color, sex, national origin, religion, or age, individuals who have experienced discrimination on the basis of disability have often had no legal recourse to redress such discrimination;

(5) individuals with disabilities continually encounter various forms of discrimination, including outright intentional exclusion, the discriminatory effects of architectural, transportation, and communication barriers, overprotective rules and policies, failure to make modifications to existing facilities and practices, exclusionary qualification standards and criteria, segregation, and relegation to lesser services, programs, activities, benefits, jobs, or other opportunities;

(6) census data, national polls, and other studies have documented that people with disabilities, as a group, occupy an inferior status in our society, and are severely disadvantaged socially, vocationally, economically, and educationally;

(7) individuals with disabilities are a discrete and insular minority who have been faced with restrictions and limitations, subjected to a history of purposeful unequal treatment, and relegated to a position of political powerlessness in our society, based on characteristics that are beyond the control of such individuals and resulting from stereotypic assumptions not truly indicative of the individual ability of such individuals to participate in, and contribute to, society;

(8) the Nation's proper goals regarding individuals with disabilities are to assure equality of opportunity, full participation, independent living, and economic self-sufficiency for such individuals; and

(9) the continuing existence of unfair and unnecessary discrimination and prejudice denies people with disabilities the opportunity to compete on an equal basis and to pursue those opportunities for which our free society is justifiably famous, and costs the United States billions of dollars in unnecessary expenses resulting from dependency and nonproductivity.

(b) Purpose.—It is the purpose of this Act—

(1) to provide a clear and comprehensive national mandate for the elimination of discrimination against individuals with disabilities;

(2) to provide clear, strong, consistent, enforceable standards addressing discrimination against individuals with disabilities;

(3) to ensure that the Federal Government plays a central role in enforcing the standards established in this Act on behalf of individuals with disabilities; and

(4) to invoke the sweep of congressional authority, including the power to enforce the fourteenth amendment and to regulate commerce, in order to address the major areas of discrimination faced day-to-day by people with disabilities.

SEC. 3. DEFINITIONS.

As used in this Act:

(1) Auxiliary aids and services.—The term "auxiliary aids and services" includes—

(A) qualified interpreters or other effective methods of making aurally delivered materials available to individuals with hearing impairments;

(B) qualified readers, taped texts, or other effective methods of making visually delivered materials available to individuals with visual impairments;

(C) acquisition or modification of equipment or devices; and

(D) other similar services and actions.

(2) Disability.—The term "disability" means, with respect to an individual—

(A) a physical or mental impairment that substantially limits one or more of the major life activities of such individual;

(B) a record of such an impairment; or

(C) being regarded as having such an impairment.

(3) State.—The term "State" means each of the several States, the District of Columbia, the Commonwealth of Puerto Rico, Guam, American Samoa, the Virgin Islands, the Trust Territory of the Pacific Islands, and the Commonwealth of the Northern Mariana Islands.

[TITLE I—EMPLOYMENT]

SEC. 101. DEFINITIONS.

As used in this title:

(1) Commission.—The term "Commission" means the Equal Employment Opportunity Commission established by section 705 of the Civil Rights Act of 1964 (42 U.S.C. 2000e-4).

(2) Covered entity.—The term "covered entity" means an employer, employment agency, labor organization, or joint labor-management committee.

(3) Direct threat.—The term "direct threat" means a significant risk to the health or safety of others that cannot be eliminated by reasonable accommodation.

(4) Employee.—The term "employee" means an individual employed by an employer.

(5) Employer.—

(A) In general.—The term "employer" means a person engaged in an industry affecting commerce who has 15 or more employees for each working day in each of 20 or more calendar weeks in the current or preceding calendar year, and any agent of such person, except that, for two years following the effective date of this title, an employer means a person engaged in an industry affecting commerce who has 25 or more employees for each working day in each of 20 or more calendar weeks in the current or preceding year, and any agent of such person.

(B) Exceptions.—The term "employer" does not include—

(i) the United States, a corporation wholly owned by the government of the United States, or an Indian tribe; or

(ii) a bona fide private membership club (other than a labor organization) that is exempt from taxation under section 501(c) of the Internal Revenue Code of 1986.

(6) Illegal use of drugs.—

(A) In general.—The term "illegal use of drugs" means the use of drugs, the possession or distribution of which is unlawful under the Controlled Substances Act (21 U.S.C. 812). Such term does not include the use of a drug taken under supervision by a licensed health care professional, or other uses authorized by the Controlled Substances Act or other provisions of Federal law.

(B) Drugs.—The term "drug" means a controlled substance, as defined in schedules I through V of section 202 of the Controlled Substances Act.

(7) Person, etc.—The terms "person", "labor organization", "employment agency", "commerce", and "industry affecting commerce", shall have the same meaning given such terms in section 701 of the Civil Rights Act of 1964 (42 U.S.C. 2000e).

(8) Qualified individual with a disability.—The term "qualified individual with a disability" means an individual with a disability who, with or without reasonable accommodation, can perform the essential functions of the employment position that such individual holds or desires. For the purposes of this title, consideration shall be given to the employer's judgment as to what functions of a job are essential, and if an employer has prepared a written description before advertising or interviewing applicants for the job, this description shall be considered evidence of the essential functions of the job.

(9) Reasonable accommodation.—The term "reasonable accommodation" may include—

(A) making existing facilities used by employees readily accessible to and usable by individuals with disabilities; and

(B) job restructuring, part-time or modified work schedules, reassignment to a vacant position, acquisition or modification of equipment or devices, appropriate adjustment or modifications of examinations, training materials or policies, the provision of qualified readers or interpreters, and other similar accommodations for individuals with disabilities.

(10) Undue hardship.—

(A) In general.—The term "undue hardship" means an action requiring significant difficulty or expense, when considered in light of the factors set forth in subparagraph (B).

(B) Factors to be considered.—In determining whether an accommodation would impose an undue hardship on a covered entity, factors to be considered include—

(i) the nature and cost of the accommodation needed under this Act;

(ii) the overall financial resources of the facility or facilities involved in the provision of the reasonable accommodation; the number of persons employed at such facility; the effect on expenses and resources, or the impact otherwise of such accommodation upon the operation of the facility;

(iii) the overall financial resources of the covered entity; the overall size of the business of a covered entity with respect to the number of its employees; the number, type, and location of its facilities; and

(iv) the type of operation or operations of the covered entity, including the composition, structure, and functions of the workforce of such entity; the geographic separateness, administrative, or fiscal relationship of the facility or facilities in question to the covered entity.

SEC. 102. DISCRIMINATION.

(a) General Rule.—No covered entity shall discriminate against a qualified individual with a disability because of the disability of such individual in regard to job application procedures, the hiring, advancement, or discharge of employees, employee compensation, job training, and other terms, conditions, and privileges of employment.

(b) Construction.—As used in subsection (a), the term "discriminate" includes—

(1) limiting, segregating, or classifying a job applicant or employee in a way that adversely affects the opportunities or status of such applicant or employee because of the disability of such applicant or employee;

(2) participating in a contractual or other arrangement or relationship that has the effect of subjecting a covered entity's qualified applicant or employee with a disability to the discrimination prohibited by this title (such relationship includes a relationship with an employment or referral agency, labor union, an organization providing fringe benefits to an employee of the covered entity, or an organization providing training and apprenticeship programs);

(3) utilizing standards, criteria, or methods of administration—

(A) that have the effect of discrimination on the basis of disability; or

(B) that perpetuate the discrimination of others who are subject to common administrative control;

(4) excluding or otherwise denying equal jobs or benefits to a qualified individual because of the known disability of an individual with whom the qualified individual is known to have a relationship or association;

(5)

(A) not making reasonable accommodations to the known physical or mental limitations of an otherwise qualified individual with a disability who is an applicant or employee, unless such covered entity can demonstrate that the accommodation would impose an undue hardship on the operation of the business of such covered entity; or

(B) denying employment opportunities to a job applicant or employee who is an otherwise qualified individual with a disability, if such denial is based on the need of such covered entity to make reasonable accommodation to the physical or mental impairments of the employee or applicant;

(6) using qualification standards, employment tests or other selection criteria that screen out or tend to screen out an individual with a disability or a class of individuals with disabilities unless the standard, test or other selection criteria, as used by the covered entity, is shown to be job-related for the position in question and is consistent with business necessity; and

(7) failing to select and administer tests concerning employment in the most effective manner to ensure that, when such test is administered to a job applicant or employee who has a disability that impairs sensory, manual, or speaking skills, such test results accurately reflect the skills, aptitude, or whatever other factor of such applicant or employee that such test purports to measure, rather than reflecting the impaired sensory, manual, or speaking skills of such employee or applicant (except where such skills are the factors that the test purports to measure).

(c) Medical Examinations and Inquiries.—

(1) In general.—The prohibition against discrimination as referred to in subsection (a) shall include medical examinations and inquiries.

(2) Preemployment.—

(A) Prohibited examination or inquiry.—Except as provided in paragraph (3), a covered entity shall not conduct a medical examination or make inquiries of a job applicant as to whether such applicant is an individual with a disability or as to the nature or severity of such disability.

(B) Acceptable inquiry.—A covered entity may make preemployment inquiries into the ability of an applicant to perform job-related functions.

(3) Employment entrance examination.—A covered entity may require a medical examination after an offer of employment has been made to a job applicant and prior to the commencement of the employment duties of such applicant, and may condition an offer of employment on the results of such examination, if—

(A) all entering employees are subjected to such an examination regardless of disability;

(B) information obtained regarding the medical condition or history of the applicant is collected and maintained on separate forms and in separate medical files and is treated as a confidential medical record, except that—

(i) supervisors and managers may be informed regarding necessary restrictions on the work or duties of the employee and necessary accommodations;

(ii) first aid and safety personnel may be informed, when appropriate, if the disability might require emergency treatment; and

(iii) government officials investigating compliance with this Act shall be provided relevant information on request; and

(C) the results of such examination are used only in accordance with this title.

(4) Examination and inquiry.—

(A) Prohibited examinations and inquiries.—A covered entity shall not require a medical examination and shall not make inquiries of an employee as to whether such employee is an individual with a disability or as to the nature or severity of the disability, unless such examination or inquiry is shown to be job-related and consistent with business necessity.

(B) Acceptable examinations and inquiries.—A covered entity may conduct voluntary medical examinations, including voluntary medical histories, which are part of an employee health program available to employees at that work site. A covered entity may make inquiries into the ability of an employee to perform job-related functions.

(C) Requirement.—Information obtained under subparagraph (B) regarding the medical condition or history of any employee are subject to the requirements of subparagraphs (B) and (C) of paragraph (3).

SEC. 103. DEFENSES.

(a) In General.—It may be a defense to a charge of discrimination under this Act that an alleged application of qualification standards, tests, or selection criteria that screen out or tend to screen out or otherwise deny a job or benefit to an individual with a disability has been shown to be jobrelated and consistent with business necessity, and such performance cannot be accomplished by reasonable accommodation, as required under this title.

(b) Qualification Standards.—The term "qualification standards" may include a requirement that an individual shall not pose a direct threat to the health or safety of other individuals in the workplace.

(c) Religious Entities.—

(1) In general.—This title shall not prohibit a religious corporation, association, educational institution, or society from giving preference in employment to individuals of a particular religion to perform work connected with the carrying on by such corporation, association, educational institution, or society of its activities.

(2) Religious tenets requirement.—Under this title, a religious organization may require that all applicants and employees conform to the religious tenets of such organization.

(d) List of Infectious and Communicable Diseases.—

(1) In general.—The Secretary of Health and Human Services, not later than 6 months after the date of enactment of this Act, shall—

(A) review all infectious and communicable diseases which may be transmitted through handling the food supply;

(B) publish a list of infectious and communicable diseases which are transmitted through handling the food supply;

(C) publish the methods by which such diseases are transmitted; and

(D) widely disseminate such information regarding the list of diseases and their modes of transmissability to the general public. Such list shall be updated annually.

(2) Applications.—In any case in which an individual has an infectious or communicable disease that is transmitted to others through the handling of food, that is included on the list developed by the Secretary of Health and Human Services under paragraph (1), and which cannot be eliminated by reasonable accommodation, a covered entity may refuse to assign or continue to assign such individual to a job involving food handling.

(3) Construction.—Nothing in this Act shall be construed to preempt, modify, or amend any State, county, or local law, ordinance, or regulation applicable to food handling which is designed to protect the public health from individuals who pose a significant risk to the health or safety of others, which cannot be eliminated by reasonable accommodation, pursuant to the list of infectious or communicable diseases and the modes of transmissability published by the Secretary of Health and Human Services.

SEC. 104. ILLEGAL USE OF DRUGS AND ALCOHOL.

(a) Qualified Individual With a Disability.—For purposes of this title, the term "qualified individual with a disability" shall not include any employee or applicant who is currently engaging in the illegal use of drugs, when the covered entity acts on the basis of such use.

(b) Rules of Construction.—Nothing in subsection (a) shall be construed to exclude as a qualified individual with a disability an individual who—

(1) has successfully completed a supervised drug rehabilitation program and is no longer engaging in the illegal use of drugs, or has otherwise been rehabilitated successfully and is no longer engaging in such use;

(2) is participating in a supervised rehabilitation program and is no longer engaging in such use; or

(3) is erroneously regarded as engaging in such use, but is not engaging in such

use; except that it shall not be a violation of this Act for a covered entity to adopt or administer reasonable policies or procedures, including but not limited to drug testing, designed to ensure that an individual described in paragraph (1) or (2) is no longer engaging in the illegal use of drugs.

(c) Authority of Covered Entity.—A covered entity—

(1) may prohibit the illegal use of drugs and the use of alcohol at the workplace by all employees;

(2) may require that employees shall not be under the influence of alcohol or be engaging in the illegal use of drugs at the workplace;

(3) may require that employees behave in conformance with the requirements established under the Drug-Free Workplace Act of 1988 (41 U.S.C. 701 et seq.);

(4) may hold an employee who engages in the illegal use of drugs or who is an alcoholic to the same qualification standards for employment or job performance and behavior that such entity holds other employees, even if any unsatisfactory performance or behavior is related to the drug use or alcoholism of such employee; and

(5) may, with respect to Federal regulations regarding alcohol and the illegal use of drugs, require that—

(A) employees comply with the standards established in such regulations of the Department of Defense, if the employees of the covered entity are employed in an industry subject to such regulations, including complying with regulations (if any) that apply to employment in sensitive positions in such an industry, in the case of employees of the covered entity who are employed in such positions (as defined in the regulations of the Department of Defense);

(B) employees comply with the standards established in such regulations of the Nuclear Regulatory Commission, if the employees of the covered entity are employed in an industry subject to such regulations, including complying with regulations (if any) that apply to employment in sensitive positions in such an industry, in the case of employees of the covered entity who are employed in such positions as defined in the regulations of the Nuclear Regulatory Commission); and

(C) employees comply with the standards established in such regulations of the Department of Transportation, if the employees of the covered entity are employed in a transportation industry subject to such regulations, including complying with such regulations (if any) that apply to employment in sensitive positions in such an industry, in the case of employees of the covered entity who are employed in such positions (as defined in the regulations of the Department of Transportation).

(d) Drug Testing.—

(1) In general.—For purposes of this title, a test to determine the illegal use of drugs shall not be considered a medical examination.

(2) Construction.—Nothing in this title shall be construed to encourage, prohibit,

or authorize the conducting of drug testing for the illegal use of drugs by job applicants or employees or making employment decisions based on such test results.

(e) Transportation Employees.—Nothing in this title shall be construed to encourage, prohibit, restrict, or authorize the otherwise lawful exercise by entities subject to the jurisdiction of the Department of Transportation of authority to—

(1) test employees of such entities in, and applicants for, positions involving safety-sensitive duties for the illegal use of drugs and for on-duty impairment by alcohol; and

(2) remove such persons who test positive for illegal use of drugs and on-duty impairment by alcohol pursuant to paragraph (1) from safety- sensitive duties in implementing subsection (c).

SEC. 105. POSTING NOTICES.

Every employer, employment agency, labor organization, or joint labormanagement committee covered under this title shall post notices in an accessible format to applicants, employees, and members describing the applicable provisions of this Act, in the manner prescribed by section 711 of the Civil Rights Act of 1964 (42 U.S.C. 2000e-10).

SEC. 106. REGULATIONS.

Not later than 1 year after the date of enactment of this Act, the Commission shall issue regulations in an accessible format to carry out this title in accordance with subchapter II of chapter 5 of title 5, United States Code.

SEC. 107. ENFORCEMENT.

(a) Powers, Remedies, and Procedures.—The powers, remedies, and procedures set forth in sections 705, 706, 707, 709, and 710 of the Civil Rights Act of 1964 (42 U.S.C. 2000e-4, 2000e-5, 2000e-6, 2000e-8, and 2000e-9) shall be the powers, remedies, and procedures this title provides to the Commission, to the Attorney General, or to any person alleging discrimination on the basis of disability in violation of any provision of this Act, or regulations promulgated under section 106, concerning employment.

(b) Coordination.—The agencies with enforcement authority for actions which allege employment discrimination under this title and under the Rehabilitation Act of 1973 shall develop procedures to ensure that administrative complaints filed under this title and under the Rehabilitation Act of 1973 are dealt with in a manner that avoids duplication of effort and prevents imposition of inconsistent or conflicting standards for the same requirements under this title and the Rehabilitation Act of 1973. The Commission, the Attorney General, and the Office of Federal Contract Compliance Programs shall establish such coordinating mechanisms (similar to provisions contained in the joint regulations promulgated by the Commission and the Attorney General at part 42 of title 28 and part 1691 of title 29, Code of Federal Regulations, and the Memorandum of Understanding between the Commission and the Office of Federal Contract Compliance Programs dated January 16, 1981 (46 Fed. Reg. 7435, January 23, 1981)) in regulations implementing this title and Rehabilitation Act of 1973 not later than 18 months after the date of enactment of this Act.

SEC. 108. EFFECTIVE DATE.

This title shall become effective 24 months after the date of enactment.

[TITLE II—PUBLIC SERVICES]

[SUBTITLE A—PROHIBITION AGAINST DISCRIMINATION AND OTHER GENERALLY APPLICABLE PROVISIONS]

SEC. 201. DEFINITION.

As used in this title:
  (1) Public entity.—The term "public entity" means—
    (A) any State or local government;
    (B) any department, agency, special purpose district, or other instrumentality of a State or States or local government; and
    (C) the National Railroad Passenger Corporation, and any commuter authority (as defined in section 103(8) of the Rail Passenger Service Act).
  (2) Qualified individual with a disability.—The term "qualified individual with a disability" means an individual with a disability who, with or without reasonable modifications to rules, policies, or practices, the removal of architectural, communication, or transportation barriers, or the provision of auxiliary aids and services, meets the essential eligibility requirements for the receipt of services or the participation in programs or activities provided by a public entity.

SEC. 202. DISCRIMINATION.

Subject to the provisions of this title, no qualified individual with a disability shall, by reason of such disability, be excluded from participation in or be denied the benefits of the services, programs, or activities of a public entity, or be subjected to discrimination by any such entity.

[PART I—PUBLIC TRANSPORTATION OTHER THAN BY AIRCRAFT OR CERTAIN RAIL OPERATIONS]

SEC. 203. ENFORCEMENT.

The remedies, procedures, and rights set forth in section 505 of the Rehabilitation Act of 1973 (29 U.S.C. 794a) shall be the remedies, procedures, and rights this title provides to any person alleging discrimination on the basis of disability in violation of section 202.

SEC. 204. REGULATIONS.

(a) In General.—Not later than 1 year after the date of enactment of this Act, the Attorney General shall promulgate regulations in an accessible format that implement this subtitle. Such regulations shall not include any matter within the scope of the authority of the Secretary of Transportation under section 223, 229, or 244.

(b) Relationship to Other Regulations.—Except for "program accessibility, existing facilities", and "communications", regulations under subsection (a) shall be consistent with this Act and with the coordination regulations under part 41 of title 28, Code of Federal Regulations (as promulgated by the Department of Health, Education, and Welfare on January 13, 1978), applicable to recipients of Federal financial assistance under section 504 of the Rehabilitation Act of 1973 (29 U.S.C. 794). With respect to "program accessibility, existing facilities", and "communications", such regulations shall be consistent with regulations and analysis as in part 39 of title 28 of the Code of Federal Regulations, applicable to federally conducted activities under such section 504.

(c) Standards.—Regulations under subsection (a) shall include standards applicable to facilities and vehicles covered by this subtitle, other than facilities, stations, rail passenger cars, and vehicles covered by subtitle B. Such standards shall be consistent with the minimum guidelines and requirements issued by the Architectural and Transportation Barriers Compliance Board in accordance with section 504(a) of this Act.

SEC. 205. EFFECTIVE DATE.

(a) General Rule.—Except as provided in subsection (b), this subtitle shall become effective 18 months after the date of enactment of this Act.

(b) Exception.—Section 204 shall become effective on the date of enactment of this Act.

[SUBTITLE B—ACTIONS APPLICABLE TO PUBLIC TRANSPORTATION PROVIDED BY PUBLIC ENTITIES CONSIDERED DISCRIMINATORY]

[PART I—PUBLIC TRANSPORTATION OTHER THAN BY AIRCRAFT OR CERTAIN RAIL OPERATIONS]

SEC. 221. DEFINITIONS.

As used in this part:
(1) Demand responsive system.—The term "demand responsive system" means any system of providing designated public transportation which is not a fixed route system.

(2) Designated public transportation.—The term "designated public transportation" means transportation (other than public school transportation) by bus, rail, or any other conveyance (other than transportation by aircraft or intercity or commuter rail transportation (as defined in section 241)) that provides the general public with general or special service (including charter service) on a regular and continuing basis.

(3) Fixed route system.—The term "fixed route system" means a system of providing designated public transportation on which a vehicle is operated along a prescribed route according to a fixed schedule.

(4) Operates.—The term "operates", as used with respect to a fixed route system or demand responsive system, includes operation of such system by a person under a contractual or other arrangement or relationship with a public entity.

(5) Public school transportation.—The term "public school transportation" means transportation by schoolbus vehicles of schoolchildren, personnel, and equipment to and from a public elementary or secondary school and school-related activities.

(6) Secretary.—The term "Secretary" means the Secretary of Transportation.

SEC. 222. PUBLIC ENTITIES OPERATING FIXED ROUTE SYSTEMS.

(a) Purchase and Lease of New Vehicles.—It shall be considered discrimination for purposes of section 202 of this Act and section 504 of the Rehabilitation Act of 1973 (29 U.S.C. 794) for a public entity which operates a fixed route system to purchase or lease a new bus, a new rapid rail vehicle, a new light rail vehicle, or any other new vehicle to be used on such system, if the solicitation for such purchase or lease is made after the 30th day following the effective date of this subsection and if such bus, rail vehicle, or other vehicle is not readily accessible to and usable by individuals with disabilities, including individuals who use wheelchairs.

(b) Purchase and Lease of Used Vehicles.—Subject to subsection (c)(1), it shall be considered discrimination for purposes of section 202 of this Act and section 504 of the Rehabilitation Act of 1973 (29 U.S.C. 794) for a public entity which operates a fixed route system to purchase or lease, after the 30th day following the effective date of this subsection, a used vehicle for use on such system unless such entity makes demonstrated good faith efforts to purchase or lease a used vehicle for use on such system that is readily accessible to and usable by individuals with disabilities, including individuals who use wheelchairs.

(c) Remanufactured Vehicles.—

(1) General rule.—Except as provided in paragraph (2), it shall be considered discrimination for purposes of section 202 of this Act and section 504 of the Rehabilitation Act of 1973 (29 U.S.C. 794) for a public entity which operates a fixed route system—

(A) to remanufacture a vehicle for use on such system so as to extend its usable life for 5 years or more, which remanufacture begins (or for which the solicitation is made) after the 30th day following the effective date of this subsection; or

(B) to purchase or lease for use on such system a remanufactured vehicle which has been remanufactured so as to extend its usable life for 5 years or more, which purchase or lease occurs after such 30th day and during the period in which the usable life is extended; unless, after remanufacture, the vehicle is, to the maximum extent feasible, readily accessible to and usable by individuals with disabilities, including individuals who use wheelchairs.

(2) Exception for historic vehicles.—

(A) General rule.—If a public entity operates a fixed route system any segment of which is included on the National Register of Historic Places and if making a vehicle of historic character to be used solely on such segment readily accessible to and usable by individuals with disabilities would significantly alter the historic character of such vehicle, the public entity only has to make (or to purchase or lease a remanufactured vehicle with) those modifications which are necessary to meet the requirements of paragraph (1) and which do not significantly alter the historic character of such vehicle.

(B) Vehicles of historic character defined by regulations.—For purposes of this paragraph and section 228(b), a vehicle of historic character shall be defined by the regulations issued by the Secretary to carry out this subsection.

SEC. 223. PARATRANSIT AS A COMPLEMENT TO FIXED ROUTE SERVICE.

(a) General Rule.—It shall be considered discrimination for purposes of section 202 of this Act and section 504 of the Rehabilitation Act of 1973 (29 U.S.C. 794) for a public entity which operates a fixed route system (other than a system which provides solely commuter bus service) to fail to provide with respect to the operations of its fixed route system, in accordance with this section, paratransit and other special transportation services to individuals with disabilities, including individuals who use wheelchairs, that are sufficient to provide to such individuals a level of service (1) which is comparable to the level of designated public transportation services provided to individuals without disabilities using such system; or (2) in the case of response time, which is comparable, to the extent practicable, to the level of designated public transportation services provided to individuals without disabilities using such system.

(b) Issuance of Regulations.—Not later than 1 year after the effective date of this subsection, the Secretary shall issue final regulations to carry out this section.

(c) Required Contents of Regulations.—

(1) Eligible recipients of service.—The regulations issued under this section shall require each public entity which operates a fixed route system to provide the paratransit and other special transportation services required under this section—

(A)

(i) to any individual with a disability who is unable, as a result of a physical or mental impairment (including a vision impairment) and without the assistance of another individual (except an operator of a wheelchair lift or other boarding assistance device), to board, ride, or disembark from any vehicle on the system which is readily accessible to and usable by individuals with disabilities;

(ii) to any individual with a disability who needs the assistance of a wheelchair lift or other boarding assistance device (and is able with such assistance) to board, ride, and disembark from any vehicle which is readily accessible to and usable by individuals with disabilities if the individual wants to travel on a route on the system during the hours of operation of the system at a time (or within a reasonable period of such time) when such a vehicle is not being used to provide designated public transportation on the route; and

(iii) to any individual with a disability who has a specific impairment-related condition which prevents such individual from traveling to a boarding location or from a disembarking location on such system;

(B) to one other individual accompanying the individual with the disability; and

(C) to other individuals, in addition to the one individual described in subparagraph (B), accompanying the individual with a disability provided that space for these additional individuals is available on the paratransit vehicle carrying the individual with a disability and that the transportation of such additional individuals will not result in a denial of service to individuals with disabilities. For purposes of clauses (i) and (ii) of subparagraph (A), boarding or disembarking from a vehicle does not include travel to the boarding location or from the disembarking location.

(2) Service area.—The regulations issued under this section shall require the provision of paratransit and special transportation services required under this section in the service area of each public entity which operates a fixed route system, other than any portion of the service area in which the public entity solely provides commuter bus service.

(3) Service criteria.—Subject to paragraphs (1) and (2), the regulations issued under this section shall establish minimum service criteria for determining the level of services to be required under this section.

(4) Undue financial burden limitation.—The regulations issued under this section shall provide that, if the public entity is able to demonstrate to the satisfaction of the Secretary that the provision of paratransit and other special transportation services otherwise required under this section would impose an undue financial burden on the public entity, the public entity, notwithstanding any other provision of this section (other than paragraph (5)), shall only be required to provide such services to the extent that providing such services would not impose such a burden.

(5) Additional services.—The regulations issued under this section shall establish circumstances under which the Secretary may require a public entity to provide, notwithstanding paragraph (4), paratransit and other special transportation services under this section beyond the level of paratransit and other special transportation services which would otherwise be required under paragraph (4).

(6) Public participation.—The regulations issued under this section shall require that each public entity which operates a fixed route system hold a public hearing, provide an opportunity for public comment, and consult with individuals with disabilities in preparing its plan under paragraph (7).

(7) Plans.—The regulations issued under this section shall require that each public entity which operates a fixed route system—

(A) within 18 months after the effective date of this subsection, submit to the Secretary, and commence implementation of, a plan for providing paratransit and other special transportation services which meets the requirements of this section; and

(B) on an annual basis thereafter, submit to the Secretary, and commence implementation of, a plan for providing such services.

(8) Provision of services by others.—The regulations issued under this section shall—

(A) require that a public entity submitting a plan to the Secretary under this section identify in the plan any person or other public entity which is providing a paratransit or other special transportation service for individuals with disabilities in the service area to which the plan applies; and

(B) provide that the public entity submitting the plan does not have to provide under the plan such service for individuals with disabilities.

(9) Other provisions.—The regulations issued under this section shall include such other provisions and requirements as the Secretary determines are necessary to carry out the objectives of this section.

(d) Review of Plan.—

(1) General rule.—The Secretary shall review a plan submitted under this section for the purpose of determining whether or not such plan meets the requirements of this section, including the regulations issued under this section.

(2) Disapproval.—If the Secretary determines that a plan reviewed under this subsection fails to meet the requirements of this section, the Secretary shall disapprove the plan and notify the public entity which submitted the plan of such disapproval and the reasons therefor.

(3) Modification of disapproved plan.—Not later than 90 days after the date of disapproval of a plan under this subsection, the public entity which submitted the plan shall modify the plan to meet the requirements of this section and shall submit to the Secretary, and commence implementation of, such modified plan.

(e) Discrimination Defined.—As used in subsection (a), the term "discrimination" includes—

(1) a failure of a public entity to which the regulations issued under this section apply to submit, or commence implementation of, a plan in accordance with subsections (c)(6) and (c)(7);

(2) a failure of such entity to submit, or commence implementation of, a modified plan in accordance with subsection (d)(3);

(3) submission to the Secretary of a modified plan under subsection (d)(3) which does not meet the requirements of this section; or

(4) a failure of such entity to provide paratransit or other special transportation services in accordance with the plan or modified plan the public entity submitted to the Secretary under this section.

(f) Statutory Construction.—Nothing in this section shall be construed as preventing a public entity—

(1) from providing paratransit or other special transportation services at a level which is greater than the level of such services which are required by this section,

(2) from providing paratransit or other special transportation services in addition to those paratransit and special transportation services required by this section, or

(3) from providing such services to individuals in addition to those individuals to whom such services are required to be provided by this section.

SEC. 224. PUBLIC ENTITY OPERATING A DEMAND RESPONSIVE SYSTEM.

If a public entity operates a demand responsive system, it shall be considered discrimination, for purposes of section 202 of this Act and section 504 of the Rehabilitation Act of 1973 (29 U.S.C. 794), for such entity to purchase or lease a new vehicle for use on such system, for which a solicitation is made after the 30th day following the effective date of this section, that is not readily accessible to and usable by individuals with disabilities, including individuals who use wheelchairs, unless such system, when viewed in its entirety, provides a level of service to such individuals equivalent to the level of service such system provides to individuals without disabilities.

SEC. 225. TEMPORARY RELIEF WHERE LIFTS ARE UNAVAILABLE.

(a) Granting.—With respect to the purchase of new buses, a public entity may apply for, and the Secretary may temporarily relieve such public entity from the obligation under section 222(a) or 224 to purchase new buses that are readily accessible to and usable by individuals with disabilities if such public entity demonstrates to the satisfaction of the Secretary—

(1) that the initial solicitation for new buses made by the public entity specified that all new buses were to be lift-equipped and were to be otherwise accessible to and usable by individuals with disabilities;

(2) the unavailability from any qualified manufacturer of hydraulic, electro-mechanical, or other lifts for such new buses;

(3) that the public entity seeking temporary relief has made good faith efforts to locate a qualified manufacturer to supply the lifts to the manufacturer of such buses in sufficient time to comply with such solicitation; and

(4) that any further delay in purchasing new buses necessary to obtain such lifts would significantly impair transportation services in the community served by the public entity.

(b) Duration and Notice to Congress.—Any relief granted under subsection (a) shall be limited in duration by a specified date, and the appropriate committees of Congress shall be notified of any such relief granted.

(c) Fraudulent Application.—If, at any time, the Secretary has reasonable cause to believe that any relief granted under subsection (a) was fraudulently applied for, the Secretary shall—

(1) cancel such relief if such relief is still in effect; and

(2) take such other action as the Secretary considers appropriate.

SEC. 226. NEW FACILITIES.

For purposes of section 202 of this Act and section 504 of the Rehabilitation Act of 1973 (29 U.S.C. 794), it shall be considered discrimination for a public entity to construct a new facility to be used in the provision of designated public transportation services unless such facility is readily accessible to and usable by individuals with disabilities, including individuals who use wheelchairs.

SEC. 227. ALTERATIONS OF EXISTING FACILITIES.

(a) General Rule.—With respect to alterations of an existing facility or part thereof used in the provision of designated public transportation services that affect or could affect the usability of the facility or part thereof, it shall be considered discrimination, for purposes of section 202 of this Act and section 504 of the Rehabilitation Act of 1973 (29 U.S.C. 794), for a public entity to fail to make such alterations (or to ensure that the alterations are made) in such a manner that, to the maximum extent feasible, the altered portions of the facility are readily accessible to and usable by individuals with disabilities, including individuals who use wheelchairs, upon the completion of such alterations. Where the public entity is undertaking an alteration that affects or could affect usability of or access to an area of the facility containing a primary function, the entity shall also make the alterations in such a manner that, to the maximum extent feasible, the path of travel to the altered area and the bathrooms, telephones, and drinking fountains serving the altered area, are readily accessible to and usable by individuals with disabilities, including individuals who use wheelchairs, upon completion of such alterations, where such alterations to the path of travel or the bathrooms, telephones, and drinking fountains serving the altered area are not disproportionate to the overall alterations in terms of cost and scope (as determined under criteria established by the Attorney General).

(b) Special Rule for Stations.—

(1) General rule.—For purposes of section 202 of this Act and section 504 of the Rehabilitation Act of 1973 (29 U.S.C. 794), it shall be considered discrimination for a public entity that provides designated public transportation to fail, in accordance with the provisions of this subsection, to make key stations (as determined under criteria established by the Secretary by regulation) in rapid rail and light rail systems readily accessible to and usable by individuals with disabilities, including individuals who use wheelchairs.

(2) Rapid rail and light rail key stations.—

(A) Accessibility.—Except as otherwise provided in this paragraph, all key stations (as determined under criteria established by the Secretary by regulation) in rapid rail and light rail systems shall be made readily accessible to and usable by individuals with disabilities, including individuals who use wheelchairs, as soon as practicable but in no event later than the last day of the 3-year period beginning on the effective date of this paragraph.

(B) Extension for extraordinarily expensive structural changes.—The Secretary may extend the 3-year period under subparagraph (A) up to a 30-year period for key stations in a rapid rail or light rail system which stations need extraordinarily expensive structural changes to, or replacement of, existing facilities; except that by the last day of the 20th year following the date of the enactment of this Act at least 2/3 of such key stations must be readily accessible to and usable by individuals with disabilities.

(3) Plans and milestones.—The Secretary shall require the appropriate public entity to develop and submit to the Secretary a plan for compliance with this subsection—

(A) that reflects consultation with individuals with disabilities affected by such plan and the results of a public hearing and public comments on such plan, and

(B) that establishes milestones for achievement of the requirements of this subsection.

SEC. 228. PUBLIC TRANSPORTATION PROGRAMS AND ACTIVITIES IN EXISTING FACILITIES AND ONE CAR PER TRAIN RULE.

(a) Public Transportation Programs and Activities in Existing Facilities.—

(1) In general.—With respect to existing facilities used in the provision of designated public transportation services, it shall be considered discrimination, for purposes of section 202 of this Act and section 504 of the Rehabilitation Act of 1973 (29 U.S.C. 794), for a public entity to fail to operate a designated public transportation program or activity conducted in such facilities so that, when

viewed in the entirety, the program or activity is readily accessible to and usable by individuals with disabilities.

(2) Exception.—Paragraph (1) shall not require a public entity to make structural changes to existing facilities in order to make such facilities accessible to individuals who use wheelchairs, unless and to the extent required by section 227(a) (relating to alterations) or section 227(b) (relating to key stations).

(3) Utilization.—Paragraph (1) shall not require a public entity to which paragraph (2) applies, to provide to individuals who use wheelchairs services made available to the general public at such facilities when such individuals could not utilize or benefit from such services provided at such facilities.

(b) One Car Per Train Rule.—

(1) General rule.—Subject to paragraph (2), with respect to 2 or more vehicles operated as a train by a light or rapid rail system, for purposes of section 202 of this Act and section 504 of the Rehabilitation Act of 1973 (29 U.S.C. 794), it shall be considered discrimination for a public entity to fail to have at least 1 vehicle per train that is accessible to individuals with disabilities, including individuals who use wheelchairs, as soon as practicable but in no event later than the last day of the 5-year period beginning on the effective date of this section.

(2) Historic trains.—In order to comply with paragraph (1) with respect to the remanufacture of a vehicle of historic character which is to be used on a segment of a light or rapid rail system which is included on the National Register of Historic Places, if making such vehicle readily accessible to and usable by individuals with disabilities would significantly alter the historic character of such vehicle, the public entity which operates such system only has to make (or to purchase or lease a remanufactured vehicle with) those modifications which are necessary to meet the requirements of section 222(c)(1) and which do not significantly alter the historic character of such vehicle.

SEC. 229. REGULATIONS.

(a) In General.—Not later than 1 year after the date of enactment of this Act, the Secretary of Transportation shall issue regulations, in an accessible format, necessary for carrying out this part (other than section 223).

(b) Standards.—The regulations issued under this section and section 223 shall include standards applicable to facilities and vehicles covered by this subtitle. The standards shall be consistent with the minimum guidelines and requirements issued by the Architectural and Transportation Barriers Compliance Board in accordance with section 504 of this Act.

SEC. 230. INTERIM ACCESSIBILITY REQUIREMENTS.

If final regulations have not been issued pursuant to section 229, for new construction or alterations for which a valid and appropriate State or local building permit is obtained prior to the issuance of final regulations under such section, and for which the construction or alteration authorized by such permit begins within one year of the receipt of such permit and is completed under the terms of such permit, compliance with the Uniform Federal Accessibility Standards in effect at the time the building permit is issued shall suffice to satisfy the requirement that facilities be readily accessible to and usable by persons with disabilities as required under sections 226 and 227, except that, if such final regulations have not been issued one year after the Architectural and Transportation Barriers Compliance Board has issued the supplemental minimum guidelines required under section 504(a) of this Act, compliance with such supplemental minimum guidelines shall be necessary to satisfy the requirement that facilities be readily accessible to and usable by persons with disabilities prior to issuance of the final regulations.

[PART II—PUBLIC TRANSPORTATION BY INTERCITY AND COMMUTER RAIL]

SEC. 231. EFFECTIVE DATE.

(a) General Rule.—Except as provided in subsection (b), this part shall become effective 18 months after the date of enactment of this Act.

(b) Exception.—Sections 222, 223 (other than subsection (a)), 224, 225, 227(b), 228(b), and 229 shall become effective on the date of enactment of this Act.

SEC. 241. DEFINITIONS.

As used in this part:
(1) Commuter authority.—The term "commuter authority" has the meaning given such term in section 103(8) of the Rail Passenger Service Act (45 U.S.C. 502(8)).
(2) Commuter rail transportation.—The term "commuter rail transportation" has the meaning given the term "commuter service" in section 103(9) of the Rail Passenger Service Act (45 U.S.C. 502(9)).
(3) Intercity rail transportation.—The term "intercity rail transportation" means transportation provided by the National Railroad Passenger Corporation.
(4) Rail passenger car.—The term "rail passenger car" means, with respect to intercity rail transportation, single-level and bi-level coach cars, single-level and bi-level dining cars, single-level and bi-level sleeping cars, single-level and bi-level lounge cars, and food service cars.
(5) Responsible person.—The term "responsible person" means—
(A) in the case of a station more than 50 percent of which is owned by a public entity, such public entity;
(B) in the case of a station more than 50 percent of which is owned by a private party, the persons providing intercity or commuter rail transportation to

such station, as allocated on an equitable basis by regulation by the Secretary of Transportation; and

(C) in a case where no party owns more than 50 percent of a station, the persons providing intercity or commuter rail transportation to such station and the owners of the station, other than private party owners, as allocated on an equitable basis by regulation by the Secretary of Transportation.

(6) Station.—The term "station" means the portion of a property located appurtenant to a right-of-way on which intercity or commuter rail transportation is operated, where such portion is used by the general public and is related to the provision of such transportation, including passenger platforms, designated waiting areas, ticketing areas, restrooms, and, where a public entity providing rail transportation owns the property, concession areas, to the extent that such public entity exercises control over the selection, design, construction, or alteration of the property, but such term does not include flag stops.

SEC. 242. INTERCITY AND COMMUTER RAIL ACTIONS CONSIDERED DISCRIMINATORY.

(a) Intercity Rail Transportation.—

(1) One car per train rule.—It shall be considered discrimination for purposes of section 202 of this Act and section 504 of the Rehabilitation Act of 1973 (29 U.S.C. 794) for a person who provides intercity rail transportation to fail to have at least one passenger car per train that is readily accessible to and usable by individuals with disabilities, including individuals who use wheelchairs, in accordance with regulations issued under section 244, as soon as practicable, but in no event later than 5 years after the date of enactment of this Act.

(2) New intercity cars.—

(A) General rule.—Except as otherwise provided in this subsection with respect to individuals who use wheelchairs, it shall be considered discrimination for purposes of section 202 of this Act and section 504 of the Rehabilitation Act of 1973 (29 U.S.C. 794) for a person to purchase or lease any new rail passenger cars for use in intercity rail transportation, and for which a solicitation is made later than 30 days after the effective date of this section, unless all such rail cars are readily accessible to and usable by individuals with disabilities, including individuals who use wheelchairs, as prescribed by the Secretary of Transportation in regulations issued under section 244.

(B) Special rule for single-level passenger coaches for individuals who use wheelchairs.—Single-level passenger coaches shall be required to—

(i) be able to be entered by an individual who uses a wheelchair;

(ii) have space to park and secure a wheelchair;

(iii) have a seat to which a passenger in a wheelchair can transfer, and a space to fold and store such passenger's wheelchair; and

(iv) have a restroom usable by an individual who uses a wheelchair, only to the extent provided in paragraph (3).

(C) Special rule for single-level dining cars for individuals who use wheelchairs.—Single-level dining cars shall not be required to—

(i) be able to be entered from the station platform by an individual who uses a wheelchair; or

(ii) have a restroom usable by an individual who uses a wheelchair if no restroom is provided in such car for any passenger.

(D) Special rule for bi-level dining cars for individuals who use wheelchairs.—Bi-level dining cars shall not be required to—

(i) be able to be entered by an individual who uses a wheelchair;

(ii) have space to park and secure a wheelchair;

(iii) have a seat to which a passenger in a wheelchair can transfer, or a space to fold and store such passenger's wheelchair; or

(iv) have a restroom usable by an individual who uses a wheelchair.

(3) Accessibility of single-level coaches.—

(A) General rule.—It shall be considered discrimination for purposes of section 202 of this Act and section 504 of the Rehabilitation Act of 1973 (29 U.S.C. 794) for a person who provides intercity rail transportation to fail to have on each train which includes one or more single-level rail passenger coaches—

(i) a number of spaces—

(I) to park and secure wheelchairs (to accommodate individuals who wish to remain in their wheelchairs) equal to not less than one-half of the number of single-level rail passenger coaches in such train; and

(II) to fold and store wheelchairs (to accommodate individuals who wish to transfer to coach seats) equal to not less than one-half of the number of single-level rail passenger coaches in such train, as soon as practicable, but in no event later than 5 years after the date of enactment of this Act; and

(ii) a number of spaces—

(I) to park and secure wheelchairs (to accommodate individuals who wish to remain in their wheelchairs) equal to not less than the total number of single-level rail passenger coaches in such train; and

(II) to fold and store wheelchairs (to accommodate individuals who wish to transfer to coach seats) equal to not less than the total number of single-level rail passenger coaches in such train, as soon as practicable, but in no event later than 10 years after the date of enactment of this Act.

(B) Location.—Spaces required by subparagraph (A) shall be located in single-level rail passenger coaches or food service cars.

(C) Limitation.—Of the number of spaces required on a train by subparagraph (A), not more than two spaces to park and secure wheelchairs nor more than two spaces to fold and store wheelchairs shall be located in any one coach or food service car.

(D) Other accessibility features.—Single-level rail passenger coaches and food service cars on which the spaces required by subparagraph (A) are located shall have a restroom usable by an individual who uses a wheelchair and shall be able to be entered from the station platform by an individual who uses a wheelchair.

(4) Food service.—

(A) Single-level dining cars.—On any train in which a single-level dining car is used to provide food service—

(i) if such single-level dining car was purchased after the date of enactment of this Act, table service in such car shall be provided to a passenger who uses a wheelchair if—

(I) the car adjacent to the end of the dining car through which a wheelchair may enter is itself accessible to a wheelchair;

(II) such passenger can exit to the platform from the car such passenger occupies, move down the platform, and enter the adjacent accessible car described in subclause (I) without the necessity of the train being moved within the station; and

(III) space to park and secure a wheelchair is available in the dining car at the time such passenger wishes to eat (if such passenger wishes to remain in a wheelchair), or space to store and fold a wheelchair is available in the dining car at the time such passenger wishes to eat (if such passenger wishes to transfer to a dining car seat); and

(ii) appropriate auxiliary aids and services, including a hard surface on which to eat, shall be provided to ensure that other equivalent food service is available to individuals with disabilities, including individuals who use wheelchairs, and to passengers traveling with such individuals. Unless not practicable, a person providing intercity rail transportation shall place an accessible car adjacent to the end of dining car described in clause (i) through which an individual who uses a wheelchair may enter.

(B) Bi-level dining cars.—On any train in which a bi-level dining car is used to provide food service—

(i) if such train includes a bi-level lounge car purchased after the date of enactment of this Act, table service in such lounge car shall be provided to individuals who use wheelchairs and to other passengers; and

(ii) appropriate auxiliary aids and services, including a hard surface on which to eat, shall be provided to ensure that other equivalent food service is available to individuals with disabilities, including individuals who use wheelchairs, and to passengers traveling with such individuals.

(b) Commuter Rail Transportation.—

(1) One car per train rule.—It shall be considered discrimination for purposes of

section 202 of this Act and section 504 of the Rehabilitation Act of 1973 (29 U.S.C. 794) for a person who provides commuter rail transportation to fail to have at least one passenger car per train that is readily accessible to and usable by individuals with disabilities, including individuals who use wheelchairs, in accordance with regulations issued under section 244, as soon as practicable, but in no event later than 5 years after the date of enactment of this Act.

(2) New commuter rail cars.—

(A) General rule.—It shall be considered discrimination for purposes of section 202 of this Act and section 504 of the Rehabilitation Act of 1973 (29 U.S.C. 794) for a person to purchase or lease any new rail passenger cars for use in commuter rail transportation, and for which a solicitation is made later than 30 days after the effective date of this section, unless all such rail cars are readily accessible to and usable by individuals with disabilities, including individuals who use wheelchairs, as prescribed by the Secretary of Transportation in regulations issued under section 244.

(B) Accessibility.—For purposes of section 202 of this Act and section 504 of the Rehabilitation Act of 1973 (29 U.S.C. 794), a requirement that a rail passenger car used in commuter rail transportation be accessible to or readily accessible to and usable by individuals with disabilities, including individuals who use wheelchairs, shall not be construed to require—

(i) a restroom usable by an individual who uses a wheelchair if no restroom is provided in such car for any passenger;

(ii) space to fold and store a wheelchair; or

(iii) a seat to which a passenger who uses a wheelchair can transfer.

(c) Used Rail Cars.—It shall be considered discrimination for purposes of section 202 of this Act and section 504 of the Rehabilitation Act of 1973 (29 U.S.C. 794) for a person to purchase or lease a used rail passenger car for use in intercity or commuter rail transportation, unless such person makes demonstrated good faith efforts to purchase or lease a used rail car that is readily accessible to and usable by individuals with disabilities, including individuals who use wheelchairs, as prescribed by the Secretary of Transportation in regulations issued under section 244.

(d) Remanufactured Rail Cars.—

(1) Remanufacturing.—It shall be considered discrimination for purposes of section 202 of this Act and section 504 of the Rehabilitation Act of 1973 (29 U.S.C. 794) for a person to remanufacture a rail passenger car for use in intercity or commuter rail transportation so as to extend its usable life for 10 years or more, unless the rail car, to the maximum extent feasible, is made readily accessible to and usable by individuals with disabilities, including individuals who use wheelchairs, as prescribed by the Secretary of Transportation in regulations issued under section 244.

(2) Purchase or lease.—It shall be considered discrimination for purposes of sec-

tion 202 of this Act and section 504 of the Rehabilitation Act of 1973 (29 U.S.C. 794) for a person to purchase or lease a remanufactured rail passenger car for use in intercity or commuter rail transportation unless such car was remanufactured in accordance with paragraph (1).

(e) Stations.—

(1) New stations.—It shall be considered discrimination for purposes of section 202 of this Act and section 504 of the Rehabilitation Act of 1973 (29 U.S.C. 794) for a person to build a new station for use in intercity or commuter rail transportation that is not readily accessible to and usable by individuals with disabilities, including individuals who use wheelchairs, as prescribed by the Secretary of Transportation in regulations issued under section 244.

(2) Existing stations.—

(A) Failure to make readily accessible.—

(i) General rule.—It shall be considered discrimination for purposes of section 202 of this Act and section 504 of the Rehabilitation Act of 1973 (29 U.S.C. 794) for a responsible person to fail to make existing stations in the intercity rail transportation system, and existing key stations in commuter rail transportation systems, readily accessible to and usable by individuals with disabilities, including individuals who use wheelchairs, as prescribed by the Secretary of Transportation in regulations issued under section 244.

(ii) Period for compliance.—

(I) Intercity rail.—All stations in the intercity rail transportation system shall be made readily accessible to and usable by individuals with disabilities, including individuals who use wheelchairs, as soon as practicable, but in no event later than 20 years after the date of enactment of this Act.

(II) Commuter rail.—Key stations in commuter rail transportation systems shall be made readily accessible to and usable by individuals with disabilities, including individuals who use wheelchairs, as soon as practicable but in no event later than 3 years after the date of enactment of this Act, except that the time limit may be extended by the Secretary of Transportation up to 20 years after the date of enactment of this Act in a case where the raising of the entire passenger platform is the only means available of attaining accessibility or where other extraordinarily expensive structural changes are necessary to attain accessibility.

(iii) Designation of key stations.—Each commuter authority shall designate the key stations in its commuter rail transportation system, in consultation with individuals with disabilities and organizations representing such individuals, taking into consideration such factors as high ridership and whether such station serves as a transfer or feeder station. Before the final designation of key stations under this clause, a commuter authority shall hold a public hearing.

(iv) Plans and milestones.—The Secretary of Transportation shall require the appropriate person to develop a plan for carrying out this subparagraph that reflects consultation with individuals with disabilities affected by such plan and that establishes milestones for achievement of the requirements of this subparagraph.

(B) Requirement when making alterations.—

(i) General rule.—It shall be considered discrimination, for purposes of, section 202 of this Act and section 504 of the Rehabilitation Act of 1973 (29 U.S.C. 794), with respect to alterations of an existing station or part thereof in the intercity or commuter rail transportation systems that affect or could affect the usability of the station or part thereof, for the responsible person, owner, or person in control of the station to fail to make the alterations in such a manner that, to the maximum extent feasible, the altered portions of the station are readily accessible to and usable by individuals with disabilities, including individuals who use wheelchairs, upon completion of such alterations.

(ii) Alterations to a primary function area.—It shall be considered discrimination, for purposes of section 202 of this Act and section 504 of the Rehabilitation Act of 1973 (29 U.S.C. 794), with respect to alterations that affect or could affect the usability of or access to an area of the station containing a primary function, for the responsible person, owner, or person in control of the station to fail to make the alterations in such a manner that, to the maximum extent feasible, the path of travel to the altered area, and the bathrooms, telephones, and drinking fountains serving the altered area, are readily accessible to and usable by individuals with disabilities, including individuals who use wheelchairs, upon completion of such alterations, where such alterations to the path of travel or the bathrooms, telephones, and drinking fountains serving the altered area are not disproportionate to the overall alterations in terms of cost and scope (as determined under criteria established by the Attorney General).

(C) Required cooperation.—It shall be considered discrimination for purposes of section 202 of this Act and section 504 of the Rehabilitation Act of 1973 (29 U.S.C. 794) for an owner, or person in control, of a station governed by subparagraph (A) or (B) to fail to provide reasonable cooperation to a responsible person with respect to such station in that responsible person's efforts to comply with such subparagraph. An owner, or person in control, of a station shall be liable to a responsible person for any failure to provide reasonable cooperation as required by this subparagraph. Failure to receive reasonable cooperation required by this subparagraph shall not be a defense to a claim of discrimination under this Act.

SEC. 243. CONFORMANCE OF ACCESSIBILITY STANDARDS.

Accessibility standards included in regulations issued under this part shall be consistent with the minimum guidelines issued by the Architectural and Transportation Barriers Compliance Board under section 504(a) of this Act.

SEC. 244. REGULATIONS.

Not later than 1 year after the date of enactment of this Act, the Secretary of Transportation shall issue regulations, in an accessible format, necessary for carrying out this part.

SEC. 245. INTERIM ACCESSIBILITY REQUIREMENTS.

(a) Stations.—If final regulations have not been issued pursuant to section 244, for new construction or alterations for which a valid and appropriate State or local building permit is obtained prior to the issuance of final regulations under such section, and for which the construction or alteration authorized by such permit begins within one year of the receipt of such permit and is completed under the terms of such permit, compliance with the Uniform Federal Accessibility Standards in effect at the time the building permit is issued shall suffice to satisfy the requirement that stations be readily accessible to and usable by persons with disabilities as required under section 242(e), except that, if such final regulations have not been issued one year after the Architectural and Transportation Barriers Compliance Board has issued the supplemental minimum guidelines required under section 504(a) of this Act, compliance with such supplemental minimum guidelines shall be necessary to satisfy the requirement that stations be readily accessible to and usable by persons with disabilities prior to issuance of the final regulations.

(b) Rail Passenger Cars.—If final regulations have not been issued pursuant to section 244, a person shall be considered to have complied with the requirements of section 242 (a) through (d) that a rail passenger car be readily accessible to and usable by individuals with disabilities, if the design for such car complies with the laws and regulations (including the Minimum Guidelines and Requirements for Accessible Design and such supplemental minimum guidelines as are issued under section 504(a) of this Act) governing accessibility of such cars, to the extent that such laws and regulations are not inconsistent with this part and are in effect at the time such design is substantially completed.

SEC. 246. EFFECTIVE DATE.

(a) General Rule.—Except as provided in subsection (b), this part shall become effective 18 months after the date of enactment of this Act.

(b) Exception.—Sections 242 and 244 shall become effective on the date of enactment of this Act.

[TITLE III—PUBLIC ACCOMODATIONS AND SERVICES OPERATED BY PRIVATE ENTITIES]

SEC. 301. DEFINITIONS.

As used in this title:

(1) Commerce.—The term "commerce" means travel, trade, traffic, commerce, transportation, or communication—

(A) among the several States;

(B) between any foreign country or any territory or possession and any State; or

(C) between points in the same State but through another State or foreign country.

(2) Commercial facilities.—The term "commercial facilities" means facilities—

(A) that are intended for nonresidential use; and

(B) whose operations will affect commerce. Such term shall not include railroad locomotives, railroad freight cars, railroad cabooses, railroad cars described in section 242 or covered under this title, railroad rights-of-way, or facilities that are covered or expressly exempted from coverage under the Fair Housing Act of 1968 (42 U.S.C. 3601 et seq.).

(3) Demand responsive system.—The term "demand responsive system" means any system of providing transportation of individuals by a vehicle, other than a system which is a fixed route system.

(4) Fixed route system.—The term "fixed route system" means a system of providing transportation of individuals (other than by aircraft) on which a vehicle is operated along a prescribed route according to a fixed schedule.

(5) Over-the-road bus.—The term "over-the-road bus" means a bus characterized by an elevated passenger deck located over a baggage compartment.

(6) Private entity.—The term "private entity" means any entity other than a public entity (as defined in section 201(1)).

(7) Public accommodation.—The following private entities are considered public accommodations for purposes of this title, if the operations of such entities affect commerce—

(A) an inn, hotel, motel, or other place of lodging, except for an establishment located within a building that contains not more than five rooms for rent or hire and that is actually occupied by the proprietor of such establishment as the residence of such proprietor;

(B) a restaurant, bar, or other establishment serving food or drink;

(C) a motion picture house, theater, concert hall, stadium, or other place of exhibition or entertainment;

(D) an auditorium, convention center, lecture hall, or other place of public gathering;

(E) a bakery, grocery store, clothing store, hardware store, shopping center, or other sales or rental establishment;

(F) a laundromat, dry-cleaner, bank, barber shop, beauty shop, travel service, shoe repair service, funeral parlor, gas station, office of an accountant or lawyer, pharmacy, insurance office, professional office of a health care provider, hospital, or other service establishment;

(G) a terminal, depot, or other station used for specified public transportation;

(H) a museum, library, gallery, or other place of public display or collection;

(I) a park, zoo, amusement park, or other place of recreation;

(J) a nursery, elementary, secondary, undergraduate, or postgraduate private school, or other place of education;

(K) a day care center, senior citizen center, homeless shelter, food bank, adoption agency, or other social service center establishment; and

(L) a gymnasium, health spa, bowling alley, golf course, or other place of exercise or recreation.

(8) Rail and railroad.—The terms "rail" and "railroad" have the meaning given the term "railroad" in section 202(e) of the Federal Railroad Safety Act of 1970 (45 U.S.C. 431(e)).

(9) Readily achievable.—The term "readily achievable" means easily accomplishable and able to be carried out without much difficulty or expense. In determining whether an action is readily achievable, factors to be considered include—

(A) the nature and cost of the action needed under this Act;

(B) the overall financial resources of the facility or facilities involved in the action; the number of persons employed at such facility; the effect on expenses and resources, or the impact otherwise of such action upon the operation of the facility;

(C) the overall financial resources of the covered entity; the overall size of the business of a covered entity with respect to the number of its employees; the number, type, and location of its facilities; and

(D) the type of operation or operations of the covered entity, including the composition, structure, and functions of the workforce of such entity; the geographic separateness, administrative or fiscal relationship of the facility or facilities in question to the covered entity.

(10) Specified public transportation.—The term "specified public transportation" means transportation by bus, rail, or any other conveyance (other than by aircraft) that provides the general public with general or special service (including charter service) on a regular and continuing basis.

(11) Vehicle.—The term "vehicle" does not include a rail passenger car, railroad locomotive, railroad freight car, railroad caboose, or a railroad car described in section 242 or covered under this title.

SEC. 302. PROHIBITION OF DISCRIMINATION BY PUBLIC ACCOMMODATIONS.

(a) General Rule.—No individual shall be discriminated against on the basis of disability in the full and equal enjoyment of the goods, services, facilities, privileges, advantages, or accommodations of any place of public accommodation by any person who owns, leases (or leases to), or operates a place of public accommodation.

(b) Construction.—
   (1) General prohibition.—
      (A) Activities.—
         (i) Denial of participation.—It shall be discriminatory to subject an individual or class of individuals on the basis of a disability or disabilities of such individual or class, directly or through contractual, licensing, or other arrangements, to a denial of the opportunity of the individual or class to participate in or benefit from the goods, services, facilities, privileges, advantages, or accommodations of an entity.
         (ii) Participation in unequal benefit.—It shall be discriminatory to afford an individual or class of individuals, on the basis of a disability or disabilities of such individual or class, directly, or through contractual, licensing, or other arrangements with the opportunity to participate in or benefit from a good, service, facility, privilege, advantage, or accommodation that is not equal to that afforded to other individuals.
         (iii) Separate benefit.—It shall be discriminatory to provide an individual or class of individuals, on the basis of a disability or disabilities of such individual or class, directly, or through contractual, licensing, or other arrangements with a good, service, facility, privilege, advantage, or accommodation that is different or separate from that provided to other individuals, unless such action is necessary to provide the individual or class of individuals with a good, service, facility, privilege, advantage, or accommodation, or other opportunity that is as effective as that provided to others.
         (iv) Individual or class of individuals.—For purposes of clauses (i) through (iii) of this subparagraph, the term "individual or class of individuals" refers to the clients or customers of the covered public accommodation that enters into the contractual, licensing or other arrangement.
      (B) Integrated settings.—Goods, services, facilities, privileges, advantages, and accommodations shall be afforded to an individual with a disability in the most integrated setting appropriate to the needs of the individual.
      (C) Opportunity to participate.—Notwithstanding the existence of separate or different programs or activities provided in accordance with this section, an individual with a disability shall not be denied the opportunity to participate in such programs or activities that are not separate or different.
      (D) Administrative methods.—An individual or entity shall not, directly or through contractual or other arrangements, utilize standards or criteria or methods of administration—
         (i) that have the effect of discriminating on the basis of disability; or
         (ii) that perpetuate the discrimination of others who are subject to common administrative control.

(E) Association.—It shall be discriminatory to exclude or otherwise deny equal goods, services, facilities, privileges, advantages, accommodations, or other opportunities to an individual or entity because of the known disability of an individual with whom the individual or entity is known to have a relationship or association.

(2) Specific prohibitions.—

(A) Discrimination.—For purposes of subsection (a), discrimination includes—

(i) the imposition or application of eligibility criteria that screen out or tend to screen out an individual with a disability or any class of individuals with disabilities from fully and equally enjoying any goods, services, facilities, privileges, advantages, or accommodations, unless such criteria can be shown to be necessary for the provision of the goods, services, facilities, privileges, advantages, or accommodations being offered;

(ii) a failure to make reasonable modifications in policies, practices, or procedures, when such modifications are necessary to afford such goods, services, facilities, privileges, advantages, or accommodations to individuals with disabilities, unless the entity can demonstrate that making such modifications would fundamentally alter the nature of such goods, services, facilities, privileges, advantages, or accommodations;

(iii) a failure to take such steps as may be necessary to ensure that no individual with a disability is excluded, denied services, segregated or otherwise treated differently than other individuals because of the absence of auxiliary aids and services, unless the entity can demonstrate that taking such steps would fundamentally alter the nature of the good, service, facility, privilege, advantage, or accommodation being offered or would result in an undue burden;

(iv) a failure to remove architectural barriers, and communication barriers that are structural in nature, in existing facilities, and transportation barriers in existing vehicles and rail passenger cars used by an establishment for transporting individuals (not including barriers that can only be removed through the retrofitting of vehicles or rail passenger cars by the installation of a hydraulic or other lift), where such removal is readily achievable; and

(v) where an entity can demonstrate that the removal of a barrier under clause (iv) is not readily achievable, a failure to make such goods, services, facilities, privileges, advantages, or accommodations available through alternative methods if such methods are readily achievable.

(B) Fixed route system.—

(i) Accessibility.—It shall be considered discrimination for a private entity which operates a fixed route system and which is not subject to section 304 to purchase or lease a vehicle with a seating capacity in excess of 16 passengers (including the driver) for use on such system, for which a solicitation is made after the 30th day following the effective date of this subparagraph, that is not readily accessible to and usable by individuals with disabilities, including individuals who use wheelchairs.

(ii) Equivalent service.—If a private entity which operates a fixed route system and which is not subject to section 304 purchases or leases a vehicle with a seating capacity of 16 passengers or less (including the driver) for use on such system after the effective date of this subparagraph that is not readily accessible to or usable by individuals with disabilities, it shall be considered discrimination for such entity to fail to operate such system so that, when viewed in its entirety, such system ensures a level of service to individuals with disabilities, including individuals who use wheelchairs, equivalent to the level of service provided to individuals without disabilities.

(C) Demand responsive system.—For purposes of subsection (a), discrimination includes—

(i) a failure of a private entity which operates a demand responsive system and which is not subject to section 304 to operate such system so that, when viewed in its entirety, such system ensures a level of service to individuals with disabilities, including individuals who use wheelchairs, equivalent to the level of service provided to individuals without disabilities; and

(ii) the purchase or lease by such entity for use on such system of a vehicle with a seating capacity in excess of 16 passengers (including the driver), for which solicitations are made after the 30th day following the effective date of this subparagraph, that is not readily accessible to and usable by individuals with disabilities (including individuals who use wheelchairs) unless such entity can demonstrate that such system, when viewed in its entirety, provides a level of service to individuals with disabilities equivalent to that provided to individuals without disabilities.

(D) Over-the-road buses.—

(i) Limitation on applicability.—Subparagraphs (B) and (C) do not apply to over-the-road buses.

(ii) Accessibility requirements.—For purposes of subsection (a), discrimination includes

(I) the purchase or lease of an over-the-road bus which does not comply with the regulations issued under section 306(a)(2) by a private entity which provides transportation of individuals and which is not primarily engaged in the business of transporting people, and

(II) any other failure of such entity to comply with such regulations.

(3) Specific Construction.—Nothing in this title shall require an entity to permit an individual to participate in or benefit from the goods, services, facilities, privileges, advantages and accommodations of such entity where such individual poses a direct threat to the health or safety of others. The term "direct threat" means a significant risk to the health or safety of others that cannot be elimi-

nated by a modification of policies, practices, or procedures or by the provision of auxiliary aids or services.

SEC. 303. NEW CONSTRUCTION AND ALTERATIONS IN PUBLIC ACCOMMODATIONS AND COMMERCIAL FACILITIES.

(a) Application of Term.—Except as provided in subsection (b), as applied to public accommodations and commercial facilities, discrimination for purposes of section 302(a) includes—

(1) a failure to design and construct facilities for first occupancy later than 30 months after the date of enactment of this Act that are readily accessible to and usable by individuals with disabilities, except where an entity can demonstrate that it is structurally impracticable to meet the requirements of such subsection in accordance with standards set forth or incorporated by reference in regulations issued under this title; and

(2) with respect to a facility or part thereof that is altered by, on behalf of, or for the use of an establishment in a manner that affects or could affect the usability of the facility or part thereof, a failure to make alterations in such a manner that, to the maximum extent feasible, the altered portions of the facility are readily accessible to and usable by individuals with disabilities, including individuals who use wheelchairs. Where the entity is undertaking an alteration that affects or could affect usability of or access to an area of the facility containing a primary function, the entity shall also make the alterations in such a manner that, to the maximum extent feasible, the path of travel to the altered area and the bathrooms, telephones, and drinking fountains serving the altered area, are readily accessible to and usable by individuals with disabilities where such alterations to the path of travel or the bathrooms, telephones, and drinking fountains serving the altered area are not disproportionate to the overall alterations in terms of cost and scope (as determined under criteria established by the Attorney General).

(b) Elevator.—Subsection (a) shall not be construed to require the installation of an elevator for facilities that are less than three stories or have less than 3,000 square feet per story unless the building is a shopping center, a shopping mall, or the professional office of a health care provider or unless the Attorney General determines that a particular category of such facilities requires the installation of elevators based on the usage of such facilities.

SEC. 304. PROHIBITION OF DISCRIMINATION IN SPECIFIED PUBLIC TRANSPORTATION SERVICES PROVIDED BY PRIVATE ENTITIES.

(a) General Rule.—No individual shall be discriminated against on the basis of disability in the full and equal enjoyment of specified public transportation services provided by a private entity that is primarily engaged in the business of transporting people and whose operations affect commerce.

(b) Construction.—For purposes of subsection (a), discrimination includes—

(1) the imposition or application by a entity described in subsection (a) of eligibility criteria that screen out or tend to screen out an individual with a disability or any class of individuals with disabilities from fully enjoying the specified public transportation services provided by the entity, unless such criteria can be shown to be necessary for the provision of the services being offered;

(2) the failure of such entity to—

(A) make reasonable modifications consistent with those required under section 302(b)(2)(A)(ii);

(B) provide auxiliary aids and services consistent with the requirements of section 302(b)(2)(A)(iii); and

(C) remove barriers consistent with the requirements of section 302(b)(2)(A) and with the requirements of section 303(a)(2);

(3) the purchase or lease by such entity of a new vehicle (other than an automobile, a van with a seating capacity of less than 8 passengers, including the driver, or an over-the-road bus) which is to be used to provide specified public transportation and for which a solicitation is made after the 30th day following the effective date of this section, that is not readily accessible to and usable by individuals with disabilities, including individuals who use wheelchairs; except that the new vehicle need not be readily accessible to and usable by such individuals if the new vehicle is to be used solely in a demand responsive system and if the entity can demonstrate that such system, when viewed in its entirety, provides a level of service to such individuals equivalent to the level of service provided to the general public;

(4)

(A) the purchase or lease by such entity of an over-the-road bus which does not comply with the regulations issued under section 306(a)(2); and

(B) any other failure of such entity to comply with such regulations; and

(5) the purchase or lease by such entity of a new van with a seating capacity of less than 8 passengers, including the driver, which is to be used to provide specified public transportation and for which a solicitation is made after the 30th day following the effective date of this section that is not readily accessible to or usable by individuals with disabilities, including individuals who use wheelchairs; except that the new van need not be readily accessible to and usable by such individuals if the entity can demonstrate that the system for which the van is being purchased or leased, when viewed in its entirety, provides a level of service to such individuals equivalent to the level of service provided to the general public;

(6) the purchase or lease by such entity of a new rail passenger car that is to be used to provide specified public transportation, and for which a solicitation is made later than 30 days after the effective date of this paragraph, that is not readily accessible to and usable by individuals with disabilities, including individuals who use wheelchairs; and

(7) the remanufacture by such entity of a rail passenger car that is to be used to

provide specified public transportation so as to extend its usable life for 10 years or more, or the purchase or lease by such entity of such a rail car, unless the rail car, to the maximum extent feasible, is made readily accessible to and usable by individuals with disabilities, including individuals who use wheelchairs.

(c) Historical or Antiquated Cars.—

(1) Exception.—To the extent that compliance with subsection (b)(2)(C) or (b)(7) would significantly alter the historic or antiquated character of a historical or antiquated rail passenger car, or a rail station served exclusively by such cars, or would result in violation of any rule, regulation, standard, or order issued by the Secretary of Transportation under the Federal Railroad Safety Act of 1970, such compliance shall not be required.

(2) Definition.—As used in this subsection, the term "historical or antiquated rail passenger car" means a rail passenger car—

(A) which is not less than 30 years old at the time of its use for transporting individuals;

(B) the manufacturer of which is no longer in the business of manufacturing rail passenger cars; and

(C) which—

(i) has a consequential association with events or persons significant to the past; or

(ii) embodies, or is being restored to embody, the distinctive characteristics of a type of rail passenger car used in the past, or to represent a time period which has passed.

SEC. 305. STUDY.

(a) Purposes.—The Office of Technology Assessment shall undertake a study to determine—

(1) the access needs of individuals with disabilities to over-the-road buses and over-the-road bus service; and

(2) the most cost-effective methods for providing access to over-the-road buses and over-the-road bus service to individuals with disabilities, particularly individuals who use wheelchairs, through all forms of boarding options.

(b) Contents.—The study shall include, at a minimum, an analysis of the following:

(1) The anticipated demand by individuals with disabilities for accessible over-the-road buses and over-the-road bus service.

(2) The degree to which such buses and service, including any service required under sections 304(b)(4) and 306(a)(2), are readily accessible to and usable by individuals with disabilities.

(3) The effectiveness of various methods of providing accessibility to such buses and service to individuals with disabilities.

(4) The cost of providing accessible over-the-road buses and bus service to individuals with disabilities, including consideration of recent technological and cost saving developments in equipment and devices.

(5) Possible design changes in over-the-road buses that could enhance accessibility, including the installation of accessible restrooms which do not result in a loss of seating capacity.

(6) The impact of accessibility requirements on the continuation of over-the-road bus service, with particular consideration of the impact of such requirements on such service to rural communities.

(c) Advisory Committee.—In conducting the study required by subsection (a), the Office of Technology Assessment shall establish an advisory committee, which shall consist of—

(1) members selected from among private operators and manufacturers of over-the-road buses;

(2) members selected from among individuals with disabilities, particularly individuals who use wheelchairs, who are potential riders of such buses; and

(3) members selected for their technical expertise on issues included in the study, including manufacturers of boarding assistance equipment and devices.

The number of members selected under each of paragraphs (1) and (2) shall be equal, and the total number of members selected under paragraphs (1) and (2) shall exceed the number of members selected under paragraph (3).

(d) Deadline.—The study required by subsection (a), along with recommendations by the Office of Technology Assessment, including any policy options for legislative action, shall be submitted to the President and Congress within 36 months after the date of the enactment of this Act. If the President determines that compliance with the regulations issued pursuant to section 306(a)(2)(B) on or before the applicable deadlines specified in section 306(a)(2)(B) will result in a significant reduction in intercity over-the-road bus service, the President shall extend each such deadline by 1 year.

(e) Review.—In developing the study required by subsection (a), the Office of Technology Assessment shall provide a preliminary draft of such study to the Architectural and Transportation Barriers Compliance Board established under section 502 of the Rehabilitation Act of 1973 (29 U.S.C. 792). The Board shall have an opportunity to comment on such draft study, and any such comments by the Board made in writing within 120 days after the Board's receipt of the draft study shall be incorporated as part of the final study required to be submitted under subsection (d).

SEC. 306. REGULATIONS.

(a) Transportation Provisions.—

(1) General rule.—Not later than 1 year after the date of the enactment of this Act,

the Secretary of Transportation shall issue regulations in an accessible format to carry out sections 302(b)(2) (B) and (C) and to carry out section 304 (other than subsection (b)(4)).

(2) Special rules for providing access to over-the-road buses.—

   (A) Interim requirements.—

      (i) Issuance.—Not later than 1 year after the date of the enactment of this Act, the Secretary of Transportation shall issue regulations in an accessible format to carry out sections 304(b)(4) and 302(b)(2)(D)(ii) that require each private entity which uses an over-the-road bus to provide transportation of individuals to provide accessibility to such bus; except that such regulations shall not require any structural changes in over-the-road buses in order to provide access to individuals who use wheelchairs during the effective period of such regulations and shall not require the purchase of boarding assistance devices to provide access to such individuals.

      (ii) Effective period.—The regulations issued pursuant to this subparagraph shall be effective until the effective date of the regulations issued under subparagraph (B).

   (B) Final requirement.—

      (i) Review of study and interim requirements.—The Secretary shall review the study submitted under section 305 and the regulations issued pursuant to subparagraph (A).

      (ii) Issuance.—Not later than 1 year after the date of the submission of the study under section 305, the Secretary shall issue in an accessible format new regulations to carry out sections 304(b)(4) and 302(b)(2)(D)(ii) that require, taking into account the purposes of the study under section 305 and any recommendations resulting from such study, each private entity which uses an over-the-road bus to provide transportation to individuals to provide accessibility to such bus to individuals with disabilities, including individuals who use wheelchairs.

      (iii) Effective period.—Subject to section 305(d), the regulations issued pursuant to this subparagraph shall take effect—

         (I) with respect to small providers of transportation (as defined by the Secretary), 7 years after the date of the enactment of this Act; and

         (II) with respect to other providers of transportation, 6 years after such date of enactment.

   (C) Limitation on requiring installation of accessible restrooms.—The regulations issued pursuant to this paragraph shall not require the installation of accessible restrooms in over-the-road buses if such installation would result in a loss of seating capacity.

(3) Standards.—The regulations issued pursuant to this subsection shall include standards applicable to facilities and vehicles covered by sections 302(b)(2) and 304.

(b) Other Provisions.—Not later than 1 year after the date of the enactment of this Act, the Attorney General shall issue regulations in an accessible format to carry out the provisions of this title not referred to in subsection (a) that include standards applicable to facilities and vehicles covered under section 302.

(c) Consistency With ATBCB Guidelines.—Standards included in regulations issued under subsections (a) and (b) shall be consistent with the minimum guidelines and requirements issued by the Architectural and Transportation Barriers Compliance Board in accordance with section 504 of this Act.

(d) Interim Accessibility Standards.—

(1) Facilities.—If final regulations have not been issued pursuant to this section, for new construction or alterations for which a valid and appropriate State or local building permit is obtained prior to the issuance of final regulations under this section, and for which the construction or alteration authorized by such permit begins within one year of the receipt of such permit and is completed under the terms of such permit, compliance with the Uniform Federal Accessibility Standards in effect at the time the building permit is issued shall suffice to satisfy the requirement that facilities be readily accessible to and usable by persons with disabilities as required under section 303, except that, if such final regulations have not been issued one year after the Architectural and Transportation Barriers Compliance Board has issued the supplemental minimum guidelines required under section 504(a) of this Act, compliance with such supplemental minimum guidelines shall be necessary to satisfy the requirement that facilities be readily accessible to and usable by persons with disabilities prior to issuance of the final regulations.

(2) Vehicles and rail passenger cars.—If final regulations have not been issued pursuant to this section, a private entity shall be considered to have complied with the requirements of this title, if any, that a vehicle or rail passenger car be readily accessible to and usable by individuals with disabilities, if the design for such vehicle or car complies with the laws and regulations (including the Minimum Guidelines and Requirements for Accessible Design and such supplemental minimum guidelines as are issued under section 504(a) of this Act) governing accessibility of such vehicles or cars, to the extent that such laws and regulations are not inconsistent with this title and are in effect at the time such design is substantially completed.

SEC. 307. EXEMPTIONS FOR PRIVATE CLUBS AND RELIGIOUS ORGANIZATIONS.

The provisions of this title shall not apply to private clubs or establishments exempted from coverage under title II of the Civil Rights Act of 1964 (42 U.S.C. 2000-a(e)) or to religious organizations or entities controlled by religious organizations, including places of worship.

SEC. 308. ENFORCEMENT.

(a) In General.—

(1) Availability of remedies and procedures.—The remedies and procedures set forth in section 204(a) of the Civil Rights Act of 1964 (42 U.S.C. 2000a-3(a)) are the remedies and procedures this title provides to any person who is being subjected to discrimination on the basis of disability in violation of this title or who has reasonable grounds for believing that such person is about to be subjected to discrimination in violation of section 303. Nothing in this section shall require a person with a disability to engage in a futile gesture if such person has actual notice that a person or organization covered by this title does not intend to comply with its provisions.

(2) Injunctive relief.—In the case of violations of sections 302(b)(2)(A)(iv) and section 303(a), injunctive relief shall include an order to alter facilities to make such facilities readily accessible to and usable by individuals with disabilities to the extent required by this title. Where appropriate, injunctive relief shall also include requiring the provision of an auxiliary aid or service, modification of policy, or provision of alternative methods, to the extent required by this title.

(b) Enforcement by the Attorney General.—

(1) Denial of rights.—

(A) Duty to investigate.—

(i) In general.—The Attorney General shall investigate alleged violations of this title, and shall undertake periodic reviews of compliance of covered entities under this title.

(ii) Attorney general certification.—On the application of a State or local government, the Attorney General may, in consultation with the Architectural and Transportation Barriers Compliance Board, and after prior notice and a public hearing at which persons, including individuals with disabilities, are provided an opportunity to testify against such certification, certify that a State law or local building code or similar ordinance that establishes accessibility requirements meets or exceeds the minimum requirements of this Act for the accessibility and usability of covered facilities under this title. At any enforcement proceeding under this section, such certification by the Attorney General shall be rebuttable evidence that such State law or local ordinance does meet or exceed the minimum requirements of this Act.

(B) Potential violation.—If the Attorney General has reasonable cause to believe that—

(i) any person or group of persons is engaged in a pattern or practice of discrimination under this title; or

(ii) any person or group of persons has been discriminated against under this title and such discrimination raises an issue of general public importance, the Attorney General may commence a civil action in any appropriate United States district court.

(2) Authority of court.—In a civil action under paragraph (1)(B), the court—

(A) may grant any equitable relief that such court considers to be appropriate, including, to the extent required by this title—

(i) granting temporary, preliminary, or permanent relief;

(ii) providing an auxiliary aid or service, modification of policy, practice, or procedure, or alternative method; an

(iii) making facilities readily accessible to and usable by individuals with disabilities;

(B) may award such other relief as the court considers to be appropriate, including monetary damages to persons aggrieved when requested by the Attorney General; and

(C) may, to vindicate the public interest, assess a civil penalty against the entity in an amount—

(i) not exceeding $50,000 for a first violation; and

(ii) not exceeding $100,000 for any subsequent violation.

(3) Single violation.—For purposes of paragraph (2)(C), in determining whether a first or subsequent violation has occurred, a determination in a single action, by judgment or settlement, that the covered entity has engaged in more than one discriminatory act shall be counted as a single violation.

(4) Punitive damages.—For purposes of subsection (b)(2)(B), the term "monetary damages" and "such other relief" does not include punitive damages.

(5) Judicial consideration.—In a civil action under paragraph (1)(B), the court, when considering what amount of civil penalty, if any, is appropriate, shall give consideration to any good faith effort or attempt to comply with this Act by the entity. In evaluating good faith, the court shall consider, among other factors it deems relevant, whether the entity could have reasonably anticipated the need for an appropriate type of auxiliary aid needed to accommodate the unique needs of a particular individual with a disability.

SEC. 309. EXAMINATIONS AND COURSES.

Any person that offers examinations or courses related to applications, licensing, certification, or credentialing for secondary or postsecondary education, professional, or trade purposes shall offer such examinations or courses in a place and manner accessible to persons with disabilities or offer alternative accessible arrangements for such individuals.

SEC. 310. EFFECTIVE DATE.

(a) General Rule.—Except as provided in subsections (b) and (c), this title shall become effective 18 months after the date of the enactment of this Act.

(b) Civil Actions.—Except for any civil action brought for a violation of section 303, no civil action shall be brought for any act or omission described in section 302 which occurs—

(1) during the first 6 months after the effective date, against businesses that employ 25 or fewer employees and have gross receipts of $1,000,000 or less; and

(2) during the first year after the effective date, against businesses that employ 10 or fewer employees and have gross receipts of $500,000 or less.

(c) Exception.—Sections 302(a) for purposes of section 302(b)(2) (B) and (C) only, 304(a) for purposes of section 304(b)(3) only, 304(b)(3), 305, and 306 shall take effect on the date of the enactment of this Act.

[TITLE IV—TELECOMMUNICATIONS]

SEC. 401. TELECOMMUNICATIONS RELAY SERVICES FOR HEARING-IMPAIRED AND SPEECH-IMPAIRED INDIVIDUALS.

(a) Telecommunications.—Title II of the Communications Act of 1934 (47 U.S.C. 201 et seq.) is amended by adding at the end thereof the following new section:

"SEC. 225. TELECOMMUNICATIONS SERVICES FOR HEARING-IMPAIRED AND SPEECH-IMPAIRED INDIVIDUALS.

"(a) Definitions.—As used in this section—

"(1) Common carrier or carrier.—The term 'common carrier' or 'carrier' includes any common carrier engaged in interstate communication by wire or radio as defined in section 3(h) and any common carrier engaged in intrastate communication by wire or radio, notwithstanding sections 2(b) and 221(b).

"(2) TDD.—The term 'TDD' means a Telecommunications Device for the Deaf, which is a machine that employs graphic communication in the transmission of coded signals through a wire or radio communication system.

"(3) Telecommunications relay services.—The term 'telecommunications relay services' means telephone transmission services that provide the ability for an individual who has a hearing impairment or speech impairment to engage in communication by wire or radio with a hearing individual in a manner that is functionally equivalent to the ability of an individual who does not have a hearing impairment or speech impairment to communicate using voice communication services by wire or radio. Such term includes services that enable two-way communication between an individual who uses a TDD or other nonvoice terminal device and an individual who does not use such a device.

"(b) Availability of Telecommunications Relay Services.—

"(1) In general.—In order to carry out the purposes established under section 1, to make available to all individuals in the United States a rapid, efficient nationwide communication service, and to increase the utility of the telephone system of the Nation, the Commission shall ensure that interstate and intrastate telecommunications relay services are available, to the extent possible and in the most efficient manner, to hearing-impaired and speech-impaired individuals in the United States.

"(2) Use of General Authority and Remedies.—For the purposes of administering and enforcing the provisions of this section and the regulations prescribed thereunder, the Commission shall have the same authority, power, and functions with respect to common carriers engaged in intrastate communication as the Commission has in administering and enforcing the provisions of this title with respect to any common carrier engaged in interstate communication. Any violation of this section by any common carrier engaged in intrastate communication shall be subject to the same remedies, penalties, and procedures as are applicable to a violation of this Act by a common carrier engaged in interstate communication.

"(c) Provision of Services.—Each common carrier providing telephone voice transmission services shall, not later than 3 years after the date of enactment of this section, provide in compliance with the regulations prescribed under this section, throughout the area in which it offers service, telecommunications relay services, individually, through designees, through a competitively selected vendor, or in concert with other carriers. A common carrier shall be considered to be in compliance with such regulations—

"(1) with respect to intrastate telecommunications relay services in any State that does not have a certified program under subsection (f) and with respect to interstate telecommunications relay services, if such common carrier (or other entity through which the carrier is providing such relay services) is in compliance with the Commission's regulations under subsection (d); or

"(2) with respect to intrastate telecommunications relay services in any State that has a certified program under subsection (f) for such State, if such common carrier (or other entity through which the carrier is providing such relay services) is in compliance with the program certified under subsection (f) for such State.

"(d) Regulations.—

"(1) In general.—The Commission shall, not later than 1 year after the date of enactment of this section, prescribe regulations to implement this section, including regulations that—

"(A) establish functional requirements, guidelines, and operations procedures for telecommunications relay services;

"(B) establish minimum standards that shall be met in carrying out subsection (c);

"(C) require that telecommunications relay services operate every day for 24 hours per day;

"(D) require that users of telecommunications relay services pay rates no greater than the rates paid for functionally equivalent voice communication services with respect to such factors as the duration of the call, the time of day, and the distance from point of origination to point of termination;

"(E) prohibit relay operators from failing to fulfill the obligations of common carriers by refusing calls or limiting the length of calls that use telecommunications relay services;

"(F) prohibit relay operators from disclosing the content of any relayed conversation and from keeping records of the content of any such conversation beyond the duration of the call; and

"(G) prohibit relay operators from intentionally altering a relayed conversation.

"(2) Technology.—The Commission shall ensure that regulations prescribed to implement this section encourage, consistent with section 7(a) of this Act, the use of existing technology and do not discourage or impair the development of improved technology.

"(3) Jurisdictional separation of costs.—

"(A) In general.—Consistent with the provisions of section 410 of this Act, the Commission shall prescribe regulations governing the jurisdictional separation of costs for the services provided pursuant to this section.

"(B) Recovering costs.—Such regulations shall generally provide that costs caused by interstate telecommunications relay services shall be recovered from all subscribers for every interstate service and costs caused by intrastate telecommunications relay services shall be recovered from the intrastate jurisdiction. In a State that has a certified program under subsection (f), a State commission shall permit a common carrier to recover the costs incurred in providing intrastate telecommunications relay services by a method consistent with the requirements of this section.

"(e) Enforcement.—

"(1) In general.—Subject to subsections (f) and (g), the Commission shall enforce this section.

"(2) Complaint.—The Commission shall resolve, by final order, a complaint alleging a violation of this section within 180 days after the date such complaint is filed.

"(f) Certification.—

"(1) State documentation.—Any State desiring to establish a State program under this section shall submit documentation to the Commission that describes the program of such State for implementing intrastate telecommunications relay services and the procedures and remedies available for enforcing any requirements imposed by the State program.

"(2) Requirements for certification.—After review of such documentation, the Commission shall certify the State program if the Commission determines that—

"(A) the program makes available to hearing-impaired and speech-impaired individuals, either directly, through designees, through a competitively selected vendor, or through regulation of intrastate common carriers, intrastate telecommunications relay services in such State in a manner that meets or exceeds the requirements of regulations prescribed by the Commission under subsection (d); and

"(B) the program makes available adequate procedures and remedies for enforcing the requirements of the State program.

"(3) Method of funding.—Except as provided in subsection (d), the Commission shall not refuse to certify a State program based solely on the method such State will implement for funding intrastate telecommunication relay services.

"(4) Suspension or revocation of certification.—The Commission may suspend or revoke such certification if, after notice and opportunity for hearing, the Commission determines that such certification is no longer warranted. In a State whose program has been suspended or revoked, the Commission shall take such steps as may be necessary, consistent with this section, to ensure continuity of telecommunications relay services.

"(g) Complaint.—

"(1) Referral of complaint.—If a complaint to the Commission alleges a violation of this section with respect to intrastate telecommunications relay services within a State and certification of the program of such State under subsection (f) is in effect, the Commission shall refer such complaint to such State.

"(2) Jurisdiction of commission.—After referring a complaint to a State under paragraph (1), the Commission shall exercise jurisdiction over such complaint only if—

"(A) final action under such State program has not been taken on such complaint by such State—

"(i) within 180 days after the complaint is filed with such State; or

"(ii) within a shorter period as prescribed by the regulations of such State; or

"(B) the Commission determines that such State program is no longer qualified for certification under subsection (f)."

(b) Conforming Amendments.—The Communications Act of 1934 (47 U.S.C. 151 et seq.) is amended—

(1) in section 2(b) (47 U.S.C. 152(b)), by striking "section 224" and inserting "sections 224 and 225"; and

(2) in section 221(b) (47 U.S.C. 221(b)), by striking "section 301" and inserting "sections 225 and 301".

SEC. 402. CLOSED-CAPTIONING OF PUBLIC SERVICE ANNOUNCEMENTS.

Section 711 of the Communications Act of 1934 is amended to read as follows:

"SEC. 711. CLOSED-CAPTIONING OF PUBLIC SERVICE ANNOUNCEMENTS.

"Any television public service announcement that is produced or funded in whole or in part by any agency or instrumentality of Federal Government shall include closed captioning of the verbal content of such announcement. A television broadcast station licensee—

"(1) shall not be required to supply closed captioning for any such announcement that fails to include it; and

"(2) shall not be liable for broadcasting any such announcement without transmitting a closed caption unless the licensee intentionally fails to transmit the closed caption that was included with the announcement."

[TITLE V—MISCELLANEOUS PROVISIONS]

SEC. 501. CONSTRUCTION.

(a) In General.—Except as otherwise provided in this Act, nothing in this Act shall be construed to apply a lesser standard than the standards applied under title V of the Rehabilitation Act of 1973 (29 U.S.C. 790 et seq.) or the regulations issued by Federal agencies pursuant to such title.

(b) Relationship to Other Laws.—Nothing in this Act shall be construed to invalidate or limit the remedies, rights, and procedures of any Federal law or law of any State or political subdivision of any State or jurisdiction that provides greater or equal protection for the rights of individuals with disabilities than are afforded by this Act. Nothing in this Act shall be construed to preclude the prohibition of, or the imposition of restrictions on, smoking in places of employment covered by title I, in transportation covered by title II or III, or in places of public accommodation covered by title III.

(c) Insurance.—Titles I through IV of this Act shall not be construed to prohibit or restrict—

(1) an insurer, hospital or medical service company, health maintenance organization, or any agent, or entity that administers benefit plans, or similar organizations from underwriting risks, classifying risks, or administering such risks that are based on or not inconsistent with State law; or

(2) a person or organization covered by this Act from establishing, sponsoring, observing or administering the terms of a bona fide benefit plan that are based on underwriting risks, classifying risks, or administering such risks that are based on or not inconsistent with State law; or

(3) a person or organization covered by this Act from establishing, sponsoring, observing or administering the terms of a bona fide benefit plan that is not subject to State laws that regulate insurance. Paragraphs (1), (2), and (3) shall not be used as a subterfuge to evade the purposes of title I and III.

(d) Accommodations and Services.—Nothing in this Act shall be construed to require an individual with a disability to accept an accommodation, aid, service, opportunity, or benefit which such individual chooses not to accept.

SEC. 502. STATE IMMUNITY.

A State shall not be immune under the eleventh amendment to the Constitution of the United States from an action in Federal or State court of competent jurisdiction for a violation of this Act. In any action against a State for a violation of the requirements of this Act, remedies (including remedies both at law and in equity) are available for such a violation to the same extent as such remedies are available for such a violation in an action against any public or private entity other than a State.

SEC. 503. PROHIBITION AGAINST RETALIATION AND COERCION.

(a) Retaliation.—No person shall discriminate against any individual because such individual has opposed any act or practice made unlawful by this Act or because such individual made a charge, testified, assisted, or participated in any manner in an investigation, proceeding, or hearing under this Act.

(b) Interference, Coercion, or Intimidation.—It shall be unlawful to coerce, intimidate, threaten, or interfere with any individual in the exercise or enjoyment of, or on account of his or her having exercised or enjoyed, or on account of his or her having aided or encouraged any other individual in the exercise or enjoyment of, any right granted or protected by this Act.

(c) Remedies and Procedures.—The remedies and procedures available under sections 107, 203, and 308 of this Act shall be available to aggrieved persons for violations of subsections (a) and (b), with respect to title I, title II and title III, respectively.

SEC. 504. REGULATIONS BY THE ARCHITECTURAL AND TRANSPORTATION BARRIERS COMPLIANCE BOARD.

(a) Issuance of Guidelines.—Not later than 9 months after the date of enactment of this Act, the Architectural and Transportation Barriers Compliance Board shall issue minimum guidelines that shall supplement the existing Minimum Guidelines and Requirements for Accessible Design for purposes of titles II and III of this Act.

(b) Contents of Guidelines.—The supplemental guidelines issued under subsection (a) shall establish additional requirements, consistent with this Act, to ensure that buildings, facilities, rail passenger cars, and vehicles are accessible, in terms of architecture and design, transportation, and communication, to individuals with disabilities.

(c) Qualified Historic Properties.—
　(1) In general.—The supplemental guidelines issued under subsection (a) shall

include procedures and requirements for alterations that will threaten or destroy the historic significance of qualified historic buildings and facilities as defined in 4.1.7(1)(a) of the Uniform Federal Accessibility Standards.

(2) Sites eligible for listing in national register.—With respect to alterations of buildings or facilities that are eligible for listing in the National Register of Historic Places under the National Historic Preservation Act (16 U.S.C. 470 et seq.), the guidelines described in paragraph (1) shall, at a minimum, maintain the procedures and requirements established in 4.1.7 (1) and (2) of the Uniform Federal Accessibility Standards.

(3) Other sites.—With respect to alterations of buildings or facilities designated as historic under State or local law, the guidelines described in paragraph (1) shall establish procedures equivalent to those established by 4.1.7(1) (b) and (c) of the Uniform Federal Accessibility Standards, and shall require, at a minimum, compliance with the requirements established in 4.1.7(2) of such standards.

SEC. 505. ATTORNEY'S FEES.

In any action or administrative proceeding commenced pursuant to this Act, the court or agency, in its discretion, may allow the prevailing party, other than the United States, a reasonable attorney's fee, including litigation expenses, and costs, and the United States shall be liable for the foregoing the same as a private individual.

SEC. 506. TECHNICAL ASSISTANCE.

(a) Plan for Assistance.—

(1) In general.—Not later than 180 days after the date of enactment of this Act, the Attorney General, in consultation with the Chair of the Equal Employment Opportunity Commission, the Secretary of Transportation, the Chair of the Architectural and Transportation Barriers Compliance Board, and the Chairman of the Federal Communications Commission, shall develop a plan to assist entities covered under this Act, and other Federal agencies, in understanding the responsibility of such entities and agencies under this Act.

(2) Publication of plan.—The Attorney General shall publish the plan referred to in paragraph (1) for public comment in accordance with subchapter II of chapter 5 of title 5, United States Code (commonly known as the Administrative Procedure Act).

(b) Agency and Public Assistance.—The Attorney General may obtain the assistance of other Federal agencies in carrying out subsection (a), including the National Council on Disability, the President's Committee on Employment of People with Disabilities, the Small Business Administration, and the Department of Commerce.

(c) Implementation.—

(1) Rendering assistance.—Each Federal agency that has responsibility under paragraph (2) for implementing this Act may render technical assistance to

individuals and institutions that have rights or duties under the respective title or titles for which such agency has responsibility.

(2) Implementation of titles.—

(A) Title i.—The Equal Employment Opportunity Commission and the Attorney General shall implement the plan for assistance developed under subsection (a), for title I.

(B) Title ii.—

(i) Subtitle a.—The Attorney General shall implement such plan for assistance for subtitle A of title II.

(ii) Subtitle b.—The Secretary of Transportation shall implement such plan for assistance for subtitle B of title II.

(C) Title iii.—The Attorney General, in coordination with the Secretary of Transportation and the Chair of the Architectural Transportation Barriers Compliance Board, shall implement such plan for assistance for title III, except for section 304, the plan for assistance for which shall be implemented by the Secretary of Transportation.

(D) Title iv.—The Chairman of the Federal Communications Commission, in coordination with the Attorney General, shall implement such plan for assistance for title IV.

(3) Technical assistance manuals.—Each Federal agency that has responsibility under paragraph (2) for implementing this Act shall, as part of its implementation responsibilities, ensure the availability and provision of appropriate technical assistance manuals to individuals or entities with rights or duties under this Act no later than six months after applicable final regulations are published under titles I, II, III, and IV.

(d) Grants and Contracts.—

(1) In general.—Each Federal agency that has responsibility under subsection (c)(2) for implementing this Act may make grants or award contracts to effectuate the purposes of this section, subject to the availability of appropriations. Such grants and contracts may be awarded to individuals, institutions not organized for profit and no part of the net earnings of which inures to the benefit of any private shareholder or individual (including educational institutions), and associations representing individuals who have rights or duties under this Act. Contracts may be awarded to entities organized for profit, but such entities may not be the recipients or grants described in this paragraph.

(2) Dissemination of information.—Such grants and contracts, among other uses, may be designed to ensure wide dissemination of information about the rights and duties established by this Act and to provide information and technical assistance about techniques for effective compliance with this Act.

(e) Failure to Receive Assistance.—An employer, public accommodation, or other entity covered under this Act shall not be excused from compliance with the requirements of this Act because of any failure to receive technical assistance under this section, including any failure in the development or dissemination of any technical assistance manual authorized by this section.

SEC. 507. FEDERAL WILDERNESS AREAS.

(a) Study.—The National Council on Disability shall conduct a study and report on the effect that wilderness designations and wilderness land management practices have on the ability of individuals with disabilities to use and enjoy the National Wilderness Preservation System as established under the Wilderness Act (16 U.S.C. 1131 et seq.).

(b) Submission of Report.—Not later than 1 year after the enactment of this Act, the National Council on Disability shall submit the report required under subsection (a) to Congress.

(c) Specific Wilderness Access.—
> (1) In general.—Congress reaffirms that nothing in the Wilderness Act is to be construed as prohibiting the use of a wheelchair in a wilderness area by an individual whose disability requires use of a wheelchair, and consistent with the Wilderness Act no agency is required to provide any form of special treatment or accommodation, or to construct any facilities or modify any conditions of lands within a wilderness area in order to facilitate such use.
> (2) Definition.—For purposes of paragraph (1), the term "wheelchair" means a device designed solely for use by a mobility-impaired person for locomotion, that is suitable for use in an indoor pedestrian area.

SEC. 508. TRANSVESTITES.

For the purposes of this Act, the term "disabled" or "disability" shall not apply to an individual solely because that individual is a transvestite.

SEC. 509. COVERAGE OF CONGRESS AND THE AGENCIES OF THE LEGISLATIVE BRANCH.

(a) Coverage of the Senate.—
> (1) Commitment to Rule XLII.—The Senate reaffirms its commitment to Rule XLII of the Standing Rules of the Senate which provides as follows:

"No member, officer, or employee of the Senate shall, with respect to employment by the Senate or any office thereof—
> "(a) fail or refuse to hire an individual;
> "(b) discharge an individual; or
> "(c) otherwise discriminate against an individual with respect to promotion, compensation, or terms, conditions, or privileges of employment on the basis of such individual's race, color, religion, sex, national origin, age, or state of physical handicap."

(2) Application to Senate employment.—The rights and protections provided pursuant to this Act, the Civil Rights Act of 1990 (S. 2104, 101st Congress), the Civil Rights Act of 1964, the Age Discrimination in Employment Act of 1967, and the Rehabilitation Act of 1973 shall apply with respect to employment by the United States Senate.

(3) Investigation and adjudication of claims.—All claims raised by any individual with respect to Senate employment, pursuant to the Acts referred to in paragraph (2), shall be investigated and adjudicated by the Select Committee on Ethics, pursuant to S. Res. 338, 88th Congress, as amended, or such other entity as the Senate may designate.

(4) Rights of employees.—The Committee on Rules and Administration shall ensure that Senate employees are informed of their rights under the Acts referred to in paragraph (2).

(5) Applicable Remedies.—When assigning remedies to individuals found to have a valid claim under the Acts referred to in paragraph (2), the Select Committee on Ethics, or such other entity as the Senate may designate, should to the extent practicable apply the same remedies applicable to all other employees covered by the Acts referred to in paragraph (2). Such remedies shall apply exclusively.

(6) Matters Other Than Employment.—

(A) In General.—The rights and protections under this Act shall, subject to subparagraph (B), apply with respect to the conduct of the Senate regarding matters other than employment.

(B) Remedies.—The Architect of the Capitol shall establish remedies and procedures to be utilized with respect to the rights and protections provided pursuant to subparagraph (A). Such remedies and procedures shall apply exclusively, after approval in accordance with subparagraph (C).

(C) Proposed remedies and procedures.—For purposes of subparagraph (B), the Architect of the Capitol shall submit proposed remedies and procedures to the Senate Committee on Rules and Administration. The remedies and procedures shall be effective upon the approval of the Committee on Rules and Administration.

(7) Exercise of rulemaking power.—Notwithstanding any other provision of law, enforcement and adjudication of the rights and protections referred to in paragraph (2) and (6)(A) shall be within the exclusive jurisdiction of the United States Senate. The provisions of paragraph (1), (3), (4), (5), (6)(B), and (6)(C) are enacted by the Senate as an exercise of the rulemaking power of the Senate, with full recognition of the right of the Senate to change its rules, in the same manner, and to the same extent, as in the case of any other rule of the Senate.

(b) Coverage of the House of Representatives.—

(1) In general.—Notwithstanding any other provision of this Act or of law, the purposes of this Act shall, subject to paragraphs (2) and (3), apply in their entirety to the House of Representatives.

(2) Employment in the house.—

(A) Application.—The rights and protections under this Act shall, subject to subparagraph (B), apply with respect to any employee in an employment position in the House of Representatives and any employing authority of the House of Representatives.

(B) Administration.—

(i) In general.—In the administration of this paragraph, the remedies and procedures made applicable pursuant to the resolution described in clause (ii) shall apply exclusively.

(ii) Resolution.—The resolution referred to in clause (i) is House Resolution 15 of the One Hundred First Congress, as agreed to January 3, 1989, or any other provision that continues in effect the provisions of, or is a successor to, the Fair Employment Practices Resolution (House Resolution 558 of the One Hundredth Congress, as agreed to October 4, 1988).

(C) Exercise of rulemaking power.—The provisions of subparagraph (B) are enacted by the House of Representatives as an exercise of the rulemaking power of the House of Representatives, with full recognition of the right of the House to change its rules, in the same manner, and to the same extent as in the case of any other rule of the House.

(3) Matters other than employment.—

(A) In general.—The rights and protections under this Act shall, subject to subparagraph (B), apply with respect to the conduct of the House of Representatives regarding matters other than employment.

(B) Remedies.—The Architect of the Capitol shall establish remedies and procedures to be utilized with respect to the rights and protections provided pursuant to subparagraph (A). Such remedies and procedures shall apply exclusively, after approval in accordance with subparagraph (C).

(C) Approval.—For purposes of subparagraph (B), the Architect of the Capitol shall submit proposed remedies and procedures to the Speaker of the House of Representatives. The remedies and procedures shall be effective upon the approval of the Speaker, after consultation with the House Office Building Commission.

(c) Instrumentalities of Congress.—

(1) In general.—The rights and protections under this Act shall, subject to paragraph (2), apply with respect to the conduct of each instrumentality of the Congress.

(2) Establishment of remedies and procedures by instrumentalities.—The chief official of each instrumentality of the Congress shall establish remedies and procedures to be utilized with respect to the rights and protections provided pursuant to paragraph (1). Such remedies and procedures shall apply exclusively.

(3) Report to congress.—The chief official of each instrumentality of the Congress

shall, after establishing remedies and procedures for purposes of paragraph (2), submit to the Congress a report describing the remedies and procedures.

(4) Definition of instrumentalities.—For purposes of this section, instrumentalities of the Congress include the following: the Architect of the Capitol, the Congressional Budget Office, the General Accounting Office, the Government Printing Office, the Library of Congress, the Office of Technology Assessment, and the United States Botanic Garden.

(5) Construction.—Nothing in this section shall alter the enforcement procedures for individuals with disabilities provided in the General Accounting Office Personnel Act of 1980 and regulations promulgated pursuant to that Act.

SEC. 510. ILLEGAL USE OF DRUGS.

(a) In General.—For purposes of this Act, the term "individual with a disability" does not include an individual who is currently engaging in the illegal use of drugs, when the covered entity acts on the basis of such use.

(b) Rules of Construction.—Nothing in subsection (a) shall be construed to exclude as an individual with a disability an individual who—
(1) has successfully completed a supervised drug rehabilitation program and is no longer engaging in the illegal use of drugs, or has otherwise been rehabilitated successfully and is no longer engaging in such use;
(2) is participating in a supervised rehabilitation program and is no longer engaging in such use; or
(3) is erroneously regarded as engaging in such use, but is not engaging in such use; except that it shall not be a violation of this Act for a covered entity to adopt or administer reasonable policies or procedures, including but not limited to drug testing, designed to ensure that an individual described in paragraph (1) or (2) is no longer engaging in the illegal use of drugs; however, nothing in this section shall be construed to encourage, prohibit, restrict, or authorize the conducting of testing for the illegal use of drugs.

(c) Health and Other Services.—Notwithstanding subsection (a) and section 511(b)(3), an individual shall not be denied health services, or services provided in connection with drug rehabilitation, on the basis of the current illegal use of drugs if the individual is otherwise entitled to such services.

(d) Definition of Illegal use of drugs.—
(1) In general.—The term "illegal use of drugs" means the use of drugs, the possession or distribution of which is unlawful under the Controlled Substances Act (21 U.S.C. 812). Such term does not include the use of a drug taken under supervision by a licensed health care professional, or other uses authorized by the Controlled Substances Act or other provisions of Federal law.
(2) Drugs.—The term "drug" means a controlled substance, as defined in schedules I through V of section 202 of the Controlled Substances Act.

SEC. 511. DEFINITIONS.

(a) Homosexuality and Bisexuality.—For purposes of the definition of "disability" in section 3(2), homosexuality and bisexuality are not impairments and as such are not disabilities under this Act.

(b) Certain Conditions.—Under this Act, the term "disability" shall not include—
(1) transvestism, transsexualism, pedophilia, exhibitionism, voyeurism, gender identity disorders not resulting from physical impairments, or other sexual behavior disorders;
(2) compulsive gambling, kleptomania, or pyromania; or
(3) psychoactive substance use disorders resulting from current illegal use of drugs.

SEC. 512. AMENDMENTS TO THE REHABILITATION ACT.

(a) Definition of Handicapped Individual.—Section 7(8) of the Rehabilitation Act of 1973 (29 U.S.C. 706(8)) is amended by redesignating subparagraph (C) as subparagraph (D), and by inserting after subparagraph (B) the following subparagraph:

"(C)
"(i) For purposes of title V, the term 'individual with handicaps' does not include an individual who is currently engaging in the illegal use of drugs, when a covered entity acts on the basis of such use.
"(ii) Nothing in clause (i) shall be construed to exclude as an individual with handicaps an individual who—
"(I) has successfully completed a supervised drug rehabilitation program and is no longer engaging in the illegal use of drugs, or has otherwise been rehabilitated successfully and is no longer engaging in such use;
"(II) is participating in a supervised rehabilitation program and is no longer engaging in such use; or
"(III) is erroneously regarded as engaging in such use, but is not engaging in such use; except that it shall not be a violation of this Act for a covered entity to adopt or administer reasonable policies or procedures, including but not limited to drug testing, designed to ensure that an individual described in subclause (I) or (II) is no longer engaging in the illegal use of drugs.
"(iii) Notwithstanding clause (i), for purposes of programs and activities providing health services and services provided under titles I, II and III, an individual shall not be excluded from the benefits of such programs or activities on the basis of his or her current illegal use of drugs if he or she is otherwise entitled to such services.
"(iv) For purposes of programs and activities providing educational services, local educational agencies may take disciplinary action pertaining

to the use or possession of illegal drugs or alcohol against any handicapped student who currently is engaging in the illegal use of drugs or in the use of alcohol to the same extent that such disciplinary action is taken against nonhandicapped students. Furthermore, the due process procedures at 34 CFR 104.36 shall not apply to such disciplinary actions.

"(v) For purposes of sections 503 and 504 as such sections relate to employment, the term 'individual with handicaps' does not include any individual who is an alcoholic whose current use of alcohol prevents such individual from performing the duties of the job in question or whose employment, by reason of such current alcohol abuse, would constitute a direct threat to property or the safety of others.".

(b) Definition of Illegal Drugs.—Section 7 of the Rehabilitation Act of 1973 (29 U.S.C. 706) is amended by adding at the end the following new paragraph:

"(22)

"(A) The term 'drug' means a controlled substance, as defined in schedules I through V of section 202 of the Controlled Substances Act (21 U.S.C. 812).

"(B) The term 'illegal use of drugs' means the use of drugs, the possession or distribution of which is unlawful under the Controlled Substances Act. Such term does not include the use of a drug taken under supervision by a licensed health care professional, or other uses authorized by the Controlled Substances Act or other provisions of Federal law."

(c) Conforming Amendments.—Section 7(8)(B) of the Rehabilitation Act of 1973 (29 U.S.C. 706(8)(B)) is amended—

(1) in the first sentence, by striking "Subject to the second sentence of this subparagraph," and inserting "Subject to subparagraphs (C) and (D),"; and

(2) by striking the second sentence.

SEC. 513. ALTERNATIVE MEANS OF DISPUTE RESOLUTION.

Where appropriate and to the extent authorized by law, the use of alternative means of dispute resolution, including settlement negotiations, conciliation, facilitation, mediation, factfinding, minitrials, and arbitration, is encouraged to resolve disputes arising under this Act.

SEC. 514. SEVERABILITY.

Should any provision in this Act be found to be unconstitutional by a court of law, such provision shall be severed from the remainder of the Act, and such action shall not affect the enforceability of the remaining provisions of the Act.

FOR FURTHER READING

The Americans with Disabilities Act: Access and Accommodations—Guidelines for Human Resources, Rehabilitation, and Legal Professionals. Delray Beach, Florida: St. Lucie Press, 1990.

Berkowitz, E. *Disabled Policy: America's Programs for the Handicapped.* New York: Cambridge University Press, 1987.

Berkowitz, M. and M. Hill, editors. *Disability and the Labor Market.* Ithaca, New York: ILR Press, 1986.

Burkhauser, Richard V. and Robert H. Haveman. *Disability and Work: The Economics of American Policy.* Baltimore: Johns Hopkins University Press, 1982.

Davis, Lennard J., editor. *The Disability Studies Reader.* New York: Routledge, Kegan Paul, 1997.

Fine, Michelle, and Adrienne Asch, editors. *Women with Disabilities: Essays in Psychology, Culture and Politics.* Philadelphia: Temple University Press, 1988.

Hartman, Tari Susan and Mary Johnson. *Making News: How to Get News Coverage for Disability Rights Issues.* Louisville, Kentucky: Advocado Press, 1994.

King, R. B. and Backer, T. E. *Overcoming Challenges: A Guide to Selective Job Placement of Workers with Disabilities.* Los Angeles: National Medical Enterprises, 1989.

Kurzweil, Ray. *The Singularity is Near: When Humans Transcend Biology.* New York: Viking, 2005.

LaPlante, M. *Data on Disability from the National Health Interview Survey, 1983–1985.* Washington, D.C.: National Institute for Disability and Rehabilitation Research, 1988.

Levitan, Sar A. and Robert Taggart. *Jobs for the Disabled.* Baltimore: Johns Hopkins University Press, 1977.

Linton, Simi. *Claiming Disability: Knowledge and Identity.* New York: New York University Press, 1998.

O'Brien, Ruth. *Crippled Justice: The History of Modern Disability Policy in the Workplace*. Chicago: University of Chicago Press, 2001.

———. *Bodies in Revolt: Gender, Disability and the Workplace*. New York: Routledge, 2005.

Oliver, Michael. *Understanding Disability: From Theory to Practice*. New York: St. Martin's Press, 1996.

Shapiro, Joseph P. *No Pity: People with Disabilities Forging a New Civil Rights Movement*. New York: Times Books, 1993.

Spechler, Jay W. *Reasonable Accommodation: Profitable Compliance with the Americans with Disabilities Act*. Delray Beach, Florida: St. Lucie Press, 1996.

Stapleton, David C. and Richard V. Burkhauser, editors, *The Decline in Employment of People with Disabilities: A Policy Puzzle*. Kalamazoo, Michigan: W. E. Upjohn Institute for Employment Research, 2003.

Stone, Deborah. *The Disabled State*. Philadelphia: Temple University Press, 1986.

Szymanski, Edna Mora and Randall M. Parker, editors. *Work and Disability: Issues and Strategies in Career Development and Job Placement,* second edition. Austin, Texas: Pro-Ed, 2003.

Thomason, Terry, John F. Burton, Jr., and Douglas E. Hyatt, editors. *New Approaches to Disability in the Workplace*. Madison, Wisconsin: Industrial Relations Research Association, 1998.

Weaver, Carolyn L., editor. *Disability and Work: Incentives, Rights, and Opportunities*. Washington, D.C., AEI Press (American Enterprise Institute), 1991.

Yelin, Edward. *Disability and the Displaced Worker*. New Brunswick, N.J.: Rutgers University Press, 1992.

INDEX

Mace, Ronald, 69, 109–110, 120, 128n1
Macy's West, 75–76
management, x, xvi, 21, 41, 65, 118, 129–154
Manpower, xvii, 33
Mao Ze Dong, 148
marketing, ix, x, xvi, 3, 7, 9, 17, 28, 47, 56, 65, 68–86, 92, 101, 118, 121, 138, 141
Marketresearch.com, 7
Marriott Foundation, 38
Martin, Casey, xvii, 85–86
Massachusetts Institute of Technology (MIT), 62, 98
Massachusetts Department of Mental Health, 120
Mattel, 69, 75, 87–88
Mazrui, Susan Palmer, xvii, 140–141
McCary, Katherine, xvii, 65–66, 143
McDonald's 7, 8, 38, 69, 75, 86
McJobs Program, 38
McKinsey and Company, 89
McMullen, David, xvii
MD. *See* muscular dystrophy
Media Access Group (WGBH), 79–80
Media Access Office, 76
media, 6, 24, 84, 88, 142
Medicaid, xv, 14, 15
"medical model," 17, 23, 52, 59
Medicare, xv, 14
Medtronic, xvii, 8, 143
Men Zhen Wen, 145–146
Merck, 52
Merrill Lynch, xvii, 51, 53, 55–56, 150
Meyer, Sarah, 63
Microsoft, xi, xiii, xiv, xvii, 18, 43, 44, 46, 53, 59, 60, 61–64, 75, 91, 96, 97, 102, 123–126, 129, 132, 133, 135, 142
Miller, Nancy D., 116
Minic, Branka, xvii, 33
Miramax, 76, 78
Mitsubishi Electric America Foundation, 64, 75
Mitsubishi, 64, 75
Monster, 61
Montone, John, 150
"moral hazard" problem, 15
Morgan Stanley, 35

Mosner, Ellen, 63
Motorola, xiii, xvii, 60, 97–101
MS. *See* multiple sclerosis
MS Society, 6, 69
Muir, Alan, xvii, 20, 24–25, 57–61, 65
multiple sclerosis (MS), 40, 114
muscular dystrophy (MD), 114
My Left Foot, 76–80

Nabisco, 71
NASA, xvii, 53–54, 60, 135
National Amusements Showcases, 80
National Association for the Advancement Colored People (NAACP), 6, 46, 84
National Association of the Deaf, 75
National Association of Women Business Owners (NAWBO), 143
National Business and Disability Council, 99
National Captioning Institute, 71
National Center for Accessible Media, 63, 80
National Institute on Disability and Rehabilitation Research, 120
National Labor Relations Act, 41
National Organization on Disability (NOD), 6, 21n, 30, 48, 61, 63
National Retail Federation, 77
National Science Foundation, 64
National Spinal Cord Injury Association (NSCIA), 5, 6, 8, 73, 75, 84–85, 139
National Technical Institute for the Deaf, 44
New York Times Magazine, 17, 132
New York Times, 17, 24, 42n1, 104, 136–137, 154nn2, 3, 4
New Yorker magazine, 20
Newsweek, 89
NGO (non-governmental organization), 6, 49, 55, 64, 89, 102, 143
niche market, ix, 17, 77, 81–83
Nickelodeon, 75
Nielsen Entertainment, xvii, 3, 7, 73, 83–84
Nike, 7, 24, 70, 85–86
NISH (National Industries for the Severely Handicapped), xv